ARSÈNAL

THE MAKING OF A MODERN SUPERCLUB

Alex Fynn and Kevin Whitcher

Vision Sports Publishing
2 Coombe Gardens,
London SW20 0QU

www.visionsp.co.uk

First published by
Vision Sports Publishing in 2008
This paperback edition published by Vision Sports Publishing in 2009

ISBN 13: 978-1905326-60-0

Editor: Jim Drewett
Copy editor: Ian Turner
Cover design: David Hicks
Proofreading: Clive Batty

Typeset by Palimpsest Book Production Limited,
Grangemouth, Stirlingshire

Printed in the UK by CPI Bookmarque, Croydon, CR0 4TD

A CIP catalogue record for this book
is available from the British Library

ARSÈNAL

THE MAKING OF A MODERN SUPERCLUB

To Sir Paul Fox for enriching my sporting life, and Tommy Mooney, a good man

Alex Fynn

For Jay and Frank

Kevin Whitcher

CONTENTS

REVIEWS FOR THE FIRST EDITION

"Many writers have tried to explain what makes Arsenal a football club that is so widely admired, even by its fiercest rivals. *Arsènal* comes closer than any previous book, offering a privileged insight into the club's fascinating blend of tradition and innovation and in particular the unique methods and motivations of its figurehead, Arsène Wenger."

Andrew Shields, sports editor, *Time Out*

"At last – a football book that reflects the spirit of the age. *Arsènal: The Making of a Modern Superclub* is a forensic account of the boardroom rumblings that have produced a world brand that sells property in London, beer in India and credit cards in Hong Kong. And 90 minutes of football on a Saturday… Its chief strength is in the depth of knowledge of Alex Fynn, a former director of Saatchi and Saatchi, and Kevin Whitcher, editor of the fanzine *The Gooner*, and the different angles from which they approach their club. This means that criticism of the club's stadium sponsorship, for example, is given in both financial terms – they could have 'protected the brand' and made a more lucrative deal – and emotional terms, namely that selling the name to Emirates is just one more way of managing the club as a business with scant regard for the fans or history."

Cameron Carter, *When Saturday Comes*

"The authors delve deep into the financial fog which currently envelops the Gunners, and attempt to predict Arsenal's likely trajectory over the next decade. The deep division in public opinion is neatly encapsulated by the book's two principled principals: Wenger and former vice-chairman David Dein… A fascinating read, which reveals the unpalatable economic realities of the modern game."

Jon Spurling, *FourFourTwo*

"Alex Fynn, recognised as 'the architect of the Premier League', has used his extensive contacts, coupled with fanzine editor Kevin Whitcher's passion and knowledge for all things Arsenal, to produce a superb book focusing on the club's transformation from a creaking domestic giant in need of a change of direction into a European powerhouse with a £200m turnover during Arsène Wenger's remarkable tenure.

"Fynn is one of the chosen few who does have access to Wenger, so his books, and his thoughts, make entertaining reading. While others have to tread carefully Fynn clearly does not and his objectivity and insights are a breath of fresh air.

"No other book does such an efficient job of covering every nook and cranny of the Wenger years. An excellent, well-crafted read."

Hampstead and Highgate Express

"Offers fascinating insights into how modern football really works."

Jewish Chronicle

"This appealing, high-class homage, not so much to the progressive London football club as to its visionary manager, father-confessor and spiritual counsellor, Frenchman Arsène Wenger......skilfully and devotedly makes out the case for his instant beatification. The liaison between Fynn, an admired and established writer, and Whitcher, editor of the club's watchdog fanzine, works seamlessly well; they understand both the ideal and the grit – the creative rhapsodic striving for beauty in a team game as well as the grim and grimy business of it."

Frank Keating, www.sportspages.com

"Between them what Alex Fynn and Kevin Whitcher don't know about Arsenal is probably not worth knowing and reading between the lines of this impressive volume there may still be more to come from this saga. What's for sure though is that this title covers a lot of background information not touched elsewhere.

"It ranges from David Dein's rise and fall together with both his deals and his clandestine dealings, kit and naming rights that are costing us dear, property speculation, superfluous stars, Wenger's ruthlessness, the rise and fall of Edelman, the scouting system, financial problems, transfer budgets, boardroom sackings, lock-downs, the advent of foreign investors, work stopping on the new stadium and much more all set against a background of Le Boss building three quite separate teams.

"It's a compelling read. Any Arsenal fan with an interest beyond just the football will enjoy it and many a Club Chairman and Director will find it seriously enlightening."

***Arsenal World* (arsenal-world.co.uk)**

"As a starting point, this book should definitely be read by all Arsenal fans; it is a clear and concisely explained journey that sits comfortably alongside the best books about the club.

***A Cultured Left Foot* (aculturedleftfoot.wordpress.com)**

ALEX FYNN AND KEVIN WHITCHER

Alex Fynn is a football consultant who has advised several clubs including Arsenal on media and marketing. *The Sunday Times* called him "the spiritual godfather of the Premier League." Kevin Whitcher is the editor of the highly influential Arsenal fanzine, *The Gooner*, and the author of *Gunning for the Double – the Story of Arsenal's 1997/98 Season*. The pair have previously collaborated on *The Glorious Game – Arsène Wenger, Arsenal and the Quest for Success*.

ALSO BY THE AUTHORS

By Alex Fynn and Kevin Whitcher
The Glorious Game

By Alex Fynn
The Secret Life of Football (with Lynton Guest)
Heroes and Villains (with Lynton Guest)
Out of Time (with Lynton Guest)
For Love or Money (with Lynton Guest)
Dream On (with H. Davidson)
Cantona on Cantona (with Eric Cantona)
The Great Divide (with Olivia Blair)

By Kevin Whitcher
Gunning for the Double – the Story of Arsenal's 1997/98 Season

ACKNOWLEDGEMENTS

It will be apparent from the text that many people contributed to this book. Of course without the assistance of a number of key individuals it could not possibly have been written. First and foremost amongst them are Arsène and Annie Wenger for permitting the periodic intrusions to their limited and precious family time and the invaluable insights provided.

Fulsome thanks are also due to Peter Hill-Wood and of course David Dein.

In addition to the key protagonists mentioned above there were a number of people, some of whom, like Tony Banfield and Alan Smith, are quoted directly, and others who wish to preserve their anonymity. We thank them all for their contributions.

Brian Dawes, Charlie Ashmore, Greville Waterman, Alex Phillips and Mel Goldberg read parts of the manuscript and their suggestions invariably improved it.

Simon Inglis, Antony Spencer, GGK, Ian Henry, Bernard Azulay, Alex Laidman, Michael Farmer, Howard Lamb and Marcia Milnes were terrific sources of information. *The Gooner* publisher Mike Francis is also owed thanks for his tolerance whilst Kevin's attention was occasionally diverted from the 'day job'.

Usually the publishers are thanked as a matter of course. In this instance this would do scant justice to the skill, commitment and consideration of both Jim Drewett and Toby Trotman. Without them there simply would not be a book. Ian Turner and Clive Batty certainly improved the writing and offered some valuable suggestions.

Back at home, thanks are due to Jay, Frank, Rhoda, Danielle and Tamara for their patience, understanding and on occasion specific help.

ACKNOWLEDGEMENTS FOR THE SECOND EDITION

With the addition of four new chapters covering the 2008/09 season, there are more thanks that have to be conveyed. To some of the main cast – Arsène Wenger, Peter Hill-Wood, David Dein, Antony Spencer and Alan Smith – it is a case of thanks again. To others, namely Ivan Gazidis, Ken Friar and Lady Nina Bracewell-Smith, an equal debt of gratitude is owed for the consideration and insights provided.

Alex Phillips, Brian Dawes and Mel Goldberg again read the manuscript and made invaluable suggestions. Ian Tanner and Ian Henry also provided insights.

Excellent sources of information for both the first edition of the book and this update included the following websites: *arseweb*, *arseblog*, *ANR*, *arsenal-world and arsenal.com*. Equally valuable sources comprised *The Gooner*, the *Deloitte Annual Review of Football Finance*, *l'Equipe*, *France Football* and the indefatigable duo of Xavier Rivoire and Philippe Auclair [aka Louis Philippe]. Thanks are also due to Arsenal TV.

Andrew Shields, Andrew Sherwood, Jem Maidment, Pat Mooney, Ian Corne and Richard Portugal admirably supported the hardback. And once again, the publishers Jim Drewett and Toby Trotman performed over and above the call of duty.

PREFACE

In 1996, the year of Arsène Wenger's arrival, Arsenal's turnover was £21 million. In 2007, after his eleventh season, it was over £200 million. Of course football has changed dramatically in the intervening period. The Premier League, Sky Television, the money, the pace of the game, the fitness of the players, the foreign stars, the money, the stadia, the fans, the kit, the merchandising, the marketing, even the rules and . . . the money. However, at Arsenal there have been more changes than almost anywhere else. Changes that are largely the result of one man's vision and philosophy. *Arsènal* recounts how the *'Boring Boring Arsenal'* of yesteryear became the great entertainers and super-club of today.

The seeds were sown with the arrival of David Dein in the boardroom in 1983 and continued apace – wondrous deeds on the field being the catalyst for dramatic change off it – taking his (temporary?) demise in 2007 in its stride. Ever onwards and upwards.

The second season in a new 21st century stadium which enabled the club to play catch up on Manchester United and overtake practically everyone else in Europe *en route* seemed a convenient time to take stock of events. With a young team and financial restrictions, expectations were that Arsenal would mark time in 2007/08. But once again Arsène Wenger confounded the sceptics.

Having revolutionised Arsenal, there is still a triumphant ending to be written. But in the meantime here is the story of how a few dedicated men and one unique individual transformed a patrician institution into one of the world's few genuine superclubs.

Alex Fynn and Kevin Whitcher, July 2008

PREFACE FOR SECOND EDITION

In the dying embers of the 1995/96 season two post-80th minute strikes from a pair of expensive Italian imports, David Platt and Dennis Bergkamp, secured a 2-1 victory over Bolton and sent Highbury into raptures at the prospect of a fifth place finish and UEFA Cup football. Thirteen years on, after the supposedly underwhelming return of Champions League and FA Cup semi-finals, Arsène Wenger's dispirited summing up of the 2008/09 campaign (that also secured a twelfth consecutive crack at the Champions League) was that "I have never worked so hard or been criticised so much."

How had events reached such an impasse? Here are four new chapters which attempt to explain, with the help of the key protagonists, the fissures in what was believed to be a love story without end and how – with both parties wary of what they might wish for – a reconciliation was effected. At least for the immediate future. Arsène Wenger's current contract expires in 2011.

Alex Fynn and Kevin Whitcher, July 2009

PROLOGUE
WHAT'S NEXT?

There is a fork in the road where Barnet Lane intersects with Totteridge Lane in north London. Habitually, the silver Mercedes bears left past the church heading for home a few hundred yards further on. Today, though, the driver takes the slip road on the right towards Mill Hill and a couple of minutes later pulls into the driveway of his destination.

Since he heard the sensational news that April afternoon, he has been turning over in his mind the possible implications, and is apprehensive as to what the next few minutes might bring.

After an affectionate greeting between two old friends, Arsène Wenger comes straight to the point. "Do you want me to resign?" he asks.

David Dein is still reeling from his, in his own words, "brutal" dismissal earlier in the day – out of the blue he had been handed a letter terminating his directorship at the club he loved after 24 years. Whilst foe and friend alike were dumbfounded by the abruptness of the sacking, in the words of one of the latter, "David was an accident waiting to happen." Emboldened as ever by the belief which transformed itself into a mantra over the years, to justify contentious decisions – "I would never do anything to harm Arsenal: I would always act in Arsenal's interest" – he had walked a tightrope ever since the move from Highbury had been prioritised over team building.

Stepping outside his specific responsibility for the playing side, his increasingly independent actions had brought him into conflict with the rest of the board. Haunted by the spectre of being overwhelmed by the huge spending power of Chelsea, Manchester United and Liverpool and his European rivals, especially Real Madrid, Barcelona, Milan and Internazionale, he was determined to ensure that Arsène Wenger had a comparable war chest. Unfortunately, his search for a wealthy benefactor, especially his clandestine wooing of the American sports entrepreneur, Stan Kroenke, was an irrevocable step too far for his colleagues. His Arsenal role had enabled him to secure an executive seat at the FA, UEFA and G14 and in his favour he encompassed the broader view that those responsibilities entailed. To the regret of the football authorities, at home and abroad, if not his fellow Arsenal directors, he was now yesterday's man. And to add to the ignominy, like a miscreant he had been forced to clear his desk and receive an escort from the Highbury House office building adjacent to the Emirates Stadium.

"No," Dein replied to Wenger's suggestion that he might resign, "I don't think that would be in the best interests of Arsenal."

It was the answer Wenger must have been hoping for. Only a few weeks before, he and his wife, Annie, had decided to stay in London (though in fact it would be some months before he would eventually get round to renewing his contract) and had settled on the new school where their daughter, Léa, would begin her secondary education. Besides, he could sense a conclusion to the most exasperating time of his Arsenal tenure. Never allowing himself to luxuriate in the euphoria of victory, it was always onwards and upwards to meet the next challenge. For the fact that, despite having the personnel capable of doing so, Arsenal had never retained the Premiership title or even once won the Champions League, Wenger blamed himself. He felt he had failed; he had certainly failed to live up to his own high expectations.

He was unconcerned about leaving a legacy. Certainly, titles and cups had been won with panache and the innovative training ground and superb playing facilities in the new stadium had been developed according to his precise specifications. But he regarded them only as a means to an end – to facilitate the chances of perpetuating the winning habit and to do so with a flourish. What mattered most was today, the next match, this season.

Paradoxically, limited in how much he could spend on wages and transfers, Wenger had been forced to concentrate on what he enjoyed above all about his job – finding and developing young talent. Now, as the 2007/08 season beckoned, anticipated revenue from his club's new home, for the first time in over two years, would give him money to sprinkle on a star or two to add to the precocious squad he had assembled.

The timing appeared propitious. He could only be optimistic, certain that the new season would see definite progress with the following campaign bringing probable fulfilment. If he left now, there would always be the nagging doubt of what might have been.

Relieved and reassured, he could now concentrate on his mission. There was work to be done and a genuinely exciting future on the horizon. Looking ahead, he had the feeling the best was yet to come.

CHAPTER ONE
CHANGE OF HEART

"Dead money", Arsenal chairman Peter Hill-Wood's renowned caustic comment about David Dein's £292,000 purchase of over 1,600 unissued shares in Arsenal Football Club in 1983, proved wildly inaccurate when, in 2007, Dein sold his shareholding (at the time consisting of less than the 16.6% stake he'd bought initially) for £75 million to Red and White Holdings Ltd. The 1983 transaction valued the club at a mere £1.8 million, even after several £1 million transfers had been undertaken, indicating the negligible importance that was then ascribed to a club's assets apart from the players. And in compiling a fortune so large that it could pay for every ticket (at an average price of over £40) for every spectator to see all of Arsenal's home matches for the duration of a season, by the time he sold, Dein had been part of a transformation in English football both on and off the field, and he felt much of it was due to his own contribution.

Yet back in the early 1980s, Dein, a successful entrepreneur through his commodity business, was just another Arsenal fan, albeit an affluent one. Living in Totteridge, both Graham Rix and Tony Woodcock were neighbours and friends, and he and wife Barbara often enjoyed socialising with them. It was a different story watching from the directors' box at a time of decline for the team. Despite three FA Cup Finals, with one outright win between 1978 and 1980, and a European Cup Winners Cup Final, there had been scant success in the league, a poor return for a side filled with gifted personnel. Moreover, in 1980 and 1981, Liam Brady and Frank Stapleton were sold to Juventus and Manchester United respectively, and although star names such as Woodcock and Charlie Nicholas were brought in to replace the former idols, the team still failed to mount a challenge for the title. Dein bought into the club at a time when English football was enduring a lengthy and tortuous trip to rock bottom, underlined by the deaths of 39 Juventus supporters as a result of trouble involving Liverpool fans before the 1985 European Cup Final in Brussels, and the subsequent ban on English clubs from UEFA's competitions for five seasons which cast a long shadow over the game.

In hindsight, one can appreciate Hill-Wood's short-term view of Dein's investment. Dein, however, was intoxicated with the increased involvement his new found status brought. His rise mirrored that of another self-made entrepreneur, property developer Irving Scholar, who took over Tottenham Hotspur in 1982. Both he and Dein had, as younger men, played in the same Sunday league, albeit for different teams, and it was a quirk that, as grammar school boys from the same part of north west London moving in the same circles, they did not come across each other. They quickly became friends once both were effectively running the clubs they loved.

There was a nice irony in their accession as successful young Jewish businessmen that they should have secured key roles as both Arsenal and Tottenham – their large numbers of Jewish fans notwithstanding – epitomised the conservative, ageist and reactionary administrations so prevalent throughout English football at that time. Akin to golf clubs, perhaps Arsenal operated a quota system on how many 'outsiders' they would allow into their inner sanctum, whilst

Tottenham had no choice in the matter, the old regime having been swept aside by a new breed who just happened to be smarter, youthful and Jewish.

From the moment Irving Scholar took over at Tottenham, he set about creating an enterprise that could fund the expensive acquisitions he felt exemplified their swashbuckling image. (He characterised his club and compared them to their greatest rivals, saying, "Whilst Arsenal would spend big money on a defender, Tottenham would spend twice as much on a forward.")

A groundbreaking merchandising business was created at White Hart Lane and Spurs floated as a plc in 1985, but not before manager Keith Burkinshaw, having accumulated two FA Cups and a UEFA Cup, walked away with the acerbic comment "There used to be a football club over there." Burkinshaw's prescient criticism proved to be accurate as Tottenham diversified into non-football areas which, instead of providing new revenue opportunities, accumulated debts that compounded the overspending on the rebuilt East Stand, eventually forcing Scholar to sell to Alan Sugar and Terry Venables in 1991. Arguably, to this date Tottenham are still struggling to achieve the success and status they acquired under Burkinshaw's stewardship.

Seeing this turn of events across town must have encouraged Dein to become more proactive. With his share purchase in 1983, he had been invited onto the board in return for the amount by which his outlay had boosted the club's coffers. One of his initial acts was to agitate for the dismissal of then manager Terry Neill, a situation Brian Clough had anticipated. Dein had been introduced to Clough by Ken Friar, the club secretary, when Nottingham Forest were the opponents at Highbury as "our new director". "Now don't you go making trouble for your manager, young man", was Clough's immediate and typical response.

It may have been an era when Bob Paisley's Liverpool were the dominating force in England and Europe, but both

Nottingham Forest and Aston Villa had shown that the Football League Championship, and indeed the European Cup, were not beyond the reach of a run-of-the-mill First Division club. Smaller than Arsenal in terms of resources, they had built successful teams due to the managerial abilities of the exceptional Brian Clough and Ron Saunders respectively. Arsenal had an excellent cup record, but in the early 1980s never challenged for the league. Terry Neill had been given the funds to buy the best but had by and large failed to produce a team that equalled the sum of its parts. When Brady and Stapleton moved on, both intimated that they were leaving for bigger clubs. Certainly, despite the rich history, there was a feeling that Arsenal were a club marking time, and perhaps had never fully recovered from the 1979/80 season that saw them play 70 matches and reach two cup finals, yet fail in both and miss out on European qualification as well.

Matters came to a head with a League Cup defeat at home to Walsall, two divisions below Arsenal, at the end of November 1983. Less than three weeks later, after two subsequent Division One losses, Neill was given his cards. The Arsenal board were historically very reluctant to dismiss managers (there had been just eleven in 60 years, two of whom had died in the post). But the manager probably knew his time was up when, shortly before the Walsall defeat, he admitted, "The players don't seem to know what it is to hunger for goals and glory. Some days I think they just want to pick up their money and go home. But we'll finish in the top six again this season. Whether or not I'll be around to see it is another matter!"

Increasingly, there were supporter protests on matchdays, demanding Neill's sacking. And Dein, so recently one of their number, empathised with the fans and argued for a change in the manager's office. "I am not a hatchet man," he said later in relation to Neill's departure, "but I like to think of myself as an action man. And where surgery was needed, I was prepared to recommend it." Neill had been concerned about the new director's relationship with the players, whilst Dein was obsessed about the club's position in the table. However, if, as Neill said, the players were content to just go through the motions, the inability to motivate them was down to him. Dein could have picked this feeling up from his mates in the squad, even if they felt the nature of their association had changed somewhat now that he was effectively one of their employers rather than a mere fan with whom they could socialise.

At the time Dein stated that Neill "was not the right person to lead us into the next decade." And despite Dein's role in his sacking, Terry Neill is today very generous about him. A regular media pundit when Arsenal are in the spotlight, Neill readily praises his erstwhile antagonist for the part he played in the transformation of the club that has occurred since he left. Moreover, there was little for the former manager to feel bitter about. The reason the players were not performing for him was unrelated to who was on the board. In his own words before the Walsall debacle, he had accepted that he had done as much as he could. The task for any manager who had known success (and four cup finals in four years at the end of the 1970s was no mean feat at a time when competition was more widespread than it is today) was to renew his resources, changing the key components before they passed their sell-by-date. Thus the Liverpool team that Bob Paisley led to European Cup glory in 1977 was very different to the one that won the championship in his final season in 1983. In the intervening years, players came and went, but the bandwagon rolled on. Retiring six months before Neill was sacked, Paisley could count 12 major trophies in a reign of similar duration to Neill's at Arsenal. One FA Cup trophy was scant return for all those years.

Neill had survived for so long because of the traditionalist view from the boardroom that regarded him as one of their own, with almost 20 years' loyal service as player, captain and manager. Besides, he was a good egg. Dein would come to fill an executive vacuum that existed at the club, in the process coming into conflict with club secretary Ken Friar, a more cautious individual by nature, who had effectively become part of the furniture, having worked his way up through the ranks since starting out in the post room as a teenager.

Dein's background was far more cut and thrust. The family business began in Shepherd's Bush Market importing exotic fruit and vegetables from the Caribbean. From these humble origins, Dein oversaw its transformation into a commodity-broking company with offices in Pall Mall. However, when he joined the Arsenal board, his enthusiasm for his business waned somewhat, in contrast to his new life at the football club that his wife has described as being akin to taking a mistress. Although Dein was ambitious enough to see the post of vice-chairman created especially for him in January 1984, the change in the boardroom didn't initially seem to beneficially affect the playing side.

It would be another two and a half seasons after Neill's exit before the new vice-chairman would begin to see real potential emerge. Don Howe – Neill's number two and the coach of the 1970/71 double side under Bertie Mee – was promoted to the post of manager, yet no significant improvement was seen as Arsenal finished sixth, followed by a fall to seventh by May 1985. During the following season, then Barcelona manager Terry Venables was sounded out about coming to Highbury.

Venables had won the Spanish league during his first season and was in the midst of a campaign that would end with a defeat on penalties in the European Cup Final. He was hot managerial property and exemplified the kind of sea change that Dein felt was imperative if the club was to show any sense of ambition. Howe got wind of what was going on and resigned in March 1986. He had earned a reputation as an excellent coach, but never really convinced as a top class manager despite subsequently carrying out the role at several clubs. Venables himself rejected the possibility of the post because he objected to it being offered behind Howe's back (and the respect he had for Howe was subsequently demonstrated when the latter became part of the England set-up when Venables was appointed national team coach in 1994). Howe's precipitous departure at least made it easier for the board. Dein later admitted, "We were having second thoughts about the long-term viability of Don Howe. He found himself in an invidious position and resigned."

So whilst chief scout Steve Burtenshaw took over as caretaker manager for the remainder of a season that saw the club finish in seventh position once again, Dein was on the hunt for a man who could actually change the culture of mediocrity at the club. It was not the only change he intended to effect. The name of Arsenal was still box office despite a solitary trophy since 1971, and Dein intended to ensure that the club profited financially as a result. In his belief that what was good for Arsenal was also good for English football he widened the scope of his ambition. There was an opportunity, he felt, to increase the potential revenue the game could earn, but also to steer such increased income towards the clubs that were most responsible for earning it. He believed the First Division was subsidising the supporting acts lower down on the Football League ladder to an unjustified degree.

In 1985 Dein was elected to the Football League Management Committee (FLMC), the only member who was not the chairman of a football club, even if in reality he was now the principal director at Arsenal. "I don't know why he's bothering with all the football politics," said Peter Hill-Wood at the time, reflecting what many now see as a further example of the short-sighted attitude of a board that was in dire need of a shake-up. Ironically, Hill-Wood would have been a more obvious candidate for the FMLC had he been interested, representing old money, the establishment and a *laissez-faire* attitude that had become synonymous with Arsenal's methods over the years. Now, though, Dein would stir up a hornets' nest in his attempts to improve the club's lot.

With Everton chairman Philip Carter, he was mandated by the FLMC to look after the television negotiations. Following the tragedies of Birmingham, Bradford and Heysel (within the space of less than three weeks) and the unforgivable loss of supporters' lives, the stock of English football had fallen so low that both ITV and the BBC were indifferent to its questionable attractions. Absent from the television screens for the first half of the 1985/86 season, league football returned only when a derisory fire-sale offer was accepted from the two broadcasters: £1.3million for the rest of the season and £6.2 million for the following two seasons. As that deal approached an end, in alliance with the other of the 'Big Five' clubs – Manchester United, Tottenham and Liverpool – Dein and Carter courted ITV.

In 1988, British Satellite Broadcasting (BSB) was preparing to launch and needed exclusive content. It was prepared to raise the rights fees for live football, providing competition for the BBC and ITV for the first time. Greg Dyke had become chairman of ITV Sport and, as a result of Irving Scholar's persistent probing at a lunch with the Big Five representatives, admitted to the Tottenham chairman that the BBC and ITV had previously worked as a cartel to hold down prices for broadcasting rights artificially. This was music to Dein's ears. "I wanted to pinch the football rights from BSB's grasp," recalled Dyke, "and he [Dein] might be able to deliver them.

He in turn wanted more money for his club and the other big clubs and I could afford to pay it."

Dyke's policy was to "go direct to the Big Five clubs of the day and offer them a minimum of a million pounds a year each for the exclusive right to broadcast their home matches. This was more than any of them had received in the past." Moreover, up to then, fees to the Football League were more evenly spread and even filtered down to encompass the lowest division. As far as Dyke was concerned, "The Football League could sell the rest of the First Division matches to whomever they wanted, but of course without the big clubs' home games, they were worth much less."

With support from Tottenham, Manchester United and Liverpool, Dein and Carter agreed to a deal which would see their five clubs do very nicely, albeit at the expense of the top flight's lesser lights as well as those in the divisions below. For £11 million a year, rising to £18 million after three years, ITV had bought the rights to show 21 live matches, as well as highlights from any other fixture in the league if they desired, as well as League Cup coverage. The rest of the league, effectively powerless with the Big Five not prepared to contemplate any alternative course of action, fell in line, with the consolation that they would also be financially better off as a result of the settlement, albeit as second-class citizens. But there was obvious indignation at the way that Dein and Carter had ensured that the Big Five were the primary beneficiaries, and both men were unsurprisingly booted off the FLMC as a consequence.

It was a set of circumstances that would have analogous repercussions almost 20 years later. On both occasions, those who felt Dein had betrayed their trust removed him from office. In 1988 he acted as he did in the belief he was serving the interests of both his club and the game in general, but was at the same time working independently of those he supposedly represented. He was a man wearing two hats – one for Arsenal and another for the Football League. He felt he had served both parties well and saw no conflict of interest. Indeed, his parting shot revealed the resentment he felt. "What other employer," he asked, "fires a man who has just brought him £44 million?"

By the time the deal was struck, Arsenal had consolidated their status as one of the Big Five through two successive seasons of progress under new manager George Graham. As a former Gunner with a good managerial apprenticeship at Millwall, he was an obvious candidate for the job. There was a vogue at the big clubs for recruiting former players as managers – Howard Kendall had done very well at Everton, emulated across Stanley Park by Liverpool's Kenny Dalglish. In a BBC *Football Focus* piece on Graham in 1986, filmed in his office at Millwall, clearly visible on the shelf behind him were books on Arsenal and *The Good Food Guide*, an indication of his tastes, perhaps even his priorities. Certainly here was a man David Dein could relate to. In the frame for pulling the trigger on Terry Neill, Dein never received the same (positive) public exposure for promoting George Graham's credentials with his co-directors.

Once at Arsenal, the new man was fortunate to inherit a very promising group of players who were emerging from the club's youth system. Reassured, and immediately putting into practice Brian Clough's dictum "in this business, you've got to be a dictator or you haven't got a chance", Graham felt free to dispose of many of the senior players who he felt might not be so malleable to his *modus operandi*. So Paul Mariner and Tony Woodcock were released before a ball had even been kicked in anger, and over the course of his first two seasons, Viv Anderson, Charlie Nicholas and Graham Rix were also shown the exit door. Captain Kenny Sansom was the last major casualty, sold against his will to Newcastle at the beginning of the momentous 1988/89 season, having been stripped of the captaincy midway through the previous campaign. (His replacement as skipper, Tony Adams, would hang on to the armband until his retirement in 2002). These were men who had been around long enough not to respond to the strict discipline that Graham wanted to instil as the best way of getting a positive response from his charges, described by defender Lee Dixon as "a sergeant-major approach to management".

When it came to contracts, Graham's toughness as a negotiator was soon established. A young Martin Keown was one stubborn individual who met his match when he held out for better terms and found himself sold to Aston Villa. Graham later showed the folly of his intransigence by re-signing Keown in 1992 on terms that made the disparity in their 1986 dealings look paltry, although it did establish a precedent. Striker Alan Smith, who Graham recruited from Leicester in 1987, recalls Graham's negotiating technique, "He liked to keep a ceiling on things which he didn't like to go over. He'd say, 'Tony Adams is on that so I'm not giving you any more.'" The bottom line though was that Graham felt he should be the top earner as he had the ultimate responsibility. "He always wanted to be on more money than the players and so as long as he was, he would be happy," says Smith. From the receiving end, Paul Merson described the manager's way of working: "It was pointless having an agent. He used to come in and say 'Right, this is what you're getting, here's your new contract. If you don't like it, see you later.'"

But it was not only the players who were affected by Graham's methods. David Dein, despite his power at the club, was still starry-eyed, delighted to be working alongside a former hero. In his twenties he had supported the side that won the 1970 Fairs Cup followed by the domestic league and cup double in 1971, of which George Graham was an integral part. But although he had helped to bring Graham back home, Dein increasingly found himself marginalised in the day-to-day dealings with the players that he had previously enjoyed, as Graham took it upon himself to deal with the contract negotiations and transfers, aided by coaching staff such as Steve Burtenshaw and Theo Foley who loyally backed up his every move. Dein reluctantly accepted the change, admitting, "I pride myself on being a good negotiator, but George has got me knocked into a cocked hat." His admiration for Graham was such that it may have impaired his judgement. When Graham called, Dein – according to colleagues – invariably responded, sometimes putting aside commercial decisions in order to involve himself with the playing side. Dein's willingness to help, however, did not endear him to Graham, who remains dismissive about the alliance between Wenger and Dein which he intimates allowed Dein "to play with his toys" in a manner you can be sure he would never have stood for.

An incident in February 1988 after Graham had been in the manager's seat for less than two years, pointed up the reality of the relationship. At the end of a press conference to promote the forthcoming friendly between Arsenal and the French national team, a friend of David Dein's and a director of the Saatchi & Saatchi advertising agency who had produced a radio campaign to promote the match on Arsenal's behalf, asked for a lift back into the West End. "Certainly," replied Dein "but I am taking George", who was just chatting to some journalists on the other side of the room. After a few minutes chit chat, Dein's friend said, "Come on David, let's go". "I can't interrupt him," said Dein. "Of course you can," said his friend. "You want to go. I want to go. He's only talking to some hacks. Tell him we're going." Dein demurred. "Ok then, I'm going to", said his friend.

So the man from Saatchi & Saatchi walked over to Graham

and said, "Apologies for interrupting Mr Graham, but it's time to go and your chauffeur is getting impatient." Whereupon Graham looked over at Dein and then without a word to either proceeded to turn his back on both Dein and the interloper to resume his conversation. How long Graham kept the vice-chairman kicking his heels is not known as Dein's friend left immediately to make his own way back to his office.

It was a stance Graham could get away with as long as he was successful, the one thing David Dein prioritised above anything else, even his personal pride. "Every time I get up in the morning and look in the mirror to shave," he said, "I see implanted on my forehead the words 'Get a winning team'."

By the end of the 1980s, Arsenal had many more options, with a flair midfield including home-grown players such as Paul Davis, David Rocastle and Michael Thomas augmented by solidity at the back. Using his knowledge of the lower divisions from his days at Millwall, Graham had been able to pick up some bargain buys that would serve the club well for years to come: Lee Dixon, Steve Bould and Nigel Winterburn, although the latter had been promoted with Wimbledon so had some top-flight experience. Arsenal's first-team squad was a step up for all of them. Even better, the mix of home-grown and cheap purchases did not command superstar wages, allowing the manager to run a tight ship. In a sense, though, Graham was making a rod for his own back, as the board, seeing what could be achieved on a modest budget, sometimes refused to provide funds when he did want to make a noteworthy signing, such as Tony Cottee from West Ham. This concept of aiming for success on the cheap resounds at the club to this day, in spite of all that has changed. It is to Graham's enormous credit then that in 1989 he wrested the league title from Liverpool.

Part of the reason that Arsenal pipped Liverpool to the title in 1989 was an event that had huge ramifications for the future of the game in England. The Hillsborough disaster that saw 96 Liverpool fans crushed to death on the occasion of an FA Cup semi-final postponed Liverpool's fixtures three weeks, with the club's players attending numerous funerals. When football resumed, the team went on an unbeaten run – including the FA Cup Final against Everton six days before facing Arsenal at Anfield in the (delayed) final league match of the season. Whether or not the players were drained from their experiences is difficult to say, but with the visitors requiring a 2–0 victory to win the title, Liverpool seemed to play within themselves, and ultimately conceded the League Championship trophy to George Graham's team through goals by Alan Smith and, sensationally in the last minute, Michael Thomas.

The only Arsenal matches David Dein voluntarily doesn't attend are those that occur during his annual winter break overseas "to recharge my batteries". In the 1980s he often stayed at his wife Barbara's family home in Florida. A keen student of American sport, he would go to see NFL games whenever possible and it was here that he first became aware of the importance and potential of the corporate market. Closer to home, Manchester United, Tottenham Hotspur and Aston Villa had paved the way in showing how executive boxes could not only produce a healthy new revenue stream but in so doing subsidise ticket prices in other areas of the ground. All very well in theory, but in practice the cost of a seat at Tottenham has always been amongst the most expensive in the top division.

Magnificent a stadium as Highbury was, hemmed in by the gardens and houses backing onto the stands, the possibilities for expansion were restricted. Additionally, the art deco facade of the East Stand was a listed building. There could have been re-construction, but it would have been a difficult task to find accommodation for boxes without alienating many of the die-hard season ticket holders. Instrumental in putting a roof on the Clock End and 53 executive boxes above it in January 1989, had Dein known what would happen later that season – namely the Hillsborough disaster and in the wake of it the Taylor Report advocating making stadiums all-seater – he might have instead considered a double-decker stand with seats above and below the executive boxes, or at least filled in the corners.

In theory, to maximise potential earnings executive boxes should have the best views in the stadium. Of course the Clock End boxholders could watch the game from a good height and get some perspective on the play, but they were still behind a goal. In an attempt to make good this deficiency, corporate packages that included seats in the West Upper were offered. Clients would dine in the Clock End complex of which the hospitality boxes were just one part. Behind the new boxes and out of sight of the pitch were an indoor five-a-side hall, a suite which was used as a pre-match restaurant and doubled up as the players' bar after the game, as well as administrative offices.

The new Clock End was officially unveiled before the Arsenal v Tottenham match, three months before Hillsborough. Once completed, the only real change that could be made was the conversion of the terracing into ad hoc seating to comply with the new legislation. There was no room to place further seating above the boxes, thereby capping Arsenal's capacity, an insoluble problem that eventually led to the abandonment of Highbury when, with more foresight, it could have accommodated a significantly larger number than the 38,500 who were ultimately able to fit in. Of more pressing concern was the fact that Arsenal were falling behind other clubs with lower attendances whose stadium improvements, especially for the corporate customer, produced a much higher per capita income than Highbury.

After making a disappointing defence of their title, Arsenal were not widely tipped to win anything in 1990/91. Yet after an amazing ride that saw them come from eight points behind Liverpool, they won the championship by a street. If two points had not been deducted for their part in a scuffle against Manchester United they would have been nine points clear at the finish, reflecting then Crystal Palace manager Steve Coppell's view that "in terms of coaching, discipline and organisation, they are the best team in the First Division". Although they registered an impressive 74 goals, it was the solidity of the backline that was most remarkable, conceding a meagre 18 times over the course of the campaign and losing only once. Despite the frustrated expectations of the previous season – after the leading the table at Christmas, they ultimately finished fourth – Graham had by and large retained faith in the existing squad, merely strengthening it with the addition of Anders Limpar, Andy Linighan and David Seaman, later augmented by further products of the youth team factory, such as Kevin Campbell and David Hillier. (Of the 16 players who won Championship medals in 1990/91, no fewer than half had emerged from the youth team, a staggering accomplishment unmatched since the days of Matt Busby at Manchester United more than 30 years before.) How times have changed – *plus ça change, plus c'est la difference*, as Arsène Wenger might comment.

Thus Graham was able to devise a playing strategy based on consistency in both selection and performance. "The beauty about being consistent," he reflected, " is that even when you have achieved it, the desire for it has still got to be there. There are not many footballers who have achieved that year in year out. We've done it over the year. Now we have to do it over the years." But it was not to be, and after two titles in three years the level of consistency, and with it league success, dropped sharply away.

As one Dein favourite, Anders Limpar, fell from grace, another emerged to replace him. (The portents were not propitious when Graham told Limpar that his lack of goals "has got nothing to do with your physical make-up, it's your mental make-up. You've got to put yourself in goal scoring positions" – a harsh criticism for a midfield player who scored 11 goals from 34 appearances in 1990/91.) A long-time admirer of Ian Wright, Dein held Crystal Palace's Chairman, Ron Noades, to his promise of first refusal if the south London club ever considered cashing in on their prime asset and thus paved the way for the player to cross town early in the 1991/92 season despite the manager already being able to field Alan Smith, Kevin Campbell, Paul Merson and Limpar in the same line-up.

The ensuing campaign was a watershed in Graham's tenure. Wright was ineligible to play in the European Cup due to the timing of his transfer, and a naive Arsenal side were taught a lesson by Sven Göran-Eriksson's Benfica at Highbury that resulted in their elimination from the competition in the club's first appearance since their debut campaign in 1971/72. Graham took on board what he had witnessed and prioritised muscle and brawn. "I love one-nil wins," he admitted to Tottenham director Douglas Alexiou.

Defending with determination and limited in ambition whilst lacking their hitherto exemplary consistency meant that, whilst never challenging in the league, Arsenal usually rose to the big occasion and became very difficult to beat in cup ties, with long balls to the lightning-fast Ian Wright often the most favoured tactic. Michael Thomas and David Rocastle were sold in the summers of 1991 and 1992 respectively, whilst Paul Davis also became surplus to requirements. Creativity had slipped down to the bottom of Graham's list of priorities for good. The flirtation was over. He was no longer prepared to pander to creative players; his ungenerous treatment of David Ginola at Tottenham a few years later was no surprise to any Limpar fan. What Graham wanted above all was work rate and he now preferred the likes of David Hillier and Danish import John Jensen as his central midfield, stolid rather than solid, with little flair and even fewer goals. Paul Merson summarised his attitude to his team as a case of "if you weren't working hard, you weren't playing" and thus creative players became something of a luxury, an irony for a manager nicknamed 'Stroller' in his playing days. It was a return to the time of 'boring, boring Arsenal', which first emerged during Billy Wright's uninspiring spell a quarter of a century before (though for Arsenal's critics they would have felt the tag most apt for the 1970/71 team who, in their view, won the title in a manner completely devoid of style). And yet under Graham it was tolerated because of the cups that were won. An FA and League Cup double in 1993 was followed by a European Cup Winners' Cup triumph a year later, but the never-say-die resilience in the knockout competitions could not sustain the week-in, week-out demands of the league and Arsenal never seriously competed again for the title under Graham after 1991. He was now the authoritarian who failed to get the best out of his players on a habitual basis. Alan Smith reflected, "He was the horrible boss who made us do horrible things but there was certainly respect there. It was only really towards the end when we'd been together too long, he was growing frustrated and we'd heard it all before, that it became really tiresome. But I would say that from 1987 till '92 it was hard work but enjoyable as we had our fair share of laughs in training."

As the players were securing their second title under Graham, the board made plans for a new North Bank stand to comply with the Taylor Report. The notion of simply placing seats on the existing terracing (the plan for the Clock End) was rejected in favour of a two-tier stand that would cost a then phenomenal £22.5 million. The plans were unveiled just as Arsenal were in the process of winning their 1991 title, a time when (with standing capacity reduced post-Hillsborough as a temporary safety measure before stadiums could be converted) the season's concluding home fixtures were all-ticket affairs, as opposed to the customary practice of queuing up and paying on the day. The club announced that season tickets for the new all-seater stand could only be purchased if fans were willing to pay either £1,500 or £1,100 for an 'Arsenal Bond'. In theory it was an imaginative way of raising the finance and was underwritten by the Royal Bank of Scotland. And yet it created a furore. Fans were used to paying £5 a match for a place on the terracing and so understandably there was a huge resentment that the only way they could remain on the North Bank was by paying over £1,000 for the right to buy a season ticket. It was bad enough that they no longer had the right to stand, but this was adding insult to injury.

As the public face of the scheme David Dein copped most of the flak, and there was a lot of it flying around. The fanzine *1–0 Down, 2–1 Up* even went as far as proposing that bricks from the North Stand should be thrown through the window of Dein's Bentley, a move that resulted in someone doing just that when he parked near a Greek restaurant in Bounds Green. Unsurprisingly this led to the threat of legal action against the fanzine and an out-of-court settlement and a subsequent front-cover apology in what *1-0 Down* termed a 'libel special' issue.

Given that the corporate boxes in the Clock End had proved popular, and with Dein's sense of ambition for the club, it was something of a mystery as to why boxes were not integrated into the new stand. At least their exclusion did not mean a reduction in the potential capacity, the structure creating 12,500 places in comparison to the mere 6,000 that would be provided by the Clock End, which simply had seats grafted onto the terracing the following season, despite the numerous restricted sightlines it produced. However, many of the bonds were not sold, leaving the Royal Bank of Scotland to pick up a large portion of the building costs. Price rises for the new bondholders' season tickets were pegged to the rate of inflation for ten years, though, and as the price of admission rose by leaps and bounds in the decade to 2003 those who did buy a bond turned out to have landed a bargain. When Arsenal were at last able to charge the market price, the cost of a bondholder's season ticket was tripled at the first opportunity.

Still, Arsenal's big move forward at the dawn of a new era was only a new stand. Having dethroned Liverpool, into the vacuum stepped Manchester United, showing all the other clubs a clean pair of heels as they quickly demonstrated that having the best team facilitated their ascent to the status of the biggest, the richest and the most profitable club in the world. Their success on the field provided the foundations for a commercial empire the like of which the world of football had never known before. And where Manchester United went, others were quick to try to follow. But Arsenal lagged behind, seemingly ill at ease in this new commercial milieu. They appeared to know their price but not their true value. And in charge of commercial matters with very little marketing experience, David Dein exemplified this attitude. As a successful salesman by day and card player and gambler by night, he had innate confidence in his own ability to strike the best deal. And he was invariably successful – up to a point.

Anxious to maintain control and to show the board good returns as a result of his own efforts, he found delegation a difficult art. Although he has denied this, he also did not easily accept the advice readily forthcoming from friends and associates alike. So when handling Arsenal's European competitions broadcasting rights (at this time there was no collective selling and the clubs managed their own rights), he favoured a tendering process, going with the highest bidder on the assumption he was getting the best market value. If he had worked with a rights specialist, the club in all likelihood would have secured a better deal but then he wouldn't have appeared as *the* rights expert to a board who didn't have a deep knowledge of the subject. But to be fair to Dein, he traded on Arsenal's status as a desirable addition to any sports agency's portfolio of clients. Indeed so keen were the German agency UFA to represent Arsenal that they guaranteed them the huge sum for the time of £1 million for their broadcasting rights in the 1991/92 European Cup. This backfired spectacularly for UFA when the English champions lost to Benfica in the second-round, and it was obliged to hand over a seven-figure rights fee for a pair of relatively low-profile ties.

In charge of the belated launch and development of the first Arsenal shop of any real substance at Finsbury Park station, Dein didn't make full use of the retail experience of a long-time friend who ran a well-known men's outfitter. "He doesn't readily take advice though he thinks he does," said his friend more in sorrow than in anger, feeling he could have done more to help Dein smooth out the inevitable wrinkles of a new retail business.

In the 1980s, neighbours Tottenham had rebuilt their East and West Stands, of which their corporate boxes were an integral part. It made Arsenal's decision not to incorporate them in the redeveloped North Bank look all the more bizarre. If over 100 boxes could be filled at White Hart Lane surely there should have been no problem in matching that at Highbury, a venue closer to the city, offering a greater number of event-like fixtures, based on the comparative success and the aggressive marketing of the Premier League. The new North Bank stand might have been an impressive structure compared with the bland ones being erected elsewhere but it was not even maximising its season-ticket revenue, as prices of the bondholder's seats were – allowing for inflation – held down for a decade whilst giving no opportunity to milk what would become a hungry hospitality market in the years that followed. It was no surprise then that as late as 1997 – five years into the life of the Premier League – Arsenal's turnover was smaller than Tottenham's, lagged behind that of Liverpool and Newcastle, and was less than a third of that of Manchester United. It was taking much longer than Dein envisaged when he was one of the prime agitators of the breakaway league for Arsenal to sit in their (in his view) rightful place at the top of the pile.

In the mid 1980s, Dein had supported Irving Scholar's advocacy which brought about the reduction in the size of the First Division to 20 clubs, the introduction of play-offs and most significantly the abolition of gate sharing, which meant the big pay days for smaller clubs became a thing of the past. By the time the FA's endorsement allowed the old First Division to break away and to create the Premier League it was back to 22 clubs, much to Dein's distaste. Only Arsenal, Manchester United and Tottenham Hotspur voted against the increase. But the die was cast.

As his implacable adversary Chelsea chairman Ken Bates put it, "David Dein was so over the moon at getting his little Premier League, he couldn't understand why Ken Bates was so supportive. We got a few things in there . . . he's only now beginning to realise what hit him." And enshrined in the constitution was one club one vote, which led irrevocably to the award of the live television contract for the new league to BSkyB, Rupert Murdoch's television arm having gathered in BSB to become the only satellite option for football. As Bates explained, "The clubs did the Sky deal [the vote was 14–6 with, amazingly, two abstentions] because we were determined to smash the Big Five dominance and we were determined to get a fair share of the money . . . if the ITV deal had gone ahead, the Big Five clubs would have been perpetuated." Outmanoeuvred, David Dein was mortified at the turn of events: " It will be seen as a black day for football . . . it was like amateur night . . . the way it was presented, the way it was negotiated beforehand and the way it was subsequently implemented . . . how can you create heroes on a minority channel?"

Further, as one of the chosen few who had previously received preferential treatment from ITV, Arsenal were not – despite all the hype of the new deal – materially better off. Compared to their sizeable share of the £18 million at stake for the last year of the ITV contract, the more democratic allocation of broadcasting funds for the member clubs of the new league (50% equally divided, 25% according to television appearances of which there was a minimum number for every club and 25% according to the position in the final table) allocated little more to Arsenal. The £35.5 million first year's payment by Sky only made a significant difference to the smaller clubs outside the Big Five, of which Everton and Tottenham were soon reduced to the ranks by their lack of playing success. So much for the reputed sum of £304 million, which was based on including an estimate of overseas rights sales that were never realised. The actual sum paid by BSkyB for its five-year contract was just under £200 million.

In effect, the Big Five self-imposed money-making restrictions on themselves – at least in terms of the huge slice of the domestic television revenue pie – when they proposed the formation of the Premier League. From their position as one of the top dogs, Arsenal for the moment were back in the pack, with the objective of ensuring that they couldn't be outflanked again.

CHAPTER TWO
TWO STEPS BACK AND ONE FORWARD

Arsenal fans might not give much thought to the dissolution of Yugoslavia that led to the war in the Balkans which claimed so many lives. But the conflict led to a sporting embargo and the football team being unceremoniously booted out of Euro 92 at the eleventh hour and replaced by Denmark. If Yugoslavia had participated, the sequence of events that led to Arsène Wenger's arrival and Arsenal's graduation to the status of one of the most popular and richest clubs in the world might never have happened. For without having seen him fire the Danes to an unexpected triumph in the tournament, it is highly unlikely George Graham would have purchased John Jensen, who inadvertently proved to be his nemesis. The Danish midfielder symbolised how the master had lost his touch in two ways. It was not only his lack of style as a central midfield player compared to his predecessors such as Thomas, Davis and Rocastle, the priority being winning the ball rather than how to use it once in possession. More pointedly, the negotiations surrounding his transfer ultimately led to Graham's dismissal in disgrace.

George Graham's downfall could not happen today. No longer do managers control the transfer and contract negotiations: after Graham's departure, David Dein (and subsequently Ken Friar) would undertake this duty on behalf of the club.

When Dein first arrived at Arsenal, he may well have harboured ambitions in this area, but his involvement on the football side was curtailed by Graham, determined to be master of all he surveyed. Sadly, the situation created opportunities for abuse: the 'brown envelope' or 'bung' culture, whereby the practice of managers receiving under-the-table payments as a cut of a transfer fee provided by a player and/or a selling club's agent was all too prevalent. However, only Brian Clough and his Nottingham Forest aides were put in the dock alongside Graham as sacrificial scapegoats. (Moreover, any verdict against Clough was academic as he was already retired.)

Graham, who received a payment of £285,000 when Jensen was signed for £1.57 million from Brondby in July 1992 (and a further payment of £140,000 when he later bought Pål Lydersen) was brought to book not by the naive football authorities but by the Inland Revenue, concerned by the untaxed earnings of the Arsenal manager. They were alerted after the story first broke late in 1994 when Simon Greenberg, then a *Mail on Sunday* journalist and more recently Chelsea's Director of Communications, was tipped off about the discrepancy between the figure that Brondby received for Jensen and the amount paid by Arsenal. The deal was set up by Norwegian agent Rune Hauge. Graham later recalled, "The meeting [with Hauge] was all very normal but the money came as a shock. I thought 'Jesus, what a Christmas present. Fantastic.' The ridiculous thing is that it wouldn't have changed my life. I was on a good salary, but greed got the better of me. I'm as weak as the next man when it comes to temptation."

There was a sense that the easy money would not be so readily available in the future and that Graham's exposure had spoilt the clandestine arrangements practised by so many of his fellow managers. One of them pointedly remarked, "We all like a drink from time to time but the trouble with George was he wanted the whole bloody brewery."

After the story came out, Graham was doomed, although he did hang on to his job for a few weeks. The fact that he had won three cups over the past two seasons doubtless prolonged his stay of execution. However, with the poor quality of the football on offer and the Highbury public enduring a fourth consecutive league campaign without having a shot at the title, the terminal rot had set in.

It is debatable whether Graham was acting in the best interests of the club when these transfers were made. Certainly Pål Lydersen never looked good enough to be a Premier League player, making a limited number of first-team appearances, none notable for anything other than his mediocrity. Still, some argued that he didn't stand out that much from many of his colleagues. Names such as David Hillier, Steve Morrow, Eddie McGoldrick, Ian Selley and Jimmy Carter are recalled by the fans as indicative of a slump in Arsenal's fortunes, although some of them did play a part in the cup successes of the time.

Alan Smith remembers the team going off the boil as Graham seemed to lose his touch, with talk in the dressing room rife. "We just thought 'this isn't happening'. We were used to top-class players at the club and this was turgid stuff." The tactics were pretty basic, described by Smith as "Wrighty, a big character, shouting for the ball and the players would hit him. It was not a creative midfield. Wrighty would get a goal and we would defend our lead. It made us a one-dimensional team." Smith recalls his time partnering Wright as "the worst of my career, although it was not his fault. But if he didn't score, invariably we didn't, which detracted from our threat. We didn't play with any width so I wasn't getting too many crosses." It was ironic that during this time, having for the most part sidelined Anders Limpar, Graham was offered Russian international winger Andrei Kanchelskis, but felt he was not what Arsenal required and allowed Manchester United to sign him. It was further evidence of a manager who had lost his way as Graham's reject gave Alex Ferguson a potent threat, in tandem with Ryan Giggs, from each flank. Smith would have loved such service, remembering, "My confidence dropped and I was at a really low ebb and that went on and on for about three years. It was totally unenjoyable and I felt like I needed to move. George would not let me go as he hadn't got a replacement."

Smith now admits that the players got wind of the bung that led to Graham's downfall before the story became public knowledge: "We thought, he's buying players like Pål Lydersen because he's getting knockbacks for it. We'd heard a whisper a few months before. One of the lads had said they'd heard it on good authority, the rumours persisted and we began to believe them. His sacking was a shock when it came, but by that stage we half sensed something was going to happen. As we weren't championship contenders, it made it easier for the board."

After the Premier League found Graham guilty of taking a bung from Rune Hauge (whose licence to practice as an agent was later withdrawn by FIFA) with the euphemism "Mr Graham did not act in the best interests of the club", Arsenal finally dispensed with his services in February 1995 and shortly after he was banned from working in football by the FA for two years. Of course, he subsequently returned to manage Leeds and, of all clubs, Tottenham. It still seems remarkable that Alan Sugar could have hired a man who, three years before his appointment as Tottenham manager, had written in his autobiography, "I will always have Arsenal's red blood running through my veins." Still, Sugar lived to regret it and after a parting of the ways in 2001, he commented, "In my time at Tottenham I made a lot of mistakes, the biggest was possibly employing him."

A stronger Arsenal board would have dismissed the manager as soon as he admitted the transgression and returned the money, which ultimately had come out of the club's coffers as part of the transfer fees theoretically paid to the selling clubs, when in fact they went into the agent's pocket. The directors left themselves open to a charge that they might have been prepared to forgive and forget by the fact that they allowed the manager to spend £6 million on three players (John Hartson, Chris Kiwomya and Glenn Helder) just days before his dismissal, none of whom subsequently remained at the club long enough to see out their contracts. After years of relative financial conservatism, the profligacy was akin to the last days of the Roman Empire, blowing the finances as the club's reputation went up in smoke. Glenn Helder actually played his debut match hours after Graham's sacking, having been signed only seven days before. Did the board really want to sack Graham, or did they do so because of the external pressure?

Meanwhile, across the Channel, after rejecting Bayern Munich, preferring to see out the last year of his contract with Monaco, a certain young coach was summarily fired after an inauspicious start to the 1994/95 French season. With Arsenal in turmoil during the last weeks of the George Graham era, at David Dein's insistence Peter Hill-Wood took Arsène Wenger to lunch at his favourite restaurant – Ziani's – a stone's throw from his Chelsea home. But with Dr Jozef Venglos the only foreign coach in the Premier League hardly presenting a good advertisement for imported expertise – he lasted less than a year before suffering the fate of the majority of Doug Ellis's hirelings – the general atmosphere in football boardrooms was not exactly liberal and Arsenal decided to make an appointment closer to home.

"I think at that moment we were nervous of hiring a foreign manager," recalls Hill-Wood. So Graham's right-hand man Stewart Houston took the reins on a caretaker basis for the remainder of the campaign. The team flirted with relegation – it must have taken the players time to adjust to the fact that 'the Coneman' (their derisory nickname for Houston stemming from his job of putting out the cones before training sessions) was now their boss – before putting a couple of key wins together over the Easter period to ease the pressure. This allowed them to concentrate on their ultimately unsuccessful defence of the Cup Winners' Cup, when they lost the final to Real Zaragoza in extra time. Houston was retained on the staff when the apparently safe pair of hands of Bruce Rioch were hired in preference to Wenger. And there was a whiff of revolution in the air that summer as two genuine superstars were acquired from Italy.

Unlike his predecessor, Bruce Rioch was only too willing to delegate to Dein and give him *carte blanche* when it came to handling transfer negotiations. Even though he had been kept at arm's length by Graham, Dein had capably demonstrated what he could do when the opportunity arose. One of his greatest coups had been the signing of Ian Wright in 1991. Dein later recalled the circumstances surrounding the move. "George Graham had identified Crystal Palace strikers Ian Wright and/or Mark Bright as being potential signings. At that time, I was speaking regularly with club chairmen, including Ron Noades from Palace. It was natural to speak about players. I was on the phone to Ron and asked him to tell me about Ian Wright and Mark Bright. Would he sell either of them? He said he was a 'reluctant seller', and that it would take a lot of money to prise one or the other away. I asked him what he called a lot of money, so he said, 'Like £2 million for Mark Bright', and that he wouldn't take 'less then £2.5 million for Ian Wright'. I asked him if that meant he would sell Ian Wright for £2.5 million. He said, 'I suppose, if it was offered it, I'd have to take it.' So I said to him, 'Ron,

I'm offering you £2.5 million for Ian Wright'. The phone went quiet. He said, 'Are you serious?' I said, 'Yes, I'm offering £2.5 million. You said you'd sell him for that, you are a man of your word, I'm offering you two and a half million.' And to his credit, he stuck by his word. He said, 'You've got yourself a deal'. And Ian Wright was at Highbury that afternoon for a medical. George Graham was having – of all things – a golf day with the press. I rang through to him on the course, and said, 'I've got good news for you: we've just signed Ian Wright.' And so George announced it to the press when he finished his golf."

"Ian Wright was almost unique," Dein later reflected. "When he came in, and Ken Friar was doing the paperwork, he said, 'Where do I sign?' We said, 'But what about your terms?' He said, 'Where do I sign?' He was not interested at all in salary or bonuses, just 'Where do I sign?' And that spoke volumes to me." By then, Dein certainly had enough experience to label the incident as atypical. But as the vice-chairman took on greater responsibility for transfers and wage negotiations, things would be different from the days when Graham would lay down the law on deals with his 'take it or leave it' approach.

The mid-1990s were a free-wheeling time with opportunistic agents and sports lawyers anxious to strike a deal at a time when exclusive representation and honouring contracts were figments of many a chairman's imagination. At home in the boardrooms of the leading Italian clubs, in the summer of 1995 Dein became aware that Internazionale were prepared to offload Dutch striker Dennis Bergkamp. Although sports lawyer and Arsenal season-ticket holder Mel Goldberg is convinced to this day he has a claim to an introduction fee, Dein felt free to deal directly with the Italians rather than go through another party because of his club's policy of only dealing with agents as players' representatives.

With club secretary Ken Friar, he flew to Milan and returned with the signature of, for the first time in Arsenal's history, a true international superstar. (Sale time in Italy obviously appealed to him as a short while later, after spending four seasons in Serie A, David Platt was signed from Sampdoria.) For once price was no obstacle: £7.5 million for Bergkamp and £4.75 million for Platt, obliterating the previous record outlay of £2.5 million for Ian Wright.

Bergkamp arrived in June 1995 aged 26, thus becoming one of the first stars to come to England with his best years still ahead of him. "I can think of no other top European club that has kept this prize [signing a world class player] from its supporters for so long," reflected author and Arsenal fan Nick Hornby, "which is why it had become ever more difficult to describe Arsenal as a top European club." No longer. "I think Arsenal took on a new aura when Dennis Bergkamp arrived," said Arsène Wenger's goalkeeping coach and former Arsenal double winner Bob Wilson. "I love the guy. I love what he has brought to the club. His stature in terms of having him at Arsenal and seeing that he likes England, likes Arsenal, has brought other players to the club."

This was Arsenal drawing a line under everything that had gone before. The boring, boring tag, the spendthrift policies and sterile football of the later Graham years, and most of all the bung scandal were all consigned to times past as the board finally gave their fans what they had been clamouring for so long: extravagant spending on world-class attackers.

Surely this is what Tottenham do? However, at the same time that Arsenal were signing Bergkamp, Spurs were busy turning themselves into the Arsenal of yesteryear, exemplified by chairman Alan Sugar's comparative parsimony and manager Gerry Francis's stunted imagination. "I can't ever see us spending £7 million on a player, I really can't," said Sugar, suggesting that Arsenal would live to regret their profligacy. Bergkamp (along with Jürgen Klinsmann whose signed shirt the Tottenham chairman wouldn't use to wash his car) exemplified in Sugar's mind the notion of 'Carlos Kickaball', a foreign mercenary who failed to deliver and would head for the exit when the going got tough. The fact that Bergkamp had a predilection for Tottenham probably passed Sugar by.

When he was a youngster, as a special treat Mr and Mrs Berkamp would take Dennis to White Hart Lane where he only had eyes for his favourite player, Glenn Hoddle. So when he was searching for an escape route out of Milan his first thought was to ask his agent, Rob Jansen, to contact Tottenham to see if there was any interest. Of course back came the answer, none whatsoever, enabling David Dein to smartly step in. Even at the eleventh hour – allegedly in the taxi taking him to Highbury to sign, Bergkamp asked Jansen to check again with Tottenham and only when he was reassured that his only London home could be in N5 did he finally commit himself to Arsenal. However, there was still one further issue to be resolved.

After the deal was done, Dein was told by Jansen that "It's nothing major but Dennis isn't too keen on flying."

"What do you mean?" said Dein. "We are aiming for Europe."

"I'm sure you'll get round it," said Jansen, making light of the situation.

Dein immediately investigated the British Airways Fear of Flying course (a two-day tutorial which culminates with the passenger sitting alongside the pilot in the cockpit as the plane takes a spin over London). As Dein was telling his new employee that there were numerous options and the course would not interfere with training, he could see the colour draining from Bergkamp's face.

"I don't like to fly, Mr Dein," said Bergkamp

"Don't worry," said Dein. "This course will help you."

"No, Mr Dein. You don't understand. I don't fly."

Arsenal's new star had been traumatised by two flying incidents, the first in 1989 when 14 Dutch Surinamese players lost their lives in a plane crash and the second as recently as the year before, when the Dutch national team were caught up in a bomb scare during the World Cup in the USA, after which he vowed never to set foot in a plane again. Although at the time Dein must have been perturbed, he might have had more serious misgivings had he envisaged the perennial European campaigns under Wenger in the years to come and consequently the many key encounters Bergkamp would miss as a result of his phobia. Today, Dein is sanguine. "We still got the bargain of all time," he says.

Whilst Rioch undoubtedly wanted Bergkamp – "He was the only foreign superstar the manager had heard of," quipped Dein – Rioch's insularity and indecisiveness might have scuppered other potential acquisitions. In a case of once bitten, twice bitten, Mel Goldberg was convinced that Bordeaux left back Bixente Lizarazu was just an unknown exotic foreign name to the Arsenal vice-chairman before he introduced him, implying that Dein in this instance was just as unworldly as his manager. Perhaps Arsenal's interest cooled when Roberto Carlos came on the market. In the event they dithered and ended up with neither. Both went to bigger clubs: Lizarazu to Bayern Munich and Carlos to Real Madrid. It was probably inevitable anyway but Dein must have felt he and his manager were not on the same wavelength.

Now though there was no time to dwell on missed opportunities. Bruce Rioch changed the team's tactics to get the ball on the floor more and build up from the back, utilising a 3–5–2 formation with Lee Dixon and Nigel Winterburn as wing backs. What was the point pumping the ball long to Ian Wright when the talents of Bergkamp and Platt had been assembled? It was a transitional season – a football cliché, but in this instance an accurate reflection of Rioch's time – laying the groundwork for future progress. Arsenal qualified for the UEFA Cup, but the fifth place finish did not satisfy the board, who expected more given the outlay to bring the two big star names to the club. Moreover, the manager had alienated certain senior players and for some reason had not signed the contract that was on the table and would have committed him for the long term.

Paul Merson recalls that Rioch appeared to be a fish out of water, he simply didn't fit in. "He couldn't handle big time players. He couldn't handle Wrighty. He used to come in and say 'I can't believe you all don't come in the same car. At Bolton [Rioch's previous managerial post] four or five of them used to come in the same car and talk about set pieces.' London's not like Bolton. He couldn't grasp the concept that Ian Wright lived an hour and 20 minutes away from the training ground and someone else lived an hour away in the other direction."

But, more critically, there were issues with his man-management style. George Graham might have seemed military to Merson, but he'd developed the players from unknowns into household names. Now they were stars, they didn't take well to a new man using the same approach that they had had to endure when they were growing up. Merson recalls a particular training session as a watershed. "One day, he said to Wrighty 'John McGinlay [his star striker at Bolton] would have scored that.' I remember now seeing Wrighty walking to the showers saying the F word to him and that was it. Wrighty was bigger than the club itself then. It was either Rioch went or Wrighty went. And Rioch went."

Dein had already targeted the man he really wanted, and after Arsène Wenger had been initially overlooked following Graham's dismissal, at Dein's behest the board believed the time was now opportune for a foreign adventure.

They were lucky to get a second chance. Peter Hill-Wood admitted, "We hadn't the nerve to do it [before hiring Rioch in preference to Wenger] and I might not have been wrong. I don't think it hurt him going to Japan." (After Arsenal's disinterest, Wenger went to manage Grampus Eight for whom he won the Japanese cup.) Indeed, there was some support for Hill-Wood's position. Wenger's former star player at Monaco, Jürgen Klinsmann, felt that "There was a different Arsène Wenger after Japan. He came back and for the first time truly believed 'I'm ready for a big club now.'"

"It was a big decision," recalls chairman Peter Hill-Wood, to reverse the one taken two years previously. However, it was quick and painless once the Arsenal trio of Dein, Hill-Wood and largest shareholder, Danny Fiszman, made the trip to Japan in the summer of 1996. An hour's discussion in Wenger's hotel room and it was handshakes all round.

Yet, as with Dennis Bergkamp, Arsène Wenger could so easily have ended up on the other side of North London. During French mid-season breaks in the late 1980s, Wenger, then the Monaco coach, would head across the Channel to absorb his annual fix of English football. "There was a different quality of passion and the way supporters lived the match was distinct from anywhere else [I had experienced] in Europe. I thought," he said, "that if one day I was given the chance to work in England, I would do it." That chance could and should have come at Tottenham.

Wenger had established a relationship with FIFA-accredited agent Dennis Roach, who had enabled him to acquire his clients Mark Hateley and Glenn Hoddle. The Monaco coach was indebted to Roach who, unbeknown to Hoddle, had changed his French destination at the last minute from Paris St Germain, enabling Wenger to snatch the man he later described as "indispensable" from under the nose of his friend and then PSG coach Gerard Houllier. Further, Roach was a good friend of Irving Scholar and was thus in a perfect position to act as a go-between. As a start, he instituted friendly matches between Monaco and Tottenham which became a regular feature of the January calendar and he organised Wenger's winter travel itinerary, with the first stop invariably White Hart Lane.

At the time, George Graham was getting his feet under the table at Arsenal, while at Tottenham David Pleat's team of talents were self-combusting – Clive Allen and Chris Waddle following Hoddle to France – as the manager committed occupational suicide by giving the tabloids the opportunity to make headlines out of his private life.

Having lived in Monaco for many years, it is the cruellest of ironies for a Tottenham fan that the biggest one of all, Irving Scholar, the most cosmopolitan and outward-looking English chairman of his time, should have passed up the golden opportunity on his doorstep. Scholar and Wenger were enthusiasts on the same wavelength regarding how their obsession should be played. Unfortunately for Wenger Scholar preferred Terry Venables as Pleat's replacement, a decision that came back to haunt him when the club went into debt and Scholar was forced to sell his shares to the Alan Sugar/Terry Venables partnership.

Although he wasn't on Tottenham's wishlist, it didn't stop Wenger's winter escapades which of course went far beyond White Hart Lane. As luck would have it, on one of his trips, lost in the bowels of Highbury, Wenger stumbled into the Ladies' Lounge (even as recently as 20 years ago, no directors' WAGs were allowed in the Arsenal boardroom). Rescued by Mrs Dein, who took him to meet her husband, the two men struck up an immediate rapport. On his own in London that night, the Deins took Wenger along to a friend's dinner party where the unexpected guest endeared himself to everyone by the panache he brought to an after-dinner game of charades. At the time, his English was only passable, but he immediately impressed David Dein with his intelligence and the Arsenal vice-chairman made a mental note of the fact that here was a different species of football man. "One for the future," Dein recalls thinking.

Having a yacht moored at Antibes on the Côte d'Azur, just along the road from Monaco, Dein became an increasingly frequent spectator at the Stade Louis II, where the post-match tradition of dinner with the Monaco coach was inaugurated and his admiration subsequently increased by leaps and bounds. Dein was convinced that if ever the Arsenal leopard was going to change its spots, he had the answer in waiting.

Although the club did not announce that Arsène Wenger would be coming until some weeks into the 1996/97 season, it became the worst kept secret in football. Rioch was dismissed days before the first league match of the new season and Stewart Houston was once again asked to take charge until Wenger's arrival. Houston then received an offer from Queens Park Rangers and jumped ship before the new number one arrived, ironically recruiting Bruce Rioch to assist him at Loftus Road in a reversal of their roles at Highbury (though apparently Houston couldn't rid himself of the habit of, from time to time, referring to Rioch as "Boss").

Pat Rice took charge for the remaining matches until Wenger had completed his obligations to Grampus 8 in Japan. His first sight of his team in the flesh was their late September elimination from the UEFA Cup by Borussia Mönchengladbach in Germany. His first match in charge was a 2–0 victory away to Blackburn two and a half weeks on. By that time, Arsenal fans had already seen the debut of a young midfielder signed on Wenger's recommendation before his arrival had been officially confirmed. ("I had to be quick because he was on the verge of signing for Ajax," he recalls. "I intercepted him when he was in Holland.") Probably only footballing francophiles were aware of the 20-year-old before he joined, but Patrick Vieira's evident talents indicated that the new boss certainly had an eye for a player.

CHAPTER THREE
A BREAK FROM THE PAST

On 12th October 1996 Arsenal took the field at Ewood Park to face Blackburn Rovers in an auspicious Premier League encounter. Auspicious because it marked Arsène Wenger's first match as the manager of Arsenal Football Club. His starting line-up that Saturday afternoon consisted of nine Englishmen, a Welshman and a Frenchman. His five substitutes were all English.

Fast forward to Sunday lunchtime on 12th August 2007. Wenger is still in his post (the second longest serving Premier League manager after Alex Ferguson) and Arsenal are about to play their opening fixture of that season's Premier League campaign, albeit in their very own 60,000-seater stadium a world away from Highbury in every sense apart from distance. The 11 starters are totally devoid of any British presence, although there is room for just one Englishman, Theo Walcott, to be squeezed onto the bench. (In fact, Arsenal's use of foreigners is the highest by far of any club from the major European leagues.)

How did it come to this? One of the great clubs of English football unable to find a place in the team for anyone from the country in which they play? The search for an answer reveals how Arsène Wenger went about creating the modern Arsenal, one so far removed from the regime during the fading years of the George Graham era that only the red shirt with white sleeves would be recognisable to those who watched the team in the early 1990s. It is the story of how Arsène Wenger built three distinct Arsenal sides, assimilating past, present and future, to procure trophies and thereby lay the foundations for future prosperity at a time of financial uncertainty. It is a unique blueprint for the making of a modern superclub, to a point where, by the time his current contract expires in 2011, Arsenal could be the world's richest club. By the conclusion of the 2006/07 season, they had risen to the heady position of third in the world money league with an annual turnover of more than £200 million (with the inclusion of its property revenues) on a net transfer spend of less than £4 million a season over the 11 campaigns that their manager had overseen. To achieve this whilst delivering seven major trophies and producing the most entertaining fare in the country can be summarised as 'the Wengerian miracle'.

The personnel Wenger inherited in 1996 were comfortable with the 3–5–2 formation that Bruce Rioch had introduced and they expressed their wish for the new boss to persevere with it. After all, they were lying second in the table on goal difference, in spite of a series of off-the-field upheavals. Over the course of less than three months, three different men had selected the first team. To add to the climate of uncertainty, club captain Tony Adams faced up to his demons and admitted he was an alcoholic to his colleagues, who probably weren't as surprised at the revelation so much as the transformation of the man who was making it. As his teammate Ian Wright commented with no ironic intent, "For Tony to admit he is an alcoholic took an awful lot of bottle."

With change and an accompanying foreboding in the air, the paramount need was for a sense of togetherness, which the new arrival effected by maintaining the existing formation as the players had requested. Had he insisted on his preferred 4–4–2 line-up, perhaps the outcome would have been even better than the third spot they attained, missing out on Champions League qualification on goal difference to Newcastle, seven points behind champions Manchester United. It would be the last time that Arsenal finished outside the top two until 2006, and the last time that Arsène Wenger would compromise on his *modus operandi*.

Still, a lot of the groundwork accomplished in Wenger's first months would bear fruit the following year, despite the players' initial hostility. This was epitomised by Tony Adams: "At first I thought, 'What does this Frenchman know about football? He wears glasses and looks more like a schoolteacher. He's not going to be as good as George [Graham]. Does he even speak English properly?'" But having got their way over their preferred system, they conceded to Wenger's newfangled preparatory methods. With a nucleus of largely English players, he concentrated on improving their physical well-being, introducing dietary changes and training that was geared towards tuning rather than testing bodies.

Sessions were much shorter than hitherto and involved much more preparatory work – stretching and jogging – to lessen the chances of injury. Regular psychological and physical examinations and continuous monitoring confirmed how effective the new methods were. During the week, the manager had to rely on his players choosing to consume copious amounts of water instead of (dehydrating) alcohol when left to their own devices. Ian Wright probably headed for the nearest takeaway as an antidote to the nourishing fare he was provided with at the training ground: "He has put me on grilled fish, grilled broccoli, grilled everything. Yuk!" Shortly after his arrival, Wenger justified his reforms: "It's silly to work hard the whole week and then spoil it by not preparing properly before the game. As a coach you can influence the diet of your players. You can point out what is wrong. Some are wrong because they are not strong enough to fight temptation and some are wrong because they do not know. As a coach I can teach the players what they do wrong without knowing it is wrong."

Perhaps it was no coincidence that the players shipped out within a year of Wenger's arrival were those who found it most difficult to adapt. John Hartson's temperament was the polar opposite of the Zen-like manager's (whilst his bulky physique suggested a liking for consuming something the manager would have disapproved of). The final straw for Wenger was probably Hartson's New Year's Day appearance as a substitute against Middlesbrough, in which he received two yellow cards for dissent and then foul and abusive language to leave his teammates a man short. On Valentine's Day the striker was sold to West Ham, with no love lost.

Paul Merson on the other hand had been rejuvenated, the inherent discipline aiding his determination to rid himself of his drug, alcohol and gambling addictions. Summing up the psychological benefits he received, Merson memorably stated, "The new manager has given us unbelievable belief." The compliments, however, were not mutual. Perhaps Wenger felt Merson had his best years behind him. To the player's surprise and despite having performed well, he was told in the summer of 1997 that an offer of £5 million from Middlesbrough had been accepted and Merson reluctantly departed the club he had joined 13 years earlier. It was unfortunate, as in his new surroundings, he would eventually fall back into his old habits. However, his selection by Glenn Hoddle for England's 1998 World Cup squad showed that his short time under Wenger had been personally rewarding.

To the outside world, it was surprising to perceive that Wenger's decision-making had a ruthless edge, that he was a manager who, ultimately, would take whatever steps he was convinced were needed in the interests of his team. Although he would never talk in negative terms, sudden transfers and loans spoke volumes, often to the bewilderment of those who were brusquely deemed superfluous. Notable later examples of players who Wenger anticipated were starting on the downward slope would be Patrick Vieira and Thierry Henry – proof that there were no exceptions, whatever their status and past contribution.

More than a decade on, and the notion that footballers used to abuse their bodies as a matter of course seems absurd, such is the omnipotence of Arsène Wenger's example. As one of many Scandinavians who adapted to the rigours of English football, Tottenham goalkeeper Erik Thorstvedt recalled the prevailing conditions pre-Wenger: "The British player eats the wrong food, drinks too much and doesn't train properly yet has this tremendous will to win." Whilst this quality was sufficient to paper over the cracks for many British managers it was never enough for Wenger. The right diet and exercise were only a means to an end, to provide the optimum conditions to enable technique to flourish. But when allied to what Wenger habitually referred to as 'desire' [for victory] then, with hindsight, his success was inevitable.

Even if, technically, many Premier League teams still fall short of continental standards, behind the scenes the influx of specialists – including psychologists, dietitians, masseurs, osteopaths – at every top-flight club was as a direct result of them absorbing Wenger's methods and beliefs. Of course, they were only adopted because they achieved results. Why should a footballer be any different from an Olympic athlete? Is he likely to perform to his potential if he enjoys a slap-up meal and a few pints the night before a big match? Merson later reflected, "No matter how great a player Thierry Henry is, if he started doing what I was doing when I was playing for Arsenal [under Graham], he probably wouldn't score another goal. When we were doing it everyone else was doing it as well, so it levelled itself out, but you can't do it any more, not in the Premier League."

Yet at the outset the resistance to a man whose ideas were so at odds with the established culture of the game in England bordered on xenophobia. Certainly, fabricated stories about Wenger's private life that led to him having to face down a melee of journalists on the steps outside Highbury in his first weeks indicated a move to belittle him and make him *persona non grata* at the earliest opportunity. Alex Ferguson didn't exactly help matters with comments like "He's a novice and should keep his opinions to Japanese football." In direct contrast to the widespread insularity he encountered – it took a while for the penny to drop – an open-mindedness and an awareness of conditions outside the United Kingdom explains exactly why Wenger was able to buy quality players at bargain prices from the overseas markets (not least France) until other managers were forced to open their eyes by the progress of the 'novice'. His first hand knowledge of continental football gave the Arsenal manager a similar advantage to that George Graham had enjoyed in his early days when he plundered the lower divisions to build his backline.

The benefits were long-term, as a critical factor in his good start was the revival Wenger inspired in the old English die-hards who had lost their 'desire' under Graham. The defence that Wenger inherited – David Seaman, Lee Dixon, Nigel Winterburn, Tony Adams, Steve Bould and Martin Keown – was stacked with experience, but the consensus between both fans and pundits was that time waits for no man and physical decline was beginning to show signs of setting in. They were won over simply because as their fitness dramatically improved so did their performances. Tony Adams put it down to physiology. "There's no one better at preparing players physically, knowing what they need to be at the peak of fitness," he said. Steve Bould stressed that he "felt so much fitter under Wenger. I wasn't injured so much. I felt a lot more supple. We would never have lasted so long without his special methods." The reactionary Little Englanders who had walked off with pretty much everything the game had to offer were reinvigorated. The defensive unit was reborn in the face of a fresh challenge, and did their stuff – as they entered their thirties – consistently enough to compete once again for the title.

And the pupils opened their teacher's eyes. Lee Dixon recalls that Wenger "was surprised how good we were as footballers and how intelligent we were. He'd thought we were like robots just doing what we were told. So when he tried to expand our game and let us go out and express ourselves, we were able to do it. When he first came he was going to let us all go." Steve Bould concurred: "He left us alone during that first season because he only arrived in September, but I think he imagined he was going to have to replace us the following summer." There is no doubt that a huge contribution to the early headway was the defenders' willingness to approach their task with a greater sense of purpose than the mere denial of opponents that George Graham required. "You were allowed to do what you wanted in many ways," recalls Nigel Winterburn. "There weren't any restrictions. He left it up to us whether we went forward or not. He trusted our judgment."

Winterburn's words point to Wenger's singular approach to coaching. There is very little instruction. Even the juvenile stand-in is not sat down, lectured and told what to do. Having prepared his troupe to perform both physically and mentally at their optimum level, the manager relies on their intelligence and skill to come up with the winning formula. As UEFA coach and former Arsenal midfielder, Stewart Robson, observes, "he develops players not by fantastic coaching but by giving them the environment to express and experiment themselves. He takes the fear out of their play by coaxing them to be more elaborate, precise and imaginative." As Wenger himself sums up, "I would say that usually to win is a consequence of the quality of play you achieve." (Although the scintillating play served up in the 2002/03 and 2007/08 seasons show that the theory isn't perfect.)

Wenger's training exercises are deployed not just to hone technique but to instil continuous thought, to get everyone into the habit of making the right choices and being able to read what their teammates are instinctively going to do. Wenger saw evidence of the success of his methods in his 2007/08 central midfield partnership of Cesc Fabregas and Mathieu Flamini: "Going forward they are technically good and very mobile. They have a good understanding and cover each other well." When everything is going to plan, positive, incisive one-and two-touch play becomes second nature, and at their zenith, competitive matches resemble training-ground exercises and vice versa. A pattern of play is unfolded: vision, movement, speed and fluidity.

During the short 20-minute drive from Totteridge to London Colney, Wenger will plan his day ahead. The actual training sessions themselves conform to a pattern although, as Wenger says, "In order that they retain their enthusiasm, the boys mustn't know exactly what's coming." And he adds, "The two criteria for a good session is that it is conducted with a good spirit and that there is the satisfaction which is derived from whole-hearted commitment." It is the highlight of his day. Nothing gives him more pleasure than being out on the pitch with his team. Training only lasts an hour and a half and he is at a loss to understand, and certainly would not tolerate, any player who does not put his heart and soul into every session. It is no co-incidence that at Arsenal no-one shirks training. Although he is omnipresent with the shrill sound of his whistle signifying the start and finish of each practice, Wenger doesn't appear to coach his charges in the strict sense of the word. The main message is to merely clarify what is expected from them.

With the incidence of midweek matches there tend to be only two rigorous sessions per week during the season. All begin with warm-up exercises and jogging which are usually delegated to Wenger's trusted technical aide Boro Primorac and assistant manager Pat Rice, followed by a number of drills, each lasting around 20 minutes, under the manager's eagle eye. Invariably the first is a control and pass examination designed to provide the aptitude and confidence to replicate the technique under match conditions. To facilitate commitment to the task in hand – there is no chance of the players knowing exactly what's in store for them and therefore being able to coast – a small-sided game follows. It is unusual in that it can feature four goals, one on each side of the pitch, with Wenger's whistle forcing swift decisions and precise shooting to locate the right target. Next comes the one-on-one test. From 30 yards, the attacker has to eliminate his marker and score as well as satisfying Wenger's stopwatch, which, according to Bob Wilson, Wenger uses "to his own beliefs, which I think are based on medical science. And if he says the exercise is going to last for eight minutes and 20 seconds, then that is exactly what happens." Kolo Toure commented, "I have Thierry Henry, Adebayor and Van Persie and if they don't score I am pleased." While all this is going on the goalkeepers are put through their own specified paces. They then join their teammates for the concluding episode: a full-scale 11-a-side game played under match conditions, which both sides do their utmost to win. It was under such circumstances that the newly acquired Thierry Henry learnt of the punishment he could expect from Premier League defenders after undergoing a no-holds-barred initiation in his own back yard at the hands, or rather the feet, of Tony Adams and Martin Keown.

The mental abilities of his charges to absorb what they

are taught without having their hand held is a key factor in Wenger's decision on who he prioritises for his top 30, his meaningful first-team contenders. Regarding Kolo Toure, he admitted, "Technically he might have been less gifted than some of his young teammates [at ASEC Mimosas in the Ivory Coast], but he had that charismatic attitude which makes a difference." The charismatic attitude is more accurately described as being smart enough to make the best use of natural ability coupled with the fervent desire to do so. Toure remembers of the Ivorian academy that gave him his first real opportunity, "I was not the best player in that group, but I was the cleverest. In football, and in life, you have to be clever. Now when I call the others I advise them what they have to do and I hope they can make it, too. If they use their brains, they will be much better than me." However, he certainly wasn't clever enough to work out what Wenger had in mind for him. It is only with hindsight he now understands how he was subtly handled. "When I came at first I did extra training every day," he remembers. "At that time he [Wenger] spoke to me every morning and afternoon. The coaches knew my qualities but told me how to do different things. They never told me what they were thinking. They just took me aside each day and gave me advice and instructions – and then I began to see what was happening [that he was being groomed for a pivotal central defensive role]."

And the element of surprise can be disconcerting. More recently, Wenger's ever-inquiring mind has discovered that by timing how quickly the players receive the ball and then lay it off, he can enhance their movement and interplay. Specifically, statistics can prove or disprove what he picks up from the touchline. He can tell Fabregas that despite the media consensus that the midfielder has put in another outstanding display, he occasionally dwelt on the ball to the detriment of a passing movement. The player may argue but the figures enable the manager to have the last word. "Technical superiority," he says, "can be measured."

The spadework for Kolo Toure's conversion from midfielder/full back to centre back was accomplished during pre-season – the most important weeks of the year for Wenger. It is surely no coincidence that Arsenal have won titles – 1998, 2002 and 2004 – the seasons following summer months with no World Cup or European Championship finals taking place. With such a high-quality cosmopolitan squad Arsenal supplies more and more internationals to these tournament finals. And so after the extension of their seasons into June or in some cases mid-July, the early part of Wenger's critical pre-season preparation has to take place without them. The manager knows from experience that it is best to give them a complete break and phase them in when he can. Nevertheless, it appears that the fatigue endured and the lack of an optimum pre-season preparation takes its toll and the team invariably fall short of its target – agonisingly so in 1999 and again in 2003 when they set the pace with scintillating football but ended up in second place.

When the manager does speak to the group, "he does it quietly in a way that makes you listen," says Toure. So no bombastic rallying call, but a calm message, delivered with an authoritative voice that manages to enthuse and persuade his players with the conviction that, as the fans put it, "Arsène knows". "He believes," says Bob Wilson, "that you can only rollock a team, have a real go at them, three or four times a season. Otherwise, the impact is lost. Similarly, at half time, he believes the words he wants to say are best expressed when the players have calmed down. And he can then make his points in a quiet, controlled manner and know there is more chance of him getting through to them." And sometimes he finds that it's not necessary for him to say anything: the players having worked out what is required by themselves. So well drilled is the squad in his way of thinking that even in the dire circumstance of potentially losing their unbeaten record to Liverpool in April 2004, Vieira and Henry did his team talk for him and the second half saw them exemplifying everything that Wenger could have wanted as they turned a demoralising deficit into a crucial victory.

He sends his team out to play chess rather than to fight. Passion should not overwhelm reason, and yet having prepared the players physically and mentally they are left to decide the best moves for themselves. Those who question the wisdom of this strategy might point to the 2005 penalty fiasco when Robert Pires and Thierry Henry conspired to miss in a bungled attempt to re-create a Johan Cruyff /Jesper Olsen Ajax spot kick from the 1980s, where the pair played a one-two before scoring. With Arsenal only being 1–0 up against Manchester City, it was a risky manoeuvre, although the manager refused to condemn his charges afterwards, perhaps because there was no further score in the match.

To the uninitiated, it may appear a conundrum how Wenger achieves so much which seems to be beyond the scope of other managers with greater resources. Whatever the secret is, there is a steady flow of requests from coaches of all nationalities and via the UEFA network (where Wenger frequently plays a leading role in the technical curricula) to visit Arsenal's training ground to try to ascertain at first hand what the 'magical' methods are. In February 2008, Diego Maradona was the latest in a long line of the great and good of the industry who wished to make their way to London Colney. When told of the Argentine maestro's request, Wenger's immediate reaction was "Why does he want to come and see me?" and the answer given to him by the messenger was "Because you are Arsène Wenger." Another of football's iconic figures, Marco van Basten, the future Holland manager, spent time at London Colney during the 2003/04 season as he prepared to return to the game as a coach. Having benefited first hand under the tutelage of the legendary Dutch manager Rinus Michels and the innovative Milan coach Arrigo Sacchi, it was a compliment that he felt he could further his education by watching the Arsenal boss at work.

However, the Wengerian masterplan could not be described as one of tactical innovation. He rarely radically alters his team's approach in the manner that other managers, such as José Mourinho are quick to do when unforeseen obstacles have to be overcome. It seems his chief tactical quandary is whether to field a 4–5–1 formation (most often deployed in the cagier, tight Champions League encounters), a 4–4–2, or its slight variation 4–4–1–1. That appears to be the extent to which any account is taken of what the opposition's strategy might be. Arsenal invariably try to play in the same manner whether up against Milan or Middlesbrough, relying on the quality of the interplay to create chances rather than any strict pre-determined positional alignments. When critical voices are raised to the effect that Wenger takes no account of the opposition, he is riled: "Do you really think," he responds, "that I have been a football manager and I do not look at the opposition at all? How can people think like that? That means I am more stupid than stupid. Of course we change our game. We always try to express our strong points. It doesn't mean we do not look at the opposition. Of course we do. It is very difficult to understand how people think that when we play in Europe, we just walk out there and do not consider who we are playing." Certainly, whatever the formation it can be very fluid, dependent on the personnel involved. The wide midfield players have licence to roam and interchange without precise managerial instructions and generally create havoc when the team is on song.

Conversely, there is a lack of flexibility to Wenger's substitutions. For anything other than time-wasting reasons approaching the 90th minute, they are invariably made for physical rather than tactical reasons. An observer who took Wenger at his word when he told him "Nobody is perfect, least of all me" ventured a leading question: 'Why do you always watch the match from the touchline?'

"Because I started my job there. I feel I have good vision. I'm used to it. I don't like the physical separation from the team," came the reply.

"But am I correct when I say that might be why sometimes the substitutions aren't right – because you can't see the overall pattern?"

"No, it's not true that your opinion is right. I can find you 50,000 different opinions in the crowd but people ignore many things I know."

"Such as?"

"Such as," replied Wenger, "I know that a guy will 'die' after an hour because I know in the last three games his high intensity dropped 30 or 40 per cent and he will not be capable to keep going." (Even so, Wenger doesn't always practise what he preaches. He still blames himself for not acting on his instincts and withdrawing Robert Pires before he ruptured his knee ligaments against Newcastle in 2004. Pires himself admits, "My injury was due to mental tiredness and [for] that I was at fault because I was not focused enough.")

"Precisely, that's my point," argued Wenger's inquisitor. "You only make substitutions for physical reasons, not tactical ones."

So the wide midfield players are withdrawn for fresh legs around the 70-minute mark and, depending on the state of play, either a central midfielder (if the team are leading) or a striker (if they are not) will be replaced, usually by a like-for-like change. There is rarely any element of surprise in the player withdrawn or the time of the switch. What improvisation that does occur is down to the ability of the players to do the unpredictable with their movement on and off the ball. Wenger can be acclaimed as an icon for the discovery, preparation and development of footballers of all ages, but he is no tactical magician. However, he certainly knew enough to realise Arsenal were better served by a 4–4–2 for his first full season.

Allied to that simple tactical change, made in the summer of 1997, Wenger's first league title was arguably the direct result of the willingness of the defensive domestic stalwarts to adapt. Another who changed his ways was Ray Parlour, who became a regular for seven seasons before following Paul Merson's exit route to Middlesbrough. Satisfied with his options for a number of key roles the manager was able to devote his transfer budget to strengthening the midfield. It seems no coincidence that in his first year, Wenger released Eddie McGoldrick, David Hillier, Andy Linighan and Ian Selley alongside Hartson and Merson, whilst acquiring a number of replacements, only one of whom (Matthew Upson) was English. Amongst the new arrivals were Marc Overmars, Emmanuel Petit and Gilles Grimandi. The first two facilitated the adaptation to a 4–4–2 system. Overmars was a speedy winger from Ajax. With his negligible defensive contribution, he would have been unsuited to the 3–5–2 of the previous campaign and was purchased in the full knowledge that such a line-up was now obsolete. Petit had been groomed by Wenger at Monaco, and was earmarked for central midfield.

So it was out with the trio of Platt, Vieira and Merson, who had been flanked when going forward by two wing backs, and in with a four of Parlour, Vieira, Petit and Overmars. Grimandi was a versatile defensive player signed along with Petit from Monaco, who joined Platt as a valuable substitute. Wenger saw the key defensive element of his 4–4–2 formation as the central players, with the midfield duo screening the centre backs. It worked particularly well with Vieira and

Petit in front of Adams and Keown, and after a team meeting midway through the 1997/98 season in which the central defenders reminded their colleagues that they needed more help from the midfield in halting opposition attacks, they initiated a long unbeaten run that culminated in the double. (And the defensive quality was maintained the following season, with Gilles Grimandi often deputising for either Petit or Vieira pointing to the manager's priority that defending through the centre was more important than on the flanks.) The price to pay was a reputation for ill-discipline and a high yellow and red card count. There was a steely side to Arsenal to accompany the silkiness of their football, but the trouble with officials that came as a consequence reprised the 'backs against the wall' mentality associated with the great teams in the club's history.

As wide players, Overmars and Parlour were inevitably more comfortable in possession than Dixon and Winterburn had been as wing backs and allowed the team to push on and hurt opponents further up the field. It was a move towards controlling matches through dominating both possession and territory. With a midfield all keen to demonstrate a positive approach, the defence passed the ball more, or brought it out themselves, instead of playing a long percentage hoof simply to relieve pressure and go for territory. It was certainly easier on the eye and the team began to earn a reputation as entertainers. So much so that as the season progressed, Overmars' attacking inclinations altered the system into a *de facto* 4–3–3. Now the chant *"Boring, Boring Arsenal"* initiated with just cause by opposition fans was purloined and lustily sung with ironic relish by Gooners. And there was hardly time to wallow in an old favourite from the Graham years, *'One-nil to the Arsenal'*, as the goals came thick and fast to render it redundant.

It is significant that, as the seasons passed, Arsenal developed their ability to hold onto the ball higher and higher up the field. By 2008 they had reached a stage where they have comfortable possession of the ball in exactly the same areas that Graham's men used to lump it up to. Now there are a number of teammates to assist in keeping possession, working the ball out of defence and through the midfield so that the opponents often withdraw into a mass of bodies within 30 yards of their goal line. This is one of two Pavlovian responses; the other is to engage in combat, to 'rough 'em up'. Consequently, the priority is to try to make greater use of width, to add variety to the attacking options when allied to the intricate interplay.

But it all began over a decade ago with an English back four bringing the ball out of defence and refusing to give it away cheaply. The *coup de grâce* came in the final home match of Wenger's first full season. With three fixtures remaining, Arsenal simply had to beat Everton to be able to celebrate a first title since 1991 in front of their own public. At 3–0 up with the clock ticking down, the red and white ribbons were already on the trophy. Arsène Wenger made a rare sentimental substitution, replacing forward Christopher Wreh (another Monaco import) with Steve Bould. The veteran slotted into central midfield and set up the fourth and final goal, playing captain and fellow central defender Tony Adams into the Everton half to beat the offside trap and smash a glorious half volley into the net with his weaker left foot. It was, in a snapshot, an example of the total football Wenger had inspired. Bould, with a reputation as a defensive destroyer who loved nothing better than the now outlawed sliding tackle from behind, producing the sweetest of passes into the path of a colleague who had cruelly been labelled a 'donkey' by the *Daily Mirror* in his earlier years.

Yet, it was not a matter of complete harmony for those presented with their medals at the conclusion of the game.

With his outspoken views on broccoli, an inevitable clash of personalities between the manager and his star striker had always loomed on the horizon. In the early part of the campaign, there was a great deal of media attention surrounding Ian Wright breaking the club goalscoring record, overtaking the 178 goals notched up by Cliff Bastin. Having achieved the feat, Wright declared he wished to move to the Portuguese club Benfica, who had made an enquiry about his availability in December. With the teenager Nicolas Anelka and the unproven Christopher Wreh as his only back-up forwards, Wenger wasn't about to sell his principal striker and did not appreciate his public comments on the matter whilst being interviewed on BBC's *Match of the Day*. Moreover this incident occurred at the conclusion of a difficult run of league matches that saw the team drop 16 points in eight outings, capped by a 3–1 home defeat to Blackburn. Wright then aggravated his situation by aggressively gesturing to fans about their lack of support during the Blackburn defeat from the dressing room windows facing the Avenell Road. He created enough of a furore for the police to be called to warn him about his behaviour.

However, Arsenal soon discovered what life without Wright would be like a month later when he suffered a hamstring injury in an FA Cup tie at Port Vale. Nicolas Anelka became the regular starter in Wright's absence as the team then embarked on an undefeated run that only ended when the title had been secured with two games to spare. This consistency was carried over to the FA Cup and the club won its second league and cup double. Anelka's ability was such that a flourishing future without Wright could be now be contemplated, a preposterous notion at the start of the season. The manager's faith in the inexperienced teenager in preference to the safer, more conservative option of the experienced campaigner became, over the years, a regular occurrence when exceptional talent, however youthful, was on call. The later departures of Patrick Vieira and Thierry Henry took place under similar circumstances.

Wright was out for several weeks, but once fit the manager resisted the temptation to recall him until the title had been wrapped up. It was a difficult time for the player, anxious to prove his fitness with selection for the England squad for the 1998 World Cup Finals imminent. He started the final two league fixtures, but it was Christopher Wreh who got the nod to partner Anelka for the final commitment of the season – the FA Cup Final against Newcastle United.

Arsenal were two up with 20 minutes left on the clock at Wembley. The first substitution had already been made: Wreh had been replaced by David Platt. With the fans clamouring for Ian Wright, there was the opportunity for a sentimental gesture (Wenger was happy enough to do it in 2004 to ensure Martin Keown qualified for a Premiership medal). As the final whistle approached, there was movement on the bench as one of the substitutes removed his training top. That he did not actually get on before the end of the match was irrelevant to the supporters, as the intended replacement was not Wright, but Gilles Grimandi. It was an unaccommodating decision, the denial of an appearance, however brief, a final dagger in the heart of a player who professed to bleed Arsenal. It soon went from bad to worse as Wright failed to make the final squad for France 98 and was forced to spend the World Cup as a television pundit. In fact, Wright had already worn the red and white shirt for the last time as during the close season he was sold to West Ham.

CHAPTER FOUR
YOUNG AT HEART

Nicolas Anelka was only 19 at the time of Wright's farewell. He was an early Highbury example of youthful promise unearthed by Wenger and turned into a superstar. Reluctantly sold by Paris St Germain in controversial circumstances in 1997 for a fee of £500,000 (Arsenal exploited the French system whereby prospects have to sign their first professional contract with the club who develop them. They cannot sign for another French club, yet there is nothing to stop them joining one abroad) he made an immediate impact in his short spell at Highbury. Largely due to Vieira and Anelka, Wenger developed a reputation as a discoverer of exceptional young stars, but until Cesc Fabregas broke through in the autumn of 2004 no comparable youthful talent emerged. Many came to the training ground in the hope that they would become good enough for the first team only to slip quietly away having failed to make the grade. The most extreme example is Anelka's countryman Jérémie Aliadière. Signed in 1999 as a 16-year-old, he did not leave the club until 2007, two years short of a testimonial. During that period, though, he made only 29 league appearances and scored just one goal. (Although Wenger has picked up some amazing potential at bargain prices, good returns have also come with more mature men.)

In fact, it could be said that Wenger's top teenage sensations emerged at Monaco. He is proud that he "put Petit in at 18, and [Lillian] Thuram at 18" and he bequeathed a healthy youth set up, including Thierry Henry and David Trezeguet. But in England it has been more a case of picking up players who had served their apprenticeships but had not yet (in his eyes) fully developed their potential. So, in the way that at Monaco he'd signed George Weah from Tonnerre Yaoundé in Cameroon at the age of 21, Patrick Vieira had played for both Cannes and Milan before he was purchased for Arsenal on Wenger's recommendation aged 20. That of course is not to gainsay the phenomenal progress they and others like them, such as Thierry Henry, Gaël Clichy and Mathieu Flamini, made under his tutelage. Perhaps in France either Wenger was lucky to have such talented youths emerging contemporaneously (as Alex Ferguson had been in the early 1990s) or other coaches didn't share the importance he attached to being able to mould young and old alike so that they could perform at their optimum level.

So to believe that his young teams are created from a burgeoning youth policy is not the complete picture, certainly as far as young Englishmen are concerned. On leaving Arsenal for Coventry in 2001, Jay Bothroyd, a star of Arsenal's youth team, commented, "Arsenal want to buy success. If a few young players come through, that's a bonus, but they are not really interested." He could have been speaking for Jermaine Pennant, Steve Sidwell, David Bentley and Matthew Upson (all of whom enjoyed Premier League success away from Arsenal, with the latter two capped as full England internationals, although none so far is a regular starter with a top four club).

The writing is generally on the wall for an Arsenal prospect if he is sent out on loan. The prospects Wenger has earmarked tend to be kept within the fold, given the odd chance from the bench or a start in the domestic cups by way of experiencing what might lie ahead. Perhaps he thinks they are best kept away from other coaches, in spite of the fact that young players generally benefit from first team experience. The hopefuls who spend time away for a few months or a season are removed from Arsenal's huge wage bill (even if at that stage of their career they do not earn that much more than their peers in other industries). More pertinently, the playing time and exposure they receive – even at a lower level than the Premiership – can enhance their value in the transfer market. A long-established member of Wenger's scouting team, Tony Banfield, explains: "At Arsenal, 15-year-olds are offered a three year contract. Then at 18, if they are good enough, they are offered a further three years. In that time, if it is felt they might not be good enough, they are sent out on loan to get more first team football, with the idea that it might improve them. When they return, if they are better they might stay, otherwise the club look to sell them on." Often the loan is turned into a permanent move as occurred with Blackburn's signing of David Bentley, whilst Birmingham bought Jermaine Pennant, Sebastian Larsson and Fabrice Muamba. And the arrangements are not always restricted to novices. Matthew Upson was over 20 when he began a series of loan spells between 2000 and 2002 at Nottingham Forest, Crystal Palace and Reading, before finally being becoming another Birmingham acquisition in 2003. Arsenal, in common with other clubs, often build a clause into such transfers as Upson's whereby they receive a percentage of any sell-on fee if a player is successful and subsequently moves on for more than his original sale price. It allows the club to continue benefiting from their initial commitment.

Occasionally the cast-off is recalled. Upson played enough matches in 2001/02 to earn a Premier League winners' medal. But the long-term outlook is bleak for those whose objective is to be regarded as an integral component of the first-team squad. Even if Jérémie Aliadière did notch up eight seasons, he had been farmed out three times before eventually getting a number of first-team appearances under his belt during his final months at Arsenal. But the surprise was that he had lasted so long. Just when it looked as if, having persevered in the face of competition from a plethora of international strikers, he might get his chance, injury intervened in the 2004 Community Shield, ruling him out for most of the season. By the time of his recovery, he had fallen back down the pecking order and eventually Wenger accepted an offer of £2 million for him from Middlesbrough in 2007. Three of the current first-team pool who have returned from their loans are Alexandre Song, Nicklas Bendtner and Justin Hoyte. Hoyte should be especially concerned as, according to the data, it is not until a player is given a number below 30 that he can feel the manager is seriously contemplating keeping him (Aliadière wore the number 30 in his last season; Hoyte sports 31).

Often cited as evidence in favour of both the academy and the loan system, Ashley Cole's progress through the ranks must be regarded as atypical. With the club ceasing to field the first-choice Brazilian-born left back Silvinho for fear of punishment due to his being registered with the football authorities using a dubious Portuguese passport, Cole was pressed into service early in 2001. He had been on loan at Crystal Palace, and just before the Silvinho predicament arose, a fee of £200,000 had been agreed to make the move permanent.

So the sweeping under the carpet of Wenger's first choice (quietly sold the following summer to Celta Vigo) opened the door to a genuine product of Arsenal's youth academy. The young man took his chance and was soon regarded as a permanent fixture. Academy head Liam Brady expressed pride that two of his former apprentices gained title medals in 2002, although goalkeeper Stuart Taylor, despite coach Bob Wilson's recommendation, was never given the opportunity to take over from David Seaman and only obtained the requisite ten appearances due to a combination of injuries to the two above him in the pecking order and a final-day substitute appearance.

The Arsenal academy has the responsibility for the development of boys between the ages of nine and 21. As it has been in existence for less than ten years, perhaps the 2001/02 season was a little premature to be expecting fully fledged first-teamers to emerge. However, by 2008, still no one had followed in Cole and Taylor's footsteps. The club's own website lists the players that the academy has produced. Johan Djourou, Fabrice Muamba, Sebastian Larsson, Arturo Lupoli and Nicklas Bendtner are cited among the more recent graduates, even if they spent their earlier years with clubs abroad. Going back a few years Jermaine Pennant, David Bentley, Steve Sidwell, Justin Hoyte, Jérémie Aliadière and Ryan Smith are mentioned. "With academy players regularly dominating the Arsenal reserve team line-ups and a steady progression of players being blooded in the senior side," states arsenal.com, "the academy production line looks set to continue and produce players to grace the Gunners' new Emirates Stadium for many years to come." If they do, it will be a genuine breakthrough.

There is no mention of Cesc Fabregas, Gaël Clichy, Abou Diaby, Denilson and Philippe Senderos, all of whom joined the club as teenagers. Theo Walcott famously came from Southampton at the age of 16. Where is the academy contribution to their development? The conclusion has to be that these kids were immediately drafted into the first-team squad due to Arsène Wenger's belief that, unlike their contemporaries, their innate ability marked them out as special (probably epitomised in his eyes by the initial impression Fabregas made on him, "At 16, to say no to Barcelona and yes to Arsenal, it was really astonishing. I was very curious to know exactly what type of kid is this to say to Barcelona 'you didn't treat me with enough consideration, I am going'.") He also believed that prolonged exposure to the coaching, even of his own staff, away from his watchful eye might fail to bring the best out of them.

Is it a coincidence that of the recent graduates listed by the club, none became established first-team players, and only three – Djourou, Hoyte and Bendtner – are still at the club (all of whom, having experienced a spell on the outside, may yet be sold rather than start on a regular basis)? A cynic might believe that the importance attached to the academy nowadays is the result of the regulations regarding quotas of home-developed players (eight out of the permitted 25 in the squad at present) necessary in UEFA competitions. Because they were teenagers when they arrived, Cesc Fabregas and Theo Walcott fulfil the necessary qualifications despite, in all likelihood, rarely coming into contact with Liam Brady and the academy coaching team. So it is never going to be difficult for Arsenal to make up the requisite numbers in the Champions League squad, even if few of them these days are English.

Relaxing at his north London home, Wenger is prepared to submit to a friendly interrogation regarding his propensity for foreign youngsters.

"It is true [that Arsenal has more foreign youngsters] – but what you always have to consider is how you produce a player. If you want to completely develop a player, ideally you take him at the age of five and you bring him right through to the first team. But the reality is that he arrives at your club [much later] at 16 or 17. If you look at the top clubs in Europe, Arsenal is producing more young players than any of them."

He is defensive when it is put to him that of all the major clubs in Europe, Arsenal has more foreigners than any other, retorting, "Yes, but what I don't understand in that is that it looks always like an accusation – why?"

"Because there would be closer identification between the fans and the team if there were more nationals, that's why," responds his questioner.

"Maybe you are right," he counters, "but I am against this idea. I think the identification should be with the quality of your display, with the spectacle you produce and the values you want to represent. And not with your passport. Maybe my thinking is not traditionalist enough, but I believe that sport can unite the world and can be an idea of what a modern society will be tomorrow. And if we regress and say 'OK, we keep all the foreign players out and the foreign coaches', I am not against that because I can go home and work at home. But I believe as well the same people, if tomorrow they have to watch the Premier League with only local players, they would be disenchanted. So it is always 'OK, we like what you play, we like what you do but we want that with English players'. I'm sorry, I'm not capable to produce it at the moment. I hope I will be one day but at the moment I cannot do it. And I do feel guilty for not doing that, but on the other hand I feel as well that for me the justice in sport is if tomorrow you live in South Africa and you grow up and you train to be a footballer in the best league in the world, that you get the chance to achieve it. That's what I think is beautiful. If somebody says 'Sorry my friend, you cannot play with the best players because you have not the right passport', for me it's not really sport."

Wenger can get away with such a view because his team is successful, overcoming the natural conservatism and insularity of supporters. His view is a more optimistic one of human nature than many experience in the stands at a match. He feels, "Fans can as well be educated. Five per cent of the most regressive sometimes expresses their opinion but it doesn't mean it's the majority. It takes time but I still believe that our fans are quite educated. I agree there is a price to pay, but at the moment the balance is not completely right because we should produce more local players, but the big clubs will always have problems now to win and to produce that. Why? Because you can only scout in a small area and the big clubs cannot only do that."

Scout Tony Banfield is adamant. "Football in Europe cannot be viewed as being English, French or German anymore – it's European," he says. "We can't go backwards. And if English kids don't reach the required level we will use those from other countries." He is however optimistic that progress will be made on the home front. "Regarding the produce of Arsenal's academy gaining first team places, it will get better. We will have players who come into the side in the future."

As a former defender now back in the fold as a youth coach, Steve Bould forecasts there will be more 'locals' in the future, citing Kieran Gibbs, Mark Randall and Henri Lansbury (despite the spelling of his first name) as local boys with the potential to make good, allowing Bould to ponder, "Maybe that eight-year cycle is coming to fruition now. Maybe the academy set up is starting to produce. Over the next few years, we might see a bundle of these kids getting in their first teams, not just here but throughout the country." These youngsters are probably the first batch to have overcome the English malaise of poor coaching in their formative years and will arrive at maturity with a sure first touch in both feet. However, Steve Bould is perhaps indulging in wishful thinking if he believes they are more likely to achieve first-team status at Arsenal than elsewhere. Although he is a biased witness, Wenger himself defends his policy: "I have tried to build an academy that will recruit young local kids. At present, we have exceptional under-14s and under-16s. Technically they are extraordinary."

One notable departure from the usual precedent of arranging loans to other English clubs has seen the placing of two teenagers in Spain. Fran Merida, plucked by Arsenal from Barcelona's academy in a similar manner as Cesc Fabregas, has been sent to Real Sociedad in the second division, whilst Mexican striker Carlos Vela, who at the time of writing had yet to kick a ball at any level for Arsenal, spent the 2006/07 with second-division Salamanca before going to top-flight *La Liga* side Osasuna. (In the case of Vela, to qualify for a UK work permit, he had to serve time in Spain.) Still to demonstrate the exceptional potential of a Fabregas, Wenger probably feels that they will learn more through being exposed to a league more conducive to their background and style of play than could be found in England and thereby have more chance to succeed than other loanees. If Merida does come out unscathed, he will be bucking the trend in a further way as he did train as one of the academy youths for a full season (rather than with the first-team squad). At least the two boys, together with their English peers, testify to Steve Bould's claim that the meticulous attention to scouting pays dividends. "First and foremost we manage to get hold of good players," says Bould. "It seems a simple starting point – recruiting the best – but it isn't so easy when every other club is trying to do the same . . . whether from abroad or in and around London."

"Do British kids have a right to play for British teams?" asks Tony Banfield. " They have to earn the right." He feels that the changing culture in affluent societies has handicapped their chances, reflecting that, "now, in working class London, kids can't play on the streets and develop themselves the way I used to. On my travels, I have developed the P formula – population plus poverty produces players." Such an equation may go some way to explaining the English exception of Wayne Rooney, who as a child played football in the roads of the working-class Croxteth area of Liverpool, where a large number of the residents were unable to find employment. Banfield confirms that, as a rule, "kids in the UK have to be nurtured in a structured manner, as they don't play on the streets. But facilities don't make players. In Africa they play in bare feet, but the quality produced now is higher than many richer countries." Of the competition to make it as a professional, he feels no sympathy for home-grown talent, stating, "It's an open market. So if you want to join Manchester United, you have to be better than a kid from France or Spain or Africa. And Spain is used as a stepping stone to the EU now for non-EU kids."

To counter the greater competition for the best players, the catchment area for Arsenal targets has increased in size. Brazil was not an unfamiliar source for seasoned players (Silvinho, Edu and Gilberto were purchased over a period of four years, whilst Barcelona's Edmilson might have joined them were it not for work-permit problems) but now the scouting system is working hard to secure teenagers from South and Central America, such as Denilson and the Mexican Vela. There is unquestionably a greater Hispanic presence at the club now, with Fabregas, Manuel Almunia, Eduardo and Merida (José Antonio Reyes and Julio Baptista providing further evidence from the recent past). David Dein says that "Arsène believes the future lies with South American and African players," although Wenger himself would not go as far as to publicly admit it. It can be assumed that he holds this belief due to the perceived superior technique of Spanish and South American prospects and greater physicality of African players. In the English game, there is little debate that an element of aerial dominance and raw power in defence is a prerequisite to success, although at Arsenal it has to be combined with technique. Further forward, there is more of a mix, as pace and skill assume greater importance.

Master of all he surveys – he fulfils the role of technical

director as well as coach and general factotum on the playing side – Wenger has built a team of scouts under the direction of Steve Rowley and Dave Holden who transverse the globe. Based in Italy, but with a territorial responsibility that extends beyond the Alps, Tony Banfield, explains: "Scouts are head-hunters looking for players who are better than those we have. At the end of each year our aim is to upgrade the playing performance of the team, physically, tactically and technically." These men are a mirror opposite of his players. "These English scouts", as Wenger explains, "have been formed here [at Arsenal] but have my way of seeing things".

One of the few foreign exceptions among Wenger's scouting network is Gilles Grimandi, whose primary remit is naturally France and the francophone overseas territories. He succinctly states, "We are able to attract the most promising prospects because we have a calling card stamped 'Arsène Wenger'." And Grimandi adds, "[Another] asset to attract youngsters is the fact that with us they know they will get the chance to play . . . it is one of our principal arguments." It was certainly one that Arsène Wenger used to Monsieur and Madame Clichy when he went to see them at their home in the south of France a few days before the FA Cup Final in 2003 to persuade them to entrust him with the development of their precocious teenage son. Gaël Clichy's club, Cannes, had been relegated to the third division and had been forced to abandon its professional status and he was now a free, though much in demand, agent. With strong competition from a number of French clubs, Damien Comolli, then a vital member of Arsène's entourage, pushed Wenger into action. As Clichy recalls, "He [Wenger] told me that Giovanni van Bronckhorst would be loaned to Barcelona and I would be the understudy for Ashley Cole. And that's exactly what happened . . . in France perhaps there are not enough chances for young players . . . there is nowhere better than England."

There is a harmonious common purpose throughout the disparate parts of the scouting networks. As Wenger explains, "The scouts and myself have regular discussions on how we assess players. We also arrange an annual get together so that the scouts can see how the first team train. We then make sure that they go and see any prospect we are interested in at training so there can be a direct comparison. Great importance is attached to what can be learned by observing a potential prospect's preparation." As he joked regarding José Antonio Reyes, "We even watched him in training. How did I do that? With a hat and a moustache." Perhaps the banal nickname of 'Clousseau' given to him on arrival by his English players was accurate after all.

This thoroughness can extend to trailing the quarry for years. Wenger adds about Reyes that he was "scouted for two years, every minute of every game." Unlike many clubs which according to Gilles Grimandi "have a tendency to pursue many leads in case they miss someone good . . . we limit our horizon and closely follow only a few. We will start at 16 or 17 and then if necessary, follow them until they are 20 . . . and perhaps one day they will sign [for us]". This attention to detail is confirmed by Tony Banfield's admission that, "Only three youngsters have been signed by the club as a result of my own scouting over 11 years, but the potential returns when you get it right justify the work I do." As an example of his own meticulous attention to detail, Grimandi reveals that "I saw Bacary Sagna on more than 30 occasions. I checked him once, then ten times, then 20 times before finally deciding he was the one we needed." In fact, Grimandi was so painstaking that by the time Sagna arrived from Auxerre in the summer of 2007, he was an atypical signing, at the end of the accepted age scale. "It is difficult to envisage taking a player of 23", says Grimandi. "It's too late. It's not worth the trouble of extending our quotas [of older players]". Wenger though is pleased that he bent the rules in this case. At Christmas 2007, he told an acquaintance that "he is one of those who has pleased me most", after Sagna became the first-choice right back.

The conclusion that can be drawn from the Arsenal academy's ten years of existence is that its function is to provide back-up players for the first-team squad, with the probability that they will eventually be sold on having failed to hold down a starting eleven spot. Liam Brady – an Arsenal man through and through – must, at times, ask himself whether much of his time has been well spent, giving the lie to David Dein's hyperbolic claim that he [Brady] "has the most important job at the club". Perhaps Wenger is too familiar with Brady's role, and feels he knows better from bitter experience. "In the beginning, I started by coaching five-to seven-year-olds at a football school, then seven-to ten-year-olds at the club [Strasbourg]," he recalls. "I then took the academy and it's there that one understands that there are young players who've not been given their chance. At the same time this is a point of decision for me. I have to see who will become a professional and who won't."

And if a player makes the grade for Wenger, "then comes the crucial period of integration into the first team. You must make a place available for a young player and it is often the most delicate of tasks, one which many clubs fail." Sometimes, it is timing rather than ability that determines the careers of Wenger's trainees. "At some stage I have to make a decision and if you do that it is not always just considering the individual – you consider an overall package. Who is in front of him? With who is he competing? Will he get in front of this guy? Is he at a level when he cannot wait anymore – if you don't do it now he will completely sink and therefore sometimes there is a gamble in there. But at the end of the day the most important thing is that the guy has a good life."

It is undoubtedly rewarding for trainees to go through their professional evolution at the academy but, so far, there seems to be little positive benefit for the future of the club itself, except on the player trading balance sheet. Even the justification that there is a lack of technique in English players seems to be countered of late by the moving on of prospects originally discovered overseas, such as Larsson and the Ghanaian-Dutch forward Quincy Owusu-Abeyie. Whether Arsenal are best served by such an approach is a moot point, but Arsène Wenger's policy of placing his trust in players of all nationalities who he can influence at first hand looks set to continue. "I always say to my players who are foreign, 'Don't just believe that you have to play well, you have to do better than people from here. If you go to a foreign country you have to give something more. If you do just what the local people do, they don't need you. So there is pressure on you to give more.'"

CHAPTER FIVE
ONWARDS AND UPWARDS

Arsène Wenger's most successful spell to date at Arsenal occurred between the 2001/02 and 2004/05 seasons, when the club landed five major trophies in four years. The pinnacle was the Premiership campaign of 2003/04 when the team accomplished the feat of going through the entire league programme without incurring a single defeat, a phenomenal feat that had only been achieved once before in England – by Preston North End in the 19th century, and they only played 22 matches compared to Arsenal's 38.

Within the 'Invincibles', there were contributors from his 1997/98 team – Patrick Vieira, Dennis Bergkamp, Ray Parlour and (albeit in more of a supporting role) Martin Keown – but for the most part a new team had been constructed largely with the chequebook, although there was no profligacy on the manager's part. In Wenger's first nine seasons at the club, the haul of titles and FA Cups was accumulated for a deficit of around £44 million (£136 million being the total spend). That he was able to attain such value for money was due to his knack of realising a high return on players whose reputations had been enhanced by his tutelage. Most notably, Nicolas Anelka (£23 million) and Marc Overmars (£25 million) brought in colossal sums from Real Madrid and Barcelona respectively, accounting for over half of the income received through transfer sales in that period. The profit from such deals enabled the club to establish itself as a major force in Europe without spending the huge amounts other teams did. If one definition of a great manager is someone who makes fewer mistakes in acquiring players, then coupled with his ability to develop youngsters, Wenger's shrewdness in the transfer market places him in this rarefied category. Moreover, his sense of timing of when to release a star has usually been spot on. Although he would not have chosen to sell Anelka, to secure Thierry Henry as a replacement for less than a third of the fee received from Real Madrid, was a masterstroke (and the remainder underwrote the construction of the sumptuous new training centre at London Colney, jokingly referred to as the 'Nicolas Anelka training ground' by former goalkeeping coach Bob Wilson). On the other hand, there is no argument that Wenger got the best years out of Overmars – his subsequent seasons were littered with injuries, with an enforced retirement four years after leaving Highbury, as well as turning a profit of over £18 million on the sale.

Later, anticipating a drop in their contribution, Wenger began to break up the Invincibles, with Patrick Vieira departing for £13.7 million in 2005 and Thierry Henry bidding *adieu* two years on for the £16.1 million paid by Barcelona. Aside from making way for younger replacements, both have subsequently missed a notable amount of playing time due to the ravages of injury. In hindsight, Wenger did well to get what he did, even if at the time some fans felt he was being short-changed, such was the contribution Vieira and Henry had made. Yet even if the supporters were sad to see their heroes move on, Wenger is ruthless when the welfare of the group is at stake, invariably being proved correct, as both the cast-aside apprentice and experienced international would reluctantly admit (though some individuals who went onto better things, such as Jermaine Pennant, David Bentley or Lassana Diarra, might argue that Wenger acted too expediently).

And so it was from the transfer fees received, together with the revenue from the Champions League, that Wenger constructed his 'second' team. The summer of 2000 saw some significant spending, as did the following close season. A characteristic of the majority of the new arrivals (including Robert Pires, Lauren and Sylvain Wiltord) was their unfamiliarity with the English game. Indeed, against Crystal Palace on Valentine's Day 2005, for the first time ever in a Premiership match, a 16-man squad totally devoid of any British players was named.

However, it wasn't all bad news for English patriots. Ashley Cole and Sol Campbell were not selected against Palace due to illness and injury respectively, and in building a new back line to succeed his inherited defence, both England internationals were key components. Whilst Cole improbably came through the ranks, Campbell had been acquired on a free transfer (personally profiting from a remunerative signing-on fee as Tottenham had foolishly allowed his contract to expire). However, two other arrivals showed that for all his acumen in the transfer market, Wenger was prone to error. Goalkeeper Richard Wright arrived from Ipswich to challenge for David Seaman's position and was selected enough times to gain a Premiership winner's medal, yet, having played in every match of the FA Cup, was dropped for the final in favour of still first choice Seaman. No one would have predicted Wright's leaving before the older keeper, but after just one season he was offered to Everton for a loss of £2.5 million. Another notable flop was Francis Jeffers, a striker who cost £8 million but failed abysmally to justify the outlay, eventually moving on at a loss of over £5 million, having played a few games with a negligible return in the goals scored column. Wenger would wait almost five years before he invested substantially in another Englishman, teenager Theo Walcott.

However, the transfer failures are mere footnotes to a rich history of coups. Henry and Pires were joined in the hall of fame by Freddie Ljungberg, Lauren, Gilberto and Kolo Toure, forming a squad with the likes of Kanu, Sylvain Wiltord and Edu in reserve producing a depth in quality unmatched in Wenger's time at the club. There was no issue with a panoply of foreign stars as the trophies were being collected in ever-increasing number. As the old guard moved on, the newcomers gelled and a relatively seamless transition took place as this new group unveiled performances that had the likes of the Dutch maestro Johan Cruyff drooling over them: "I watch Arsenal all the time and I admire their style. If they win playing football the way only they know how then Europe would be proud to have such champions."

The period was highlighted by the securing of two league records. Firstly, they put together a sequence of 23 away matches without suffering a defeat (in tandem with being unbeaten at home after December 2001) that effectively ensured the 2001/02 title. The run was ended in October 2002 by a late winner from a 16-year-old Everton substitute called Wayne Rooney. However, Wenger's men surpassed even this exploit by remaining unbeaten home and away for 49 games, beginning in May 2003 and continuing for 17 months until October 2004 when once again Arsenal's nemesis proved to be Rooney (now a Manchester United player). He scored the second goal, as well as earning a contentious penalty for the first in the 2–0 league defeat at Old Trafford. After both setbacks, the team took time to recover, dropping points that would ultimately cost them their chance of retaining the league titles secured in putting the runs together.

In 2002, the Everton defeat bequeathed a series of four losses in eight league outings. As Arsenal only lost six times over the course of the entire campaign, finishing five points behind champions Manchester United, it was a lethal slump. Similarly, two years on, 12 points were then dropped from 18 available after starting the season like a runaway train, continuing their invincibility of the previous campaign. The steady stream of missed opportunities allowed the free-spending Chelsea to overtake them and become the dominant team in England, with Arsenal again finishing runners-up.

In both seasons, as defending champions, it seemed a case of picking up where they had left off before the summer break. A 4–1 humbling of Leeds at Elland Road early in the 2002/03 season elicited fulsome praise from fans, media, pundits and even opponents. Wenger described his team as "danger everywhere, tremendous spirit, a privilege to watch. It was total football." "It was demoralising. They just pass and move, pass and move. You find yourself working for nothing," said Olivier Dacourt of Leeds. "They are better than the Manchester United team who won the treble and they are even better than Real Madrid. I'm sure Arsenal would beat them." As Real were at the time the Champions League-winning self-styled 'Galacticos' featuring Zinedine Zidane, Ronaldo, Luis Figo and Raúl amongst others, it was certainly a rare accolade from a vanquished foe.

The sense of a supreme side at the peak of its powers was such that the media – with its collective tongue firmly planted in its cheek – asked Wenger whether it would be possible for the team to go unbeaten for an entire season. "It will be difficult but we can do it," was the unexpected reply. "It was done by Milan and I can't see why we cannot do it this season. Other teams think exactly the same but they don't say it because they're scared of looking ridiculous." Or indeed setting themselves up for a large dose of hubris, although

Wenger had the last laugh when his team did actually achieve the feat in May 2004. Recalling the scenario some years later, he said, "When you win and [then] you have lost a game you think, 'Maybe we could have done better there.' But when you do not lose any games you do not have those questions. We lost the title in 2003 but we had done the double the year before. I asked the players after the summer break what had gone wrong. They said, 'It's because of you, Boss.' I said, 'Yes, OK, but why do you really think you lost.' They said again, 'No, Boss, it was because of you. You put so much pressure on us by saying we would go the whole season unbeaten.' I said to them, 'All right then, but I'm going to say it again. You can go through the whole season without losing. I believe in you.' Normally when you win the title the team loses the next match. It happens every year. But that year [2004] we had won the title with some games to go and when we played as champions they made sure they did not lose. It meant the seed had been planted in their minds. It took a while to come but in the end they achieved what they didn't think was possible."

"I think in that period when we were going on the pitch, we knew that we were going to win the game," recalls Patrick Vieira. "I think Arsène created at this moment the belief that we were the best and even when we were 1–0 or 2–0 down we knew that we were going to win the game or take a point. So we really believed that we were the best. The way we were playing, the way we believed in each other was unbelievable."

Yet the backlash after the long unbeaten runs were brusquely terminated raised the question of how a group so seemingly resolute and unconquerable can suddenly fall away in such an alarming fashion merely because they lose a game. Certainly Arsène Wenger has a case to answer. Perhaps the reason lies in the coaching or rather the lack of it. The focus is on maximising ability, improving skills, developing into better technicians. "He makes an average player into a good player, a good player into a very good player and a very good player into a world-class player," according to David Dein, but he doesn't specifically teach them how to win. As a result of enhancing the attributes Wenger holds dear – pace, power, skill, creative thinking and desire – victory should be the natural consequence, the end product. And with such productive end results winning has become accepted as the norm. Losing is not contemplated and therefore everyone – players and coaches alike – are dumbfounded when it happens. The 'unbelievable belief' coined by Paul Merson has a flip side when the faith is punctured. There seems no fallback position from which to regroup. A collective trauma invades the group. It is as if they have forgotten how to lose, or at least how to react positively to defeat, so unexpected is it.

Wenger may be a master manager, but it seems that he has no solutions when the unthinkable happens, no way of countering the doubt when infallibility is disproved. His words may sound re-assuring ("I think you will be surprised by my team's reaction. They will react strongly on Tuesday," he said after the Everton defeat in October 2002, only to see his side lose at home to Auxerre in the Champions League) but they seem full of self-delusion, at least if the response of the players is anything to go by. Bizarrely, given his teams endure so few setbacks, they are tarnished with an Achilles' heel of mental fragility, which is often brought up by Alex Ferguson, implying that he doesn't suffer from the same chronic condition. Could it be that a more pragmatic manager might have actually restored equilibrium more quickly in the autumns of 2002 and 2004 and provided a very talented group with the strength of purpose to go on and win League Championships rather than FA Cups the following May? In response, Wenger might justifiably argue that a more pragmatic manager might not be able to create a team that could go unvanquished for so long in the first place. However, for supporters and manager alike it's difficult to close the book on the ones that got away.

Wenger himself admits, "I am very critical with myself. I believe as well when you do not lose for 49 games it's such a long period, when you keep always the team under tension. When you get there and suddenly you lose the game you start here again and you say to your players and they think, 49 games, we will never make that again. And you have to tell them, 'Now my friends, we climb back there again and you do 50.' And they say, 'Come on, give us a breather a little bit, we just did 49 games.' So what I mean is defeat is very difficult to take. When I was very young it was very difficult to take because it was such a big disappointment. And then you hate so much to lose. When you are more experienced, you anticipate all the problems and the difficulties you will face because you know the consequences. You can anticipate the confidence will go down, the motivation goes down, the understanding in the team will be less good, less spontaneous and you have to respond to all that. The longer the period goes the more difficult it is to act as if nothing has happened. It depends as well on the cycle of the team. If the cycle of the team goes to an end and they have done that 49 games and they lose, subconsciously they think, we have done our best. If it's a young team, the next game, they go again."

In 2002/03, while Wenger was awaiting to discover the final component of his new back four (Kolo Toure would solve the missing link), the team seemed bereft of the figure of calmness and authority conspicuous by its absence since Tony Adams retired. Martin Keown was in the twilight of his career and Pascal Cygan, brought from Lille, had proved disappointingly inconsistent. With their own high standards slipping both David Seaman and Sol Campbell were looking increasingly vulnerable. The late, late strike by Rooney for Everton had established an unfortunate precedent. Away to Liverpool, Newcastle, Aston

Villa and Bolton, leads were lost and points sacrificed. Even at Highbury, Manchester United perpetuated the pattern by coming from behind to gain a 2–2 draw. That game saw Sol Campbell dismissed with the consequence that he missed the run-in, including a home defeat to Leeds that confirmed the trophy presentation would take place at Manchester United's next game. Such was the alarming loss of confidence in their ability to hold onto a lead that a fortnight after the title concession, the FA Cup Final against Southampton witnessed the unedifying sight of Robert Pires taking the ball to the corner flag in the closing stages to use up time. This was anything but total football. It was a sad reflection on the heights they had scaled earlier in the season but they realised that in the cold light of day they might end up empty-handed. Regardless of the manager's philosophy, the players determined the entertainment was over. They were going to make sure that they had a tangible reward for their efforts.

The summer break and a productive 2003 pre-season got the show back on the road. Not only did the team rediscover its touch but it went on to post the record breaking 49-match unbeaten run and land another title in the process. "My ambition was always to go a whole season without losing," said Wenger. For him and all purists the league reigns supreme. There is only one answer to the question of which is the best team – the league champions. The league is the only competition that represents the strength and depth of the domestic game. It is football in its purest, fairest form. Everybody plays everybody else, home and away; three points for a win, one for a draw and none for a defeat. There are no bonus points. Away goals are not worth more. There is no extra time, replays, penalty shoot-outs, golden or silver goals. So 2003/04 was the finest Arsenal season ever: played 38, won 26, drew 12, lost 0. It was arguably also the finest league season ever by an English club.

What made the exploit all the more remarkable was that it was accomplished by playing offensively. The team went out with a philosophy to subdue their opponents by skilful interplay. It was a heady mix of abilities that ensured the team could appear audacious, even wanton (Henry, Pires and Vieira even became known as the three musketeers) but crucially, the screening qualities of Gilberto in central midfield allowed his teammates to boldly go out on a limb and additionally he would often cover for a defender caught out of position if an attack did break down suddenly. He performed a similar role to the one he had carried out for Brazil in winning the 2002 World Cup, and had he not needed a period of assimilation, Arsenal could well have secured three league titles in a row. It may be no coincidence that on the two occasions Arsenal's first choice selection lost to English opposition that season (Manchester United in the FA Cup and Chelsea in the Champions League) Gilberto was absent due to illness. His calm comportment compensated for the element of defensive composure the club had lost with the retirement of Tony Adams.

Thus the scene was set for some of the finest approach work, passing and movement that English supporters had ever set eyes upon as all and sundry were taken apart. Often the side were applauded off the field away from home by opposition fans who were knowledgeable enough to appreciate that they were witnessing something extraordinary. A 5–1 sixth round FA Cup drubbing for Portsmouth drew a standing ovation from all four sides of Fratton Park. Such was the admiration and so many the plaudits that once they had secured the title, it felt as if thousands of non-Arsenal supporters (with certain obvious abstentions from Manchester and parts of London) were actually willing them to go on and finish unbowed. It was a rare time when exhibitions of such purity transcended the traditional parochial resentment that is endemic to football fans. After overhauling Nottingham Forest's 42-match unbeaten run Brian Clough said, "Arsenal are nothing short of incredible." And then, true to form, "They could have been nearly as good as us." For good measure, he added that they "caress a football the way I dreamed of caressing Marilyn Monroe." And although obviously biased, Dennis Bergkamp's view, "This is the closest I have seen to the Dutch concept of total football" must be taken at face value. And such excellent notices were not restricted to England. "When I travel abroad," said Wenger, "it made a major impact because people know how difficult it is to play a whole season unbeaten." For football purists, it bettered the near perfection of Arsenal's 1990/91 title in two respects. George Graham's team suffered a single defeat in the 38 outings, and Wenger's side were renowned more for what they did going forward than in defence. It was an irony then that, having secured their status as champions, they took their foot off the pedal and ended up with a goal less than Graham's team, totalling 73 by the end of the season. However, when the Invincibles met their denouement, lightning struck again and a serious challenge for the title was not mounted until the team had been rebuilt.

There was undoubtedly a sense of injustice at the turn of events that saw the unbeaten run come to an end at Old Trafford on 24th October 2004, a venue where incidents often play a pivotal role in the outcome of Arsenal's season. They justifiably felt hard done by due to Rooney's penalty award (the key moment of the game, a late second goal being largely academic) and the perceived thuggery of their opponents. Weak refereeing allowed Gary Neville, Ruud van Nistelrooy (subsequently banned for three matches for a challenge missed by the referee) and Rio Ferdinand to make their presence felt in exchanges where the existence of a ball seemed incidental. The hostility was a hangover from the previous season's encounter at the same venue, when the away team rounded on Van Nistelrooy at the final whistle, so perturbed were they by his theatrics and unsporting play in earning a last minute penalty which he subsequently missed. The FA determined though, by the fines and bans they handed out to Arsenal personnel, that United were more sinned against than sinners.

With their unbeaten run ended, once inside the tunnel the Arsenal players let their opponents know how unfairly they felt they had been treated, resulting in an argument between the two managers. Ferguson, at the door of the visitors' dressing room told Wenger to control his players, before some post-match refreshment was thrown at the United manager, although precisely what it was is dependent on which tabloid version of events that became known as 'Soupgate' and 'Pizzagate' is to be believed. What is in no doubt is that such was the extent of the melee, United's security staff had to separate representatives of the two clubs. Wenger probably felt that he had been stitched up by his *bête noire* so there was never any likelihood of him admitting that maybe there should be some internal self-questioning and recrimination. Unfortunately, this holier-than-thou position ceded the moral argument to Ferguson, who was able to claim with some justification, his own reputation as a bad loser notwithstanding, "To not apologise for the behaviour of [his] players is unthinkable. It's a disgrace. But I don't expect him ever to apologise." The hubbub aside, most critically, Arsenal failed to just accept that they had been the victims of poor refereeing and downright unlucky, and move on. Rather, a team that (as two years before) was lauded as one of the best ever club sides the world had ever seen, allowed the incident to undermine them and a more resilient Chelsea to take the initiative and establish a convincing lead in the title contest.

The players take their cue from the manager. Arsène Wenger is a modest, self-effacing philosopher who finds it easy enough to move on from triumph, never resting on his laurels or enjoying his success. "With your club it is a love story that you expect will last forever and also accept that you could leave tomorrow," he reflects. Which is perhaps why he agonises over defeats, running over in his mind the factors that produced the unexpected. But he doesn't roll with the punches. Recovery takes too long, and his team seems to follow his lead. Although aware of the dangers – "the face of the manager," he admits, "is a mirror to the health of his team" – too much time and energy are expended on self-pity. Even the Invincibles' season was nearly halted in its tracks after elimination from the FA Cup and the Champions League in the space of four days. In their subsequent league fixture at home to Liverpool, they found themselves 2–1 down at the interval. It took what was arguably Thierry Henry's finest performance in an Arsenal shirt to turn the game around and get the quest for the Premiership back on track with a 4–2 victory.

The defence that season was improved by two changes, addressing the salient weaknesses that allowed the 2002/03 title to slip away. German international Jens Lehmann replaced the fading Seaman, whilst Kolo Toure, previously a utility player who had featured at both full-back positions as well as in midfield, was moved to partner Sol Campbell in the centre of the defence. His versatility endeared him to the manager – "I think about him as a centre back or right back, but sometimes I think this guy could make a centre forward. When he plays closer to the goal – in midfield or up front – he always creates chances and it's too tempting when I think about it." Given the importance to Wenger of keeping possession and ability on the ball – not least in defence – it is no coincidence that both Lauren and Ashley Cole played the earlier part of their careers further forward before being converted to full backs. Compared with Lee Dixon and Nigel Winterburn, the pair gave the team a great deal more threat going forward, even if defensively, they were not as tenacious as their predecessors, although Cole did improve to such an extent that he was eventually touted as one of the outstanding left backs in world football. Tony Banfield reveals "Technique and body shape are critical in all positions for Arsène. He wants full backs who can defend and when they go forward cross the ball like a winger. He doesn't just put people in boxes." It is Wenger's way to envisage how changing positions can lead to optimum performance. Other examples are Thierry Henry, a winger converted to a centre forward, Emmanuel Petit, a centre back moved to midfield and Freddie Ljungberg switched from a striker to wide midfield. The only downside is that the prioritisation of possession, with seemingly suicidal passes made within the team's own penalty area, can see some moments that frighten the living daylights out of fans who would sometimes prefer to see the ball hoofed to safety *à la* George Graham's men of old. Fortunately the current crop are adept enough not to get caught out too often.

Perhaps then, Wenger's Arsenal should have performed better than they have in their ten consecutive Champions League campaigns. The first two (1998/99 and 1999/2000) were effectively sacrificed by the decision to play their home matches at Wembley. The sell-out crowds confirmed Arsenal had outgrown their Highbury home, but the neutral venue didn't faze, and in some cases may even have inspired, opponents and they did not survive the group stage (although at least on the second occasion, their third place led to UEFA Cup involvement and the opportunity for Highbury to host European nights once again as the team progressed to the final and defeat on penalties to Galatasaray).

The unfamiliarity of the larger stadium and its bigger pitch dimensions counted against the 'home' side. Wembley undoubtedly held back the team's progress on the European platform, not least in upsetting the manager's well-honed pre-match routine, developed to maximise the players' focus on the job in hand and minimise extraneous distractions. Attention to detail went as far as ensuring adult movies were out of bounds (the night before a game, home or away, Premiership or Champions League, is spent at a hotel). "Films can be distracting," Wenger believes. "I feel that once you are together you want your players to focus on the game, not on anything else." Of the porn ban, he recalls, "I said we don't do that and that was it, nobody said a word. I could control that, but now, if players come with a computer and want to take a porn film you cannot control it any more. Things change. Before they only had the television in the hotel."

At the time of the decision to use Wembley, Wenger had been in the job less than two years and did not wield the power he has since appropriated. For some time now he has done it his way. Particular care is taken with the peculiar circumstances of European competition. Home or away, the routine is the same. The players train at London Colney the day before a match and spend that night in a hotel before making their way to the stadium after their pre-match meal – consumed precisely three hours before kick-off – by coach. Even for away trips, the only variation is the length of the flight involved (travelling is a necessary evil and even domestic journeys of any distance involve flying to minimise journey time). For Champions League away fixtures the party fly from Luton in the afternoon after training in the morning, relax in the evening and return as soon as possible after the following day's match. The opportunity for a training session at the actual venue is not taken up, a rare Wenger procedure that has not been copied. Whether or not there is an advantage to be gained from becoming accustomed to the stadium and the pitch is debatable, but for the manager, it is a variation, a distraction he doesn't need. The hours before a game – be it an afternoon or evening kick-off – involve nothing more strenuous than a stroll or a jog.

So, with such a precise programme is there any flexibility to accommodate any idiosyncrasies? Dennis Bergkamp, so integral to the team, was not going anywhere by plane, and although television's *The A-Team* got around the phobia of BA Barracus with the aid of sedatives, fact was not about to imitate fiction. Initially, Bergkamp made the trip to the more accessible grounds by car, boat and train, sometimes using all three modes of transport on one journey. The furthest he travelled in Arsenal's cause was probably when he played against Fiorentina in Florence in 1999. On that occasion, his contribution did not appear affected by the journey in a game Arsenal should have won but for a missed spot-kick. However, the time taken and the physical condition of the player on arrival soon had Wenger reluctantly deciding he was better off without him. The consequence was the equivalent of losing probably his key man to suspension or injury every other European match, with the adverse affect on selection and tactics. For so many seasons Bergkamp's link-up play was a prerequisite and the team often struggled when he was not on the pitch. He contributed so much towards the domestic trophies that one wonders whether Arsène Wenger would have signed him if he had known he would be handicapped in this way in European competition. Of course, in 1995 when Bergkamp arrived in London to play for Bruce Rioch's Arsenal, the Champions League format was still in its infancy and had yet to evolve into the prestigious money-making phenomenon it is today. Very few clubs, if any, with serious European aspirations would sign a non-flyer now.

Perhaps this might explain why there was no great clamour for the player's services as he grew older and accepted the unsentimental year-at-a-time renewals that became Wenger's policy for over-30s. In effect, such contracts were the manager's way of saying "You might be useful to me for another season, but if necessary I can survive without you and I won't stand in your way if you want to leave." Most players take the option of free agency, a move and a good salary to see out their days elsewhere, with the added bonus of a better chance of a first-team starting place. But Bergkamp was happy at Arsenal, his family were settled in Hadley Wood in Hertfordshire, and he was wealthy enough not to concern himself with diminished earning power. Besides, unlike many in his trade he wasn't materialistic. As he said when he arrived at Highbury, "I never believed in star status," and so easily adapted to the cameo role of the bit-part player. Ironically, Arsenal came closest to winning the Champions League in his final year at the club, by which time he had been phased out of the starting line-up, with compatriot Robin van Persie, José Antonio Reyes and Emmanuel Adebayor all ahead of him in the queue for the strikers' positions.

In Europe that season of 2005/06, Wenger often fielded a 4–5–1, leaving Thierry Henry to forage alone in attack whilst withdrawing his second striker into the midfield. It was a relatively new approach on the manager's part and the team was visibly more compact in the centre when not in possession. The notion of the second striker playing off the front man in the way Bergkamp sometimes did was dispensed with; this was no 4–4–1–1. It had been employed in the previous season's FA Cup Final (with Bergkamp as the lone front man) in desperation due to Wenger's conviction that his team was 'physically gone' and in his view there was no alternative. On that occasion, Lady Luck was probably Arsenal's outstanding contributor in a victory over Manchester United, secured via a penalty shoot-out after 120 tortuous minutes that was ill-deserved. So although Wenger will never go so far as to prepare a plan to deny his rivals, dire circumstances and the Champions League can force a more cautious approach, a rare concession of sorts. Of course the choice over when and where to involve Bergkamp was in the past now he was playing out his final year in a supporting capacity, which may have influenced the decision to deploy a line of five across the centre. The battle for midfield control often determines the outcome of European encounters. In past seasons, Arsenal were too dependent on Patrick Vieira and it was asking too much of one man to win the midfield battle almost single-handedly. Despite Vieira's heroics, there simply weren't enough tackles being made. Similarly, in defence, there was not enough quality support and cover to aid Sol Campbell. So when Henry and Pires flourished, they did so as a result of their own gifts and in spite of the system which was often fire-fighting rather than providing them with a solid platform on which they could freely express themselves.

When in possession with 4–5–1, there was no lack of flair, but the extra body in midfield aided the backline, and Arsenal were able to compile a Champions League record for not conceding a goal that spanned 12 fixtures. It was as if the manager, having reached a semi-final with Monaco in 1994, had finally remembered how to tackle the particular exigencies of the competition. Arsenal had tried and failed so many times to make the last four that he could not be credited with a tactical masterstroke after all this time, but rather, just trying something less adventurous that Henry, although not liking the role, could see the sense of: "[In the Champions League] we always played against teams who wanted to play positively apart from Juventus. We persevered with 4–5–1 and it worked well."

By not needing to alter the team between home and away legs, Arsenal developed a greater harmony and advanced to the final, taking the notable scalps of Real Madrid and Juventus *en route*. Bergkamp's last competitive duty for the club was for the final against Barcelona in Paris. With plenty of time to recover from the short trip by Eurostar, he was available for selection. However, it was no surprise that he only made the bench, and with stamina a priority due to the reduction to ten men after only 18 minutes with Jens Lehmann's dismissal (in tandem with the sacrifice of Robert Pires to make way for Manuel Almunia to keep goal) there was no chance of him making a valedictory appearance. Arsenal lost the final 2–1, Bergkamp a mere spectator. It was sad that he should be joined by Pires to watch the concluding 72 minutes, who it later transpired had also made his last bow in an Arsenal shirt.

The match turned out to be a watershed. Not only would the team never again grace their historic Highbury home, but three more of those who appeared would be joining Pires in bidding farewell. Sol Campbell, Ashley Cole and José Antonio Reyes never played for the club again. Following the loss of Patrick Vieira and before him Ray Parlour, could the dressing room now come to terms with the absence of so many key men? Could Arsène Wenger rebuild once again? And would he have to do it without his captain and star player?

CHAPTER SIX
TURNING OVER

May 17th 2006. In the changing room of the vanquished Champions League finalists, Thierry Henry walked over to Arsène Wenger. "I looked him straight in the eye and I simply said, 'I am staying,'" Henry reported. Arsène Wenger shook his hand and replied, "I knew it. I was certain." And yet, Henry had made up his mind only moments before. (The first that his wife, Clare, or his friend, David Dein, knew of the decision was on the plane returning to England.)

If the preceding 90 minutes of action had unfolded in a different manner, he might have made his own final appearance in an Arsenal shirt. Having resolved his quandary, it was easy to deny that possibility. "It was a decision made from the heart," he said later, "and if on losing I decided to stay, how much stronger would the feeling have been if we had won?" He went on to explain: "Despite everything wonderful that I envisaged [at Barcelona] it was not as strong as the relationship with my club. I wanted to be seen like a [Paolo] Maldini. When someone spoke about Arsenal, they spoke about me and when they spoke about me, they were speaking about Arsenal." The decision to stay may have been influenced by a very generous loyalty bonus paid upfront that became apparent when the club's accounts for the period were published.

The final had not been played in a good spirit. Henry, in particular, had been singled out for gratuitous attention from opponents who most observers believed would soon be his teammates. He was surprised and disillusioned at their behaviour. Equally disillusioned was Robert Pires. From his perspective, his sacrificial substitution that allowed Manuel Almunia to fill in for the dismissed goalkeeper Jens Lehmann made his mind up about leaving for *La Liga*'s Villarreal. "I try not to live with regrets," he reflected later. "I had to make a choice and, at that moment, it was painful to do it but I felt that regarding what happened during the final, I lost Arsène Wenger's confidence. I wasn't thinking about it before but, for me, it has been the trigger. It was the Champions League final in France, in front of all the family, all the French. So, for me, it has been the signal. He [Wenger] had plenty of options. I don't know who I would have substituted but, for me, it was the fatal blow."

If Arsenal had a full complement on the pitch, they would certainly have been able to push Barcelona much harder and might even have emerged victorious. Their confident start showed they were not in awe of their opponents and with two attacking formations the outcome could have remained in doubt until the very end. If Henry had lifted the trophy, he would have been able to depart reassured that he had given his side as much as he could, and that he was not leaving them in the lurch at a critical time of change. And Pires might have been content to accept the kind of arrangement Dennis Bergkamp had in his latter years. He wanted to feel appreciated, even if he felt he wasn't going to start every game as a matter of course (a situation already occurring due to the competition for places and his own advancing years).

Losing Pires was a blow, but Henry's decision to stay was crucial. Scheduled to move to their new home in the summer of 2006, Arsenal needed to provide value for money to a much larger audience of 60,000, of whom 9,000 would be asked to pay – on a fortnightly basis – the kind of sums that buy the best seats at a World Cup Final. In short, top of the bill stars who would both entertain and ensure the club contests the big prizes were essential, especially as they were not going to open the new ground as European champions.

Two days after the defeat in Paris, a press conference was called at which Thierry Henry, Arsène Wenger and David Dein all looked very pleased with themselves as it was announced that the number 14 shirt would continue to be worn by its present occupant. With a year remaining on his existing deal, Arsenal were in no position to let him see it out and leave for nothing in 2007. So it had came down to a choice of Henry either signing a new contract or moving on so that the club could receive substantial recompense on their investment.

David Dein later revealed "We turned down two world-record deals from Spanish clubs. You don't have to be a rocket scientist to work out who they were." (At the time the highest ever fee was the £47 million paid by Real Madrid for Zinedine Zidane to secure his services from Juventus in 2001.) When Dein added that "Our message was clear – he wasn't for sale. I'd like to think he heard that", one suspects that he can only have been talking about the past, as in 2006 Henry was most definitely on the market until pen had been put to paper to secure his services until 2010.

That Henry did decide to remain was a huge shot in the arm for both the club and its supporters. "I had two aims at the start of the week" said the manager, "to win the European Cup and then to make Thierry stay. I only managed one of those but, for the future of the club, that's certainly the best one. I believe this season has created a special bond inside the team and there is much more to come. Wednesday night reinforced that feeling among the players and if you want to continue that progression it would rely on Thierry's decision. It is basically an insurance for the future." This despite Wenger later admitting "It's not difficult to anticipate [that his performances would fall away as he got older] but I still signed him on a long contract because Thierry Henry has so many qualities that he could have played behind the striker as well. Or on the wing."

If there was understandable euphoria at the time, hindsight provides a different perspective. The reality is that, even though Henry was terrific box office, he cast a shadow over the club, one that inhibited the development of an ever-increasing number of young teammates. His contribution in the final season at Highbury, his first as club captain after the 2005 sale of Patrick Vieira to Juventus, had been monumental. Not only did he lead the side to a Champions League final, his Premiership goals (27 in 32 appearances) ensured that the club finished fourth and guaranteed their participation for the next competition. Certainly, a first season at their new opulent home without Champions League football would have been a bitter disillusion – more so in that it would have been Tottenham who would have ousted them if the last day results had worked out in their favour. "If Thierry went to a club like Barcelona or Real Madrid he would just be a prince," said David Dein. "Here he knows he is a king." And therein lay the seeds of malaise.

Life began at their new home with many of the more experienced heads having departed, and along with Jens Lehmann, Gilberto Silva and later William Gallas, Henry was outnumbered by callow young men barely out of their teens. He spoke positively of his role as an elder statesman, but so often his body language conveyed a completely different message. If a pass went astray, or was not made in his direction, he would often glare witheringly at the guilty party in the manner of a disapproving parent. Cesc

Fabregas later admitted, "Henry intimidated us. He is a great player but it was not easy to play alongside him." Even for an unworldly personality such as José Antonio Reyes, whose command of English was practically non-existent, Henry's disdain was all too apparent. Little wonder he couldn't wait to get back to his homeland and – ironically – the more accommodating regime of Fabio Capello at Real Madrid. It would be too late for Reyes, but after Henry, Fabregas emphasised that "Now it is different."

As the weeks went by at the Emirates, opponents quickly surmised that if they were able to stifle the home team with weight of numbers in and around their own danger area they could cope with the threat. Arsenal's desire to hold onto the ball until a gilt-edged chance was fashioned meant a lack of penetration. This was in spite of dominating possession and due in the main to prioritising Henry when, perhaps, it would have been better either going it alone or finding a better-placed colleague.

If Henry had gone and Pires had stayed, the team would have been able to play with more cohesion and fluidity, with a greater number of players weighing in with goals and assists. As Henry was injured for much of the campaign, the supporters became accustomed to seeing, on a regular basis, an Arsenal side without him. Indeed, some of the team's most satisfactory performances took place when he was on the sidelines. The Carling Cup run that culminated in a losing final against Chelsea showed the squad possessed real potential that was now ready for promotion. That final – Arsenal's last visit of ten made to Cardiff's Millennium Stadium in the seven years that Wembley was out of action marked the start of an 11-day period in which their involvement in all three cup competitions came to a sorry end. An FA Cup fifth-round replay at Blackburn saw an extra-time exit, before PSV visited north London the following midweek and concluded their host's European adventures for the season, despite the gamble of Henry entering the fray during the second half when patently not in physical shape to do so.

In fairness to Henry, there was every indication that he was never fully fit at any stage of the season and at the beginning of December, Wenger took the decision to rest him on the eve of the Emirates' first north London derby. There were back page headlines stating that Henry had taken the news very badly and argued with his manager before storming out of the training ground in a fit of pique. That version of events was vehemently denied by the player. "No one actually knows what we said to each other and still they are speculating," Henry said. "Nothing that has been said in the paper is true. I did leave the training ground disappointed on Friday because I wanted to play against Spurs. Nobody forced me to not play. It was a discussion that we had and I was upset because I don't like to not play. I want to be on the pitch. But sometimes you have to be honest with yourself and listen to your body." In Wenger's view, "August 15th finished Henry", a reference to France coach Raymond Domenech's insistence on playing the striker for the entirety of a friendly against Bosnia–Herzegovina. "He came out from an exhausting season that finished with a final in the Champions League and the final in the World Cup – which he both lost – and on top of that he didn't get the FIFA World Player of the Year. It was difficult to swallow because he knew he arrived close to 30 and that was the year for him. He didn't get rewarded and it was a killer for him. He was physically and mentally exhausted." After a summer devoid of a decent rest, Wenger knew the vital importance of not rushing back his star forward. Henry was not even considered for the first leg of the critical Champions League qualifier against Dinamo Zagreb, even though it took place over four weeks after he picked up his runners-up medal in Berlin. "We do not play with players who are not at a certain level of preparation," stated Wenger, a hint that was patently ignored by Domenech.

By the beginning of December, Wenger had seen enough to know his captain was way below par. He was still scoring goals and registering assists, but the familiar burst of pace was sadly absent. Nevertheless, despite his better judgment he continued to select him until their spat brought matters to a head. Wenger decided to bite the bullet and admit that physically the club's record scorer, though not yet even 30, might have fallen victim to the immutable law of diminishing returns. And to expect a continuation of season after season of 25 goals and 20 assists (which had come to be taken for granted by Arsenal fans) was unrealistic.

Henry probably didn't help his cause with his newspaper column in *The Sun* on the day of the Tottenham game as he began his enforced rest. He said, "Our situation at Arsenal is like a boxer going in the ring, a lightweight going up against a heavyweight. You can have a surprise sometimes but, more often than not, the heavyweight will last longer over 12 rounds. The depth of the squad is nowhere near the others. I am not having a go at the board or the manager. It is just a fact. There will always be teams that have more money than you. But you can rest assured Arsène Wenger will try to – once again – land a few bargains in January. Even using the loan system, there are top-class players who would jump at the chance of first-team football. One player who springs to mind is Chelsea's Shaun Wright-Phillips. If he could be picked up on loan, I'm sure he could do a great job, given half a chance." Arsène Wenger doubtless did not take kindly to Henry telling him how to do his job. So when quizzed on Henry's comments, his terse response – "I don't know, you should ask him," – hinted that his captain was operating outside his remit. Less diplomatic was an unnamed international colleague who told the French press that the striker is "an enormous bighead who cannot take criticism".

In truth, after what turned out to be his final appearance in an Arsenal shirt against PSV, Henry could have been pressed back into service for the final weeks of the campaign, but as there was little likelihood of failing to ensure a top-four finish and Champions League qualification, nor on the other hand of challenging for the top two positions, Wenger took the opportunity to assess the prospects for the following season rather than field one he had already decided was expendable. Henry's sudden sale in the summer to Barcelona for £16.1 million took supporters by surprise in much the same way as had Vieira's to Juventus two years earlier, not least because the day before the news of the deal become public, Henry took part in the launch of Arsenal's commercial relationship with Ebel watchmakers, a very ironic piece of timing.

Henry's own willingness to leave the UK may have been influenced by the break-up of his marriage, news of which came out after the move. He reportedly told friends, "Lots of things have changed recently and I had to get away from everything English, including my wife unfortunately. It's a very sad time for all of us, but you've got to know when to move on." The feeling had been growing that perhaps he had been too hasty in rejecting Barcelona's advances. Certainly, a year earlier the Catalans had believed they had their man, whom they anticipated – after their double of the Champions League and *La Liga* – would set them up wonderfully for the defence of their titles. They felt they had been badly let down by Henry. A year on and Ferran Sorriano, Barcelona's vice-president in charge of all economic activities, was prepared to try again, but only after Henry had indicated a change of heart. The departure of his close friend, David Dein, on the one hand and the close professional ties with the Dein family on the other – Dein's eldest son Darren is

Henry's commercial adviser, and his daughter Sascha, who had worked in Barcelona, acted as a conduit – facilitated the rapprochement between the two parties. As Arsène Wenger recalls, "He's a very intelligent guy. And he said, 'Listen, I have two or three years at the top, top, top. We have a very good young side but I do not want to wait for success. And so I want to go somewhere where I can get immediate success because in two, three years that will not be possible anymore for me.'" Barcelona received the assurances they sought and the transfer was speedily concluded. Yet Wenger emphasised: "It was his decision. Like it was his decision to stay. But when he wanted to leave I didn't want to stand in his way because if he feels deeply like that as the captain of the club I want to do what he wants."

An ill-timed correlation among some of the more mature players who have left Arsenal in recent years was that they seemed to become injury prone with their new clubs. Certainly this applied to both Vieira and Henry (the former missing spells through injury at both Juventus and subsequently Internazionale and the latter experiencing a stop-start first season at Barcelona). More seriously, Edu and Robert Pires both missed almost their entire first seasons with their new Spanish clubs as a result of pre-season injuries. Going further back, Marc Overmars and Emmanuel Petit also had problems remaining fit at Barcelona. Whether Wegner anticipated falling performance levels or they were just unfortunate coincidences only he can say. With hindsight, his judgment on when to let older heads move on is rarely at fault, even if there is a good deal of head scratching at the time.

Undoubtedly the longer Wenger manages, the greater is his own preference for youth (and physical capability) over experience, although he acknowledges the gap in his team's armour created by the potential mental fragility that this can bring. Which begs the question, is his policy a consequence of Hobson's choice (with a limited available budget) or a genuine conviction that it is the only way to achieve optimum results in a sport that is becoming ever faster and placing greater physical and psychological demands on its participants?

Despite the company line that Arsène Wenger's transfer budget was unaffected by the board scrambling around to raise funds to build their new home, the facts tell a very different story. The summer of 2001 was the last period when substantial sums (£22.5 million on three players) were spent in the close season. The outlay in the following three summers totalled less than £15 million – and that amount was recouped by Vieira's transfer alone. Wenger did buy Sevilla's José Antonio Reyes in January 2004 for an initial payment of £10.5 million, although there was not enough in the kitty to complete the purchase of Robin van Persie from Feyenoord, whose move, despite only costing £2.75 million, had to be postponed for six months. Perhaps if Van Persie had arrived earlier, the Invincibles side may have able to extend their prowess to the FA Cup or Champions League, where they fell agonisingly short. It was a matter of keeping the ship afloat rather than trying to keep up with the liners disappearing over the horizon, a policy that sunk Leeds United.

So the manager had to gamble on potential rather than relying on reputation, prospects who would be unlikely to reach the standard of Vieira, Henry and Pires as rapidly, if at all. As a consequence for two seasons the club was well off the pace at the top of the Premiership, yet ironically Wenger was inured against criticism by the move that had created the handicap in the first place. There was little danger of lack of demand to attend for the final season at Highbury, whilst the novelty of the Emirates also produced full capacity. So despite the extra 22,000 places (a good portion of which were in the highly priced middle tier) as many were coming through the turnstiles as would have if the team they were coming to see were the Invincibles reprised.

The only real imposition placed on the manager as he replenished his resources was the prerequisite of year-on-year involvement in the Champions League for the income it guaranteed. He pulled it off, but certainly flirted with danger as qualification became a serious distraction in Highbury's home stretch, Arsenal only squeezing past Tottenham and into fourth place on the last match day. Points were certainly sacrificed as more and more of the players pencilled in for his future plans were blooded: the defence that was put out after the turn of the year often featured 24-year-old Kolo Toure as its oldest head.

During the Invincibles season, Wenger was questioned about the optimum age for footballers.

"I'm convinced that up front now you need to be young," he began.

"Up front? I remember last year," said his interviewer, "you talked about the optimum ages throughout the team. Can you tell me how you feel about that now? How old does a goalkeeper have to be?"

"Between 30 and 35"

"And a central defender?"

"I would say best age 26 to 34. Midfield between 26 and 32 and a striker between 24 and 30. Those are the top ages."

"But you're breaking those rules with some of the young players aren't you?"

"Exceptional talents break the rules – that means they play early – they make their own rules. I do not say that these players do not play before [they reach the optimum age] but they are at the top of their potential during this period. But before, because they have an exceptional talent they play already."

"What about some of the other key qualities for each of these departments in the team?" Wenger was asked.

"Well I would say at the back it's concentration, apart from all the quality you look for . . ."

"In an athlete?"

"You need to be an athlete everywhere, but I must say for me the top quality for a defender is concentration level."

"Don't you only get that though when you get older?"

"Yes, because you get more cautious, and he is a fireman, a defender, he always predicts the worst and tries to have a position where he can correct it. So that's easier when you get older. When you're young you live off the cuff. Midfield – a technical level and up front pace."

"And you would say that you have that throughout the team at the moment?" his questioner continued.

"Well we have qualities I feel are very exciting and overall a very good technical level and a very good athletic level. Then I think we have above that a great spirit in the club and in the team."

With the financial restrictions placed upon him, Wenger's shopping had to be even smarter, which meant procuring less-established players than he might have picked up in more affluent times. The mark of a typical signing during this time was their anonymity, even those who were already internationals. So instead of Kanu, possessor of a Champions League winner's medal, 2006 saw Emmanuel Adebayor join from Monaco – an unused substitute in the 2004 final with a loser's medal for watching his vanquished teammates. Who in the English game was familiar with Abou Diaby or Bacary Sagna from Auxerre? Even internationals like Alex Hleb and Eduardo had fans wondering about their pedigree. The one exception was William Gallas, an atypical signing as the likelihood of Wenger hiring a 29-year-old apart from a goalkeeper under normal circumstances are almost non-existent. However, David Dein was determined that if Ashley Cole was going to Chelsea it must be at the cost of weakening their squad rather than making a minuscule dent in their owner's bank balance. A more characteristic purchase who arrived at the same time as Gallas but with far less fanfare was the 18-year-old Brazilian Denilson from São Paulo.

Of course, the debatable decision to dispense with experience was a matter of choice for Wenger. Starting with Dennis Bergkamp, the policy of only offering single-year contract extensions to the over-30s was introduced. Thus, a player in his late 20s knew that any deal he signed would be the last to give him any long-term security. If the new approach meant the loss of Robert Pires and Sylvain Wiltord (who was offered a two-year contract as a 29-year-old, but rejected it in order to be able to leave on a free transfer) then so be it. The manager was prepared to forego a potential transfer fee rather than subsidise for any length of time someone who he felt had his best days behind him. On occasion, Wenger's intransigence strained relationships. While Dennis Bergkamp was prepared to accept what was on offer and come back for more at yearly intervals, others wanted and felt they deserved greater security. It became apparent from January 2004 onwards that Wiltord would leave in the summer and, once he had recovered from injury, he was marginalised in much the same way Ian Wright had been several years earlier. As Wiltord went on to enjoy three title-winning seasons with Lyon, there is certainly an argument to be made that Wenger would have been better served by retaining him in spite of his age, rather than investing heavily in his youthful replacement, José Antonio Reyes, who ultimately flattered to deceive.

Wenger though had different priorities. He had to ensure that if, financially, things did not work out, he had a young group who would grow older together and that, in the worst case scenario, would have some sell-on value. "My priority will always be to keep the players I already have," he says, "because above all I believe in the virtues of teamwork. And one can only maintain and develop the players by communicating a culture, a culture which passes from generation to generation." In the short term, trophies would actually be a bonus. It was a delicate balancing act, operating with a miniscule budget compared to his rivals whilst keeping his team competitive enough to ensure Champions League football, with its attendant (and essential) income.

The corollary at the start of the 2006/07 season was a largely inexperienced squad. The opening skirmishes at the Emirates saw Henry and Ljungberg start, although their injury woes soon gave the fans a glimpse of the future. Aside from Gilberto and William Gallas, the oldest outfield squad members were 25-year-olds Tomas Rosicky and Kolo Toure. So much for Wenger's optimum ages. By his own criteria, only William Gallas was playing at the peak of his powers. His qualifying assessment, "because they have exceptional talent they play already", was still to be proved.

Compared to the past there were a high number of home draws in the first half of the Premiership campaign – five in the first nine fixtures. A pattern emerged as a result of unworldliness on the one hand and exceptional stamina and fitness on the other. Either Arsenal scored first, and went on to a comfortable victory, or conceded the lead and then salvaged a draw, often equalising right at the death as the visitors visibly wilted under the pressure. But it was often naivety – specifically a lack of concentration – that sometimes handicapped them when they fell behind. Still, the omens were good. As the team gradually became accustomed to their new surroundings, results improved. The concluding ten league matches saw only five points dropped, compared with twice as many from the first nine. They even came from behind to beat eventual champions Manchester United, and taken in conjunction with a victory at Old Trafford, the conviction grew that, with greater consistency, this young side could challenge their free-spending rivals.

Wenger believes that "the elevation of the general physical level has made the game faster and therefore you need a minimum high standard of physical ability to survive, even if you have experience and talent. So, instead of driving at 100 miles an hour football is now 150 miles an hour. So at 150 mph you can use your experience, but you must be [physically] capable of driving at 150 mph. The physical level of any team in the Premier League compared to ten years ago is higher. Because every new generation is better prepared. And the measurement of the physical performances of the players has kicked out some players who were not at the level."

Certainly the Arsenal squad for the first seasons at the Emirates, with at least two players for every position, was numerically as strong as any other. However, due to the lack of experience, there was less quality in depth. So, needing to overturn a 1–0 deficit against PSV in the home leg of the Champions League game, Wenger fielded Gilberto at centre back whilst the raw Johan Djourou remained on the bench. In central midfield there were two teenagers. No one questioned the selection of the precocious Fabregas, but was Denilson the right partner? Up front Emmanuel Adebayor, yet to notch his first Champions League goal, was partnered by Julio Bapista who, outside of the Carling Cup, had scored a total of two goals since his arrival on loan from Real Madrid. Arsenal's scorer on the night? A PSV player putting through his own net. It was not enough. In desperation, Wenger was forced to send on an unfit Thierry Henry for his final appearance in a futile attempt to score a second goal. PSV qualified thanks to a late equaliser.

With every passing transfer window since Wenger splashed out on Theo Walcott, Adebayor and Abou Diaby in January 2006, Arsenal's supporters became increasingly frustrated at the small amount of chequebook activity, not least because with the club at last on more solid financial ground and the board's pronouncements of available funding, the only restraint on the manager is his own parsimony. Many fans believe the squad is simply not strong enough, doubting Wenger's faith in the younger players, or indeed that certain of the older ones that he has signed (such as Pascal Cygan) were ever good enough in the first place. What is revealing about the youthful inflow is that, in spite of not paying huge sums to get them, Arsenal's 2006/07 wage bill (£89.7 million) was similar in size to that of Manchester United, though at just over 50% of turnover is way below the Premiership average (Chelsea write their own rules with staff costs of over £100 million). The message seems to be that even if Arsène Wenger now chooses not to shop at Harrods, once he has bought what he wants, he is determined to hang onto it if he can (without undermining the club's wage structure).

With a combined budget for transfer activity and player wages, the Arsenal manager knows his limits, though they have been considerably extended as a result of the high rise in income: the Emirates effect. If former managing director Keith Edelman is taken at his word ("Arsène has got sufficient funds for any signing he wishes to make") Wenger chooses not to spend everything he has available to him. Towards the end of the 2006/07 season, Peter Hill-Wood, Danny Fiszman and Arsène Wenger met up for dinner at Wiltons, a renowned West End restaurant. Hill-Wood recalls, "At the end of the dinner, we were talking about a new contract for him. And Danny said, 'Arsène, if we gave you £100 million to spend, what would you do?' And this was exactly his remark. 'I'd give it back.' Good, nice to hear it."

It is apparent that the manager places more importance on keeping happy those he has taken time and energy to find and develop than he does taking a chance on expensive new additions. "I will always stick to the same policy," Wenger explains, "but if there is a guy who could one day reach out to another level and will cost a fortune, we could nevertheless buy him." It would be inaccurate to claim that Wenger used to sign current stars, as really only Marc Overmars, Davor Suker, Sol Campbell and William Gallas ever arrived with well-established reputations that the manager was never going to markedly enhance. But it could certainly be argued that Arsenal had more success when there was stiffer competition for places, with experienced campaigners often unable to get a start. At no point in their careers at the club could the likes of Kanu, Sylvain Wiltord, Edu, Gilles Grimandi and Oleg Luzhny claim that they had a first-team place nailed down. That resource disappeared with the stadium move and cries for its return have seemingly fallen on deaf ears.

Is it possible that, in reaction to what Wenger has referred to as "financial doping" (a veiled attack on certain clubs' extravagant spending) he has decided to build a team in a completely different way, declining to engage in any auction? Could he be reluctant to spend his budget by way of proving a point? Namely, anyone can buy success, but there is another way: constructing a side stuffed full with players produced by his own coaching methods. "You may forget that one of the joys of team sports is the development of a group who have been together for some time," reflects Wenger. "Take the example of this young Arsenal team [2007/08]. They have grown up together which means they have also suffered together and shared the pain. When you think about the disappointments of last season, I feel in spite of everything it was a turning point. We held on. We never gave up and we always fought. I said to myself, 'There is something special there, a mental strength that will surprise people when it goes well.'"

Granted, the approach is almost certainly a result of (financial) necessity being the mother of (youthful) invention, but how many other managers could have produced a team on such meagre resources that sells out a 60,000 stadium on a habitual basis? And not only that, but wherever in the world they play, Arsenal attract crowds as glamour opposition, a consequence of the regular broadcasting of their Premiership adventures and the sheer entertainment value they provide. So now Milan or Real Madrid versus Arsenal is an 80,000-plus sell-out as a live event with millions more around the world watching the television spectacular. Indeed, the Arsenal versus Milan Champions League first leg in February 2008 had more commentary teams covering the game in the flesh than any previous match in the competition's history outside the final. Wenger's young team are top of the bill, as he concurs: "I think we are more respected in Europe because of eight or nine consecutive seasons in the Champions League. Everywhere we go it looks like it is a big, big game. We had to gain respect and we are [now] looked upon as a big scalp." (Gooners still chuckle at Zinedine Zidane's response when a journalist asked him if he almost joined Tottenham earlier in his career. The answer – "Who?" – would never have been given about Arsenal.)

The significance of Europe is uppermost in Wenger's mind. Firstly, continued participation goes a long way towards underpinning his budget. Secondly, in his own mind, the absence of the Champions League trophy is a gaping hole in his CV that he is determined to fill in before his work at Arsenal is complete. "I want to win the Champions League but it's step by step," he says. "And to win not once but two or three times, to go into the history of European football." And if he can do it with his 'third' Arsenal side, it will be the supreme achievement, against all the odds.

CHAPTER SEVEN
MOVE ALONG NOW

In the summer of 1998 Arsenal announced that their upcoming Champions League matches would not be staged at their own home. As newly crowned Premiership champions the club, for the first time since 1991, had qualified for the rebranded European Cup. In the intervening seven years the competition had undergone a dramatic makeover. So much so that Arsenal were apparently unwilling to meet the stipulated commercial criteria demanded by UEFA. The broadcasters and sponsors who underwrote the competition and provided the huge financial rewards required literally hundreds of tickets, hospitality and parking spaces. Highbury might not have been ideal, but with a little effort and imagination the obligations could have been fulfilled. Somehow, the venue that could not cope in 1998 and 1999 was subsequently able to host six campaigns when the club's original choice of Wembley Stadium began the process of reconstruction. The club bit the bullet and moved a couple of hundred Highbury season-ticket holders from their prime West Stand seats. They also had to leave the first four pitchside rows empty, presumably irritating more fans, so that the perimeter advertising boards of the Champions League sponsors could have the necessary impact. As a result, capacity was reduced to 35,500.

But the main reason behind the decision to sacrifice a large measure of home advantage and play at Wembley in 1998 was that the directors knew only too well that more and more potential revenue was being lost with every successive home fixture. Moving the Champions League matches to a venue that could accommodate over 70,000 would give them a firm idea of how many people might be prepared to pay to watch the team if more tickets were available. And of course they could make more money if their hunch proved correct.

The trio of group-stage opponents – Dynamo Kiev, Panathinaikos and Lens – were hardly the stuff of legend to fire the imagination of the Gooner multitude, so as insurance against the potential embarrassment of banks of empty seating, prices were heavily discounted, with thousands available at £10. And it worked, as all three matches easily sold out. However, the downside of the exercise was that Arsenal went out, finishing third despite the questionable standard of the opposition, group winners Dynamo Kiev excepted. At least the following season, there was less disgrace in being eliminated by Barcelona and Fiorentina, although the exit was still a terrible letdown after creditable away draws against both clubs. Arsenal had not bargained for the opposition, without exception, raising their game, stimulated by the prospect of playing at one of the historic homes of football. Although these appear in the Arsenal record books as home fixtures, there was no question that effectively they took place at a neutral venue.

At least the third match of the group against unglamorous Swedish opponents provided the reassurance that Arsenal could fill the high capacity whoever they were playing. "What really opened my eyes," Arsène Wenger later reflected "was that when we played against [AIK] Solna in the Champions League at Wembley we sold 74,000 seats and the opponent wasn't anybody exceptional." "Why?" asked David Dein rhetorically. "Because we had 20,000 seats at £10. We simply have to have a bigger stadium. We are at a disadvantage [at Highbury]. You go to Old Trafford and they've got over 60,000 of their own fans behind them. People want to see us. Now is the time to act." Ultimately, from a marketing point of view at least it was an invaluable experiment, albeit at the cost of effectively delaying the team's learning process on the continent by a couple of seasons.

To even begin to satisfy their potential customers, the board would have to look at leaving Highbury for good. The Wembley experience created an about turn in the directors' plans. Chairman Peter Hill-Wood recalls, "We had a board meeting and decided to look at building a new stadium and we agreed unanimously we wouldn't move, and then we changed our mind. I think you've always got to be prepared to do that." To David Dein the marble halls were history. "We are treading water," he said. "What we are doing now [by being at Highbury] is to keep putting prices up in order to try to meet overheads and you now have a different supporter profile. And that in my opinion is not right."

Worried about the impending drain on resources that building a new stadium would entail and how it might affect the playing side, Dein continued to press for other options with Wembley at the top of his list of candidates. He wanted Arsenal to consider returning to Wembley with its re-opening scheduled for 2003. He felt that if Wembley became Arsenal's permanent home it would in time become a stronghold, just as it had been for England for decades. Of course the stadium would be owned by the FA, still staging cup finals and England internationals, and Arsenal would be its partner by virtue of providing the bulk of its turnover. It was an unusual concept – with matchday and event income more than covering the fixed and variable costs of building and administration providing the unlikely scenario of relegation was avoided.

However, when it came for support for his Wembley plan

Dein was soon in a minority of one. "I think that the rest of the board felt that [Dein's] judgment was quite wrong," said Peter Hill-Wood. "Whether he had a different agenda to the rest of us is a moot point. We were convinced that we had to have our own stadium. To be tenants of the FA at Wembley with an ever-increasing rental didn't make any financial sense." It would have been unheard of for a top-tier British club not to own their own home, although a common arrangement in Italy where a stadium is often owned by the local authority and sometimes hosts more than one team, such as Rome's Stadio Olimpico (shared by Roma and Lazio) and the San Siro (home of AC Milan and Internazionale). The vice-chairman's view was based on a belief that the immediate here and now was what counted and, if successful, the future would take care of itself.

His co-directors did consider buying Wembley outright. "We actually made a bid before the FA bought it [from Wembley plc]," confirms Hill-Wood. "It would not have been the right answer but we were serious about it." This was a bizarre standpoint considering the club's poor playing results at the national stadium. Arsenal were prepared to ignore the maxim that to have a successful business you first have to have a successful team. Apart from the attendances, Wembley had provided little evidence it could replace the stronghold that was Highbury. However, the argument was soon academic. The old venue hosted its final match in autumn 2000, with the FA aiming to replace the existing structure and re-open for business within three years. A seemingly never-ending succession of construction, financial and legal problems resulted in the new Wembley eventually staging its first match several months after the Emirates was up and running.

Another option for Arsenal was to locate near the M25 motorway in Hertfordshire, which would have allowed for easier access by car, and little in the way of 'NIMBY' objections or construction constraints. However, while parking problems would have been mitigated, there would have been fewer links to public transport and due to its lack of proximity to the West End and the City, the corporate hospitality market, not least for midweek matches, would have been more difficult to attract.

The club were persuaded to change their focus away from greenfield sites by Antony Spencer, a partner of land agents Anthony Green and Spencer. Initially involved with the board as a conduit for the Eurostar development at Kings Cross – Eurostar wanted to incorporate Arsenal in their plans for a new station – Spencer quickly recognised that there were insoluble problems with that concept and switched his attention to coming up with an alternative even closer to home. Superimposing an exact to scale footprint of the Wembley Stadium site on the London N5 section of the A–Z, the possibility of Ashburton Grove leapt off the page at him. A triangle of land sandwiched between the London to Glasgow railway line, the Hornsey Road and Queensland Road, housing a council waste depot and several small businesses, the site was just about big enough for a stadium but obtaining planning permission would be problematic to say the very least.

With Arsenal pursuing a number of different options, now including Finsbury Park, Spencer, having become even more convinced that his idea was viable – despite initially been told by the board not to be ridiculous, it was a built-up area – eventually persuaded them to allow him to present his proposal. The thrust of his presentation was that "Arsenal should move to Arsenal", 500 yards down the road. As Spencer later reflected, "If the planning rules had been strictly enforced, the site would never have been selected as it was a designated industrial site [prohibiting leisure development]." But he knew that Islington Council were desperate to keep the club in the borough and the fact that they owned 80 per cent of the site might just make the pipe dream a reality.

With Arsenal only interested in finding a new home, Spencer had to alert them to the necessity of incorporating regeneration as a fundamental plank in the project if they were ever going to get permission for an inner London stadium. It took a while for a meeting of minds. He eventually convinced them that "they were being taken for a walk in the park" regarding their preferred site of Finsbury Park (a contact of Spencer's at the Government Office For London told him, "they're crazy if they think they're going to build a football stadium in a park"). What Spencer brought to the party was the power of his argument as a committed supporter and his expertise as a property developer. He persuaded the board that he was a pragmatist who practised the art of the possible. Long after the Emirates was up and running, acting Managing Director Ken Friar was finally able to generously give Spencer his due. "We wouldn't have been able to do it [re-locate to Ashburton Grove] without his foresight. It was under our noses and we couldn't see it. Not only did he find it for us but he spent the next few years putting it together."

Having settled on Ashburton Grove, a scheduled opening date within four years – August 2004 – was announced, which was hopelessly optimistic given the unchartered territory that had to be navigated in the planning and construction of a 60,000 capacity football stadium in an inner London borough, not to mention the relocation of the waste transfer station.

As progress proceeded apace, Danny Fiszman was intrigued to learn how Spencer was proving so adroit in acquiring the necessary land from the small businesses on the site. He persuaded Spencer to take him to one of his meetings. As they got out of Spencer's car, Fiszman said to him, "Antony, haven't you forgotten something?" meaning his briefcase containing the necessary offer documents. "Oh yes," said Spencer, and went to the boot of his car and took out a baseball bat. Fiszman blanched, remembering only the previous week that Spencer had given him a DVD of *The Sopranos*. Spencer laughed, put the bat – which belonged to his baseball-playing son and just happened to be in his car that morning – back, retrieved his briefcase and they went to their appointment. Afterwards, recalling the reaction of the vendor, who said, "It's not every day somebody comes in to buy your property surrounded by two stinking rubbish dumps with rats running round everywhere. You'd [the Arsenal duo] better sit down and have a cup of tea." Spencer told Fiszman that his *modus operandi* was polite perseverance. No force necessary.

Unfortunately by this time Danny Fiszman's relationship with David Dein was not so cordial. Fiszman had bought into the club in 1992 when Dein, in need of investment in his commodity company, had sought a sympathetic purchaser for a significant chunk of his 42 per cent holding who would agree to voting with him on key decisions. As the decade progressed, Dein required further funds to plough into an ultimately fruitless and highly costly legal attempt to recover a bad debt related to his non-Arsenal business. Effectively, Fiszman became a cash machine for the vice-chairman, as he purchased outright more and more of the shares he held jointly with Dein. Most significantly, control of a block of shares transferred in 1996 enabled Fiszman to overtake Dein as Arsenal's largest shareholder. In December 1999, Dein sold what remained of the jointly held shares to Fiszman, leaving Dein with a 16.2 per cent stake (compared with Fizman's 28 per cent).

Then the pair fell out. The specific reason why the two men argued remains the subject of speculation to this day, even to chairman Hill-Wood, who maintains, "I don't know [why they fell out]. I'd be very interested. Danny has never said anything to me about it. He's very discreet." When it was put to Dein that money issues might be the cause of his relationship with Fiszman breaking down, he dismissed the notion. Certainly there is a case for believing they may have disagreed about the stadium issue to such an extent that their previously harmonious state could never be repaired. It was the biggest decision the club had ever made. And Fiszman gaining the support of the other directors for Ashburton Grove was something Dein may have taken as a personal affront.

With the new stadium and its concomitant commercial and financial ramifications prioritised, David Dein's remit became confined to the playing staff (which over the years, whatever his other specific responsibilities, had always been his primary concern). With only a supporting role on the main project, to make matters worse for Dein, Keith Edelman was drafted in as managing director to replace Ken Friar. With choppy waters ahead, the club needed a harsh dose of financial reality and Edelman fitted the bill perfectly. In name, Edelman may have been succeeding Friar, but he effectively became Arsenal's first full-time chief executive. He was the antithesis of Dein, far more businessman than football man. Maybe so, but contracts with builders and bankers rather than the football authorities were now the order of the day.

In December 2001, the green light for the venture was given by Islington Council. Looking back, Peter Hill-Wood describes turning the dream into reality as "an amazing feat. We had a lot of people criticise the local planners and the council and all that. We had a lot of support from Islington and there were people there who had the vision to see that this was a regeneration scheme that was going to be of great benefit to Islington. We did it for the sake of Arsenal but you've got to weigh that up with the benefits that you contribute locally otherwise you're not going to get consent." The board had finally embraced Antony Spencer's regeneration vision. As part of the agreement the area had to be revitalised with 2,500 new residential units, a waste transfer station to replace the one previously sitting where the new stadium's pitch is now as well as bridges and walkways to facilitate the flow of pedestrian traffic on matchdays. Arsenal had to acquire the land at no little cost, relocate over 50 existing businesses that had to – in some cases unwillingly – make way for the development. As football stadium expert Simon Inglis commented, "For all the team's prowess on the pitch, 20 years ago the idea of Arsenal taking the lead role in the regeneration of Islington would have seemed absurd. And yet it is now claimed that the club has become in effect the largest private residential developer in the borough. It is an extraordinary turnaround." The actual building cost of the stadium, by the appointed contractor Sir Robert McAlpine, was £225 million – a figure dwarfed by a total bill of over £430 million. Just how many Thierry Henrys would that sort of money buy?

Actually, about eight and half at the peak of his powers, if Chelsea's enquiries for him during his Arsenal career are to be taken at face value, prompting the observation from Dein that "the Russians have parked their tanks on our lawn and are firing £50 notes at us." As one of the approaches came at half-time during an Arsenal – Chelsea match in late 2004, Dein mentioned it to Danny Fiszman, who said, "Tell them to f*** off!" "I have," responded Dein. At another time, Dein reportedly began a meeting with Chelsea's hierarchy by walking into the room announcing, "Thierry Henry's not for sale." It was the kind of attitude that endeared him to the supporters, although he was speaking on behalf of a board who might not always have shared his view, depending on the size of the offer, as the financial constraints of Ashburton Grove began to envelop everything and everyone.

The board were looking beyond a time when Arsène Wenger, or indeed any of them, would still be around. The manager had been able to spend substantially in the summers of 2000 and 2001 and the purchases he made then would set him up for a time when the purse strings were tightened:

Arsenal would go on to win five major trophies in four seasons between 2002 and 2005, with salaries rather than transfers the predominant expense. In making their decision to go ahead with Ashburton Grove the board were prepared to risk the present for the future, but walked a financial tightrope in order to do it, emboldened by a manager who told them he could, if necessary, make do, mend and still bring them success. Hill-Wood pays tribute to Wenger's realism about the financial circumstances in which he was operating, confirming, "He has always been very happy with it [his budget]. He's never come to us and said, 'I want to buy X, he's going to cost us £50 million', because he understands the figures well enough to know that we can't afford £50 million."

At one point it looked as if the board were going to have to stump up a lot more if the new stadium project was not going to be stymied. One particular piece of land on the east side of the Caledonian Road turned out to be an essential piece of the jigsaw. Its acquisition from a supermarket chain (who had initially intended to build a huge store, but were beset with planning difficulties of their own), reached an impasse. They were prepared to sell but their price was high, and they weren't budging. Whilst Arsenal's trio of Fiszman, Edelman and Friar took stock of their position, there were rumours that there were other parties about to enter the fray. So to ensure they were not gazumped the Arsenal board had to act quickly, pay up and pay the full price.

Demolition work began in 2002. However, while this process was comparatively straightforward, in April 2003 tools were downed as the club, overwhelmed by legal and planning obstacles, faced a cash-flow problem. McAlpine had to redeploy workers with no indication as to when they might be able to return. A revised timetable had already been put in place anticipating a completion date of August 2005, but now that was postponed once again to the start of the 2006/07 season. Later Hill-Wood admitted, "We weren't cash positive at Highbury for some years. We weren't actually generating cash and businesses survive on cash-flow." There were a lot of boardroom man hours put in to salvage the plans, and the relevant trio of directors pressed on, but the ramifications were felt down the line as the club, in the words of the chairman, "muddled through financially".

Negotiations to award Dennis Bergkamp a one-year contract were dragged out endlessly by the club, to the frustration of both the player and his agent. When it was later suggested to Arsène Wenger that there were faults on both sides, he was candid enough to exonerate the player. "Dennis Bergkamp was always, I must say, faultless. He was always strongly determined to stay and made big sacrifices (a significant drop in salary) in order to do so. But when a player goes from 34 to 35 you don't know if he will make the whole season. It [the problem] was on the club side. We didn't know how far we could go financially because we didn't know how many games he would play." Wenger then added his own *mea culpa*: "I must say he [Bergkamp] has produced much more this season [2003/04] than physical tests would have told you. And that's all credit to him." And there were other economies that must have been difficult for Wenger to swallow. The preseason training camp in Austria involved travelling with a budget airline (although that would have been academic to the non-flying Dutchman). It was as well that the French stars who were in the process of renegotiating contract extensions could not make the trip due to their participation for *Les Bleus* in the Confederations Cup. The ignominy might have had them electing to ply their trade elsewhere.

What irony then that, from such a makeshift position, Wenger achieved his finest ever league season despite, after initial encouragement, being refused any of his earmarked reinforcements. Perhaps he didn't think he would have to make such sacrifices. In February 2004, he revealed his frustration when questioned about the state of play.

"There's an English expression – fool's errand – where they send you somewhere and they already know that you can't find the answer," it was put to Wenger. "Last summer David Dein went and had a look at [José Antonio] Reyes and Harry Kewell and also [Cristiano] Ronaldo. But you didn't have any money even though the chairman [had] said that the building of the new stadium wouldn't deprive you of money."

"Last year, the situation was a little bit different," replied Wenger. "We had not completed the financing of the stadium so we had to be cautious. We wanted to go step by step, complete the signing of the stadium and then plan the future because we can improve, can prepare the team for 2006 and get the income in the future years, so we didn't want to go into any risky situation before we had done that."

"You're very loyal, but I would put it a different way," continued his questioner. "Would you say that, at a certain time, the directors – excluding yourself and David Dein – prioritised the stadium over the team, and they felt that you would make bricks out of straw."

"Well I believe that the club was at the moment of history where you have to go a step further if you want to become one of the biggest clubs in the world," Wenger responded. "You can always argue how much or not how much but if you want to go a step further, considering the potential of the club, a new stadium was needed. Even if in the short term you had to be more cautious with the team . . . what the board thought is that we had already a good team and that with the good work going on we could improve it because we have good youngsters."

"Did they know that or did you tell them that?"

"I told them that we had good youngsters," said Wenger, "and that we could still compete at the top level this season

[2003/04]. And it motivated the team as well because they knew – 'Come on, we have to be up for it' – because everybody bought and we didn't buy, so maybe it gave us a little bit more awareness that we had to dig deep and everybody pull together."

"You made a virtue out of a necessity."

"Yes, exactly, because I feel always that the team was still very young and that it could improve."

In the summer of 2003 Ronaldo joined Manchester United after impressing Alex Ferguson in a pre-season friendly with his then club Sporting Lisbon, whilst Kewell left Leeds for Liverpool. Reyes eventually joined Arsenal the following January from Sevilla, although his transfer fee would be paid in instalments. Dein described the situation as "like being in a boxing ring with one hand tied behind my back". He would emerge from board meetings around this time "with my eyeballs rolling" and was in no doubt that Arsène Wenger shared his frustration.

CHAPTER EIGHT

BUDDY, CAN YOU SPARE ME £260m?

How does an organisation with a turnover of £91 million, posting pre-tax losses of more than £22 million, raise £357 million? Answer: with three men – Danny Fiszman, Ken Friar and Keith Edelman – working like dogs, putting in some very long days and nights, to convince a group of banks to share the risk. When tools were downed and the Ashburton Grove site closed in 2003, Danny Fiszman (as he later revealed to a group of concerned fans) would wake up in the mornings with his bedsheets soaked in sweat. And if in 2008 chairman Peter Hill-Wood admitted "If we had our time again we would not have been so ambitious," (implying that he felt the club could have spent less extravagantly on fixtures and fittings), how low must everyone have felt in the dark ages of the cash-flow crisis of five years before? Showing remarkable fortitude, for the oppressed trio it was back to the drawing board to try to negotiate the obstacles that had halted their plans.

At the time, Leeds United were giving Premier League clubs a bad name as they vaingloriously chased the dream of becoming a European superpower. The heady taste of a run to a Champions League semi-final in 2001was so coercive that they went on a spending spree on players' wages and transfers which eventually took them out of the Premiership and into administration. Without their own continued Champions

League involvement Arsenal might have been tempted to go down the same road, putting themselves even further in hock whilst attempting to build a new home. "Many banks wouldn't look at funding because Leeds had just got into financial trouble," Edelman confirmed. "The banking market wasn't very excited at the prospect of building a new stadium."

At least, though, the club were able to raise some funds on their own. In 2000, a new share issue brought media group Granada (now ITV) into the fold with a 9.99% stake and as equal partners in Arsenal Broadband, a joint venture formed to exploit new media rights. In return, the club received £77 million in two stages: £47 million when the deal was struck, and a further £30 million due when planning approval for the new stadium was granted. "Organisationally, we've moved from a club to a business," Edelman later observed, an unwitting indictment on the *ancien régime* when Dein was pulling the strings. "When I joined in 2000, we had no money at all. Arsenal had put in over £150 million of equity [into the new stadium budget], so we had to do some very large transactions. The Granada deal was the cornerstone [facilitating other long-term agreements]." True, but did the club have to cede so much decision-making to another company who now controlled a large measure of their broadcasting and merchandising rights?

In 2004, a kit deal worth £55 million over seven years was struck with Nike. Crucially, the entire amount was paid upfront. Two years earlier, Nike had handed over five times as much for a 13-year agreement with Manchester United. Further, the existing shirt sponsorship deal with mobile phone operator O2 was markedly inferior to the sums both Manchester United and Chelsea received from their sponsors. In the intervening period, the football industry had not only expanded substantially, but Arsenal had shown that they were capable of matching United on the field. Yet the need for a cash injection not only forced them to sell themselves short, they undermined the long-term value of their business and handed an immediate significant competitive advantage to their chief rivals. Unlike Arsenal, Manchester United were able to invest their Nike income on the team.

Some time later Keith Edelman reflected, "We started to change our culture four to five years ago, to make people think forward and with a bit more entrepreneurialism. We wanted them to think more commercially, and be more customer-focused." A laudible sentiment, but there was still some way to go before the club could give Procter & Gamble a run for their money. To rub salt into their self-inflicted wounds, just a few miles away a serious contender had emerged to threaten the North/South duopoly.

With Chelsea in dire financial straits, in July 2003 the club's owner Ken Bates had sold out lock, stock and empty barrel to Russian billionaire Roman Abramovich. At great expense, Stamford Bridge had been metamorphosed into Chelsea Village, with a hotel and residential apartments as part of the development. Anticipating new revenue streams, money was spent in the transfer market and on wages, bringing the club success for the first time since Osgood and company were kings of the King's Road in the 1970s, but also taking it well into the red.

Arsenal had two pivotal fixtures against Chelsea in 2004. In February, they defeated them 2–1 in the league at Stamford Bridge. As their opponents that day eventually finished as runners-up to them, it was a vital result. However, in April at Highbury, the men Abramovich's fortune had assembled turned the tables in the Champions League. There had always been rich men in football but no one had ever spent so much money so quickly and to such effect as Roman Abramovich. It was a financial blue tidal wave that the Arsenal board could not have foreseen as they made their bid to keep up with

Manchester United. How could anyone compete with a business model, or to be more accurate the lack of one, which allows trading losses of tens of millions of pounds on an annual basis? After the *belle époque* of the Invincibles, Arsenal quickly found the task beyond them. Only by also throwing money around did once profitable Manchester United, now debt-ridden as consequence of the Glazer takeover, manage to eventually prevent the title going to the *nouveau riche* of West London for a third consecutive occasion in 2007.

At Highbury on the other hand, so much depended on one man to keep producing the goods. He was only an employee and there was no guarantee that he would stay around indefinitely. The contract Arsène Wenger signed in 2001 only ran until the end of the 2004/05 season. When renewal time came around in the autumn of 2004 he was probably the hottest managerial property in world football and could have named his price at any of several choice destinations if he had decided to depart the following summer. "We said we would like him to extend his contract with us till we got to the stadium," said Peter Hill-Wood. "Of course we would like him to stay longer. We made no secret of the fact that he was seen by everybody as very important to the development of the new stadium." It was probably no coincidence that Arsène Wenger signed his contract in 2001 shortly after planning permission for the new home was granted. And it was signed in the full knowledge that the days of big spending were over, at least in the short term, unless he could fund purchases by sales, a procedure that had served him well up to that point.

Fortunately Wenger himself, all too aware of how the hardship of Highbury was adversely affecting his plans, was as keen as anyone to move to a bigger place. "The heart wants to stay at Highbury," he admitted, "but the brain wants to go somewhere else." The board may have felt confident in his loyalty, but what if results took a serious downturn and eventually his position became untenable? Worse, what if ill health struck? It was a huge leap of faith, but one that appeared to pay immediate dividends. Who is to say that the euphoria enveloping the club as Wenger's wonders were posting their unbeaten run did not play a part in convincing the sceptics that maybe Arsenal were an atypical business in a fickle industry and worth a calculated flier by the banks?

In February 2004, the Premiership pacesetters proudly announced that they had borrowed £260 million from a consortium of banks (registered in Scotland, Ireland, Portugal, Germany and Belgium, their multinational grouping reflecting the cosmopolitan make-up of the club). McAlpine got back to work with the objective of ensuring their task would be completed by 2006. "The important thing about this deal," Managing Director Keith Edelman explained, "is that the risk of filling the stadium has been taken by the banks, not by Arsenal Football Club. The stadium is owned by Ashburton Properties Ltd and the banks are taking the risk around that, so if the stadium does not fill out it is down to the stadium company and not Arsenal. However, I don't think anyone would go into this deal thinking that is a possibility." "The risk is taken by the stadium company," Peter Hill-Wood added, "so that if something went wrong the bank would end up owning the land [but not the football club]. But it is not going to go wrong."

The loan was structured for repayments to be completed by 2018, with millions shelled out in interest in the meantime. Hill-Wood was sanguine despite the financial commitment. "It's OK to get into debt to build a new stadium if you think that the financial models you've worked on give you the opportunity to repay those debts over a given period," he asserted. "We've worked it out and the banks have agreed with the financial model that we will be able to repay the loan over the long term."

The board had by a process of osmosis become property

experts, an unintended vocation described as "much more profitable than running a football club" by Peter Hill-Wood, not entirely tongue in cheek. "There's a lot more residential potential that we can develop, including of course the existing stadium [Highbury Square] which will be turned into flats". There would be 700 apartments (the pitch would be transformed into a communal garden for the estate) at a starting price of £250,000-plus for a one-bedroom flat. Anticipating the potential profit, the board decided they would control the development themselves, rather than sell the area with planning permission as they would eventually do with parcels of land they owned on the other two sites that were part of the regeneration. So it was that Arsenal Holdings plc's "principal activities" were described as "professional football club and property development". The board's seamless transition into property experts begged the question of why they couldn't learn more about how to maximise revenue from their core business, such as the naming rights for the new stadium.

With work back on course, in 2004 the temptation to accept an offer from Emirates Airline proved irresistible: a sum of £100 million was initially announced (later revised down to £90 million) for the stadium naming rights for 15 years and the shirt sponsorship for eight years from 2006. However, the new stadium already had an identity before Emirates arrived on the scene. The club themselves had referred to their new home as Ashburton Grove, the name of a street ultimately removed from the map due to the changes in the landscape forced by the council's compulsory purchase orders on the club's behalf. Once it was realised that the use of Ashburton Grove might actually threaten to undermine the value of the stadium's naming rights they had sold, the club abruptly refrained from any mention of it in their public pronouncements. Yet the cat was already out of the bag, and there were many purists who felt that, after years of playing at Highbury, 'the home of football' as the sign above the North Bank gates in Gillespie Road proclaimed, Arsenal had sold their soul. Further, they objected to having to call their new home after an airline and continued using Ashburton Grove, some ultimately shortening it to either Ashburton or the Grove when talking about the place. *The Gooner* fanzine, the club's best-selling independent supporters' magazine, operated a policy of not referring to the stadium by what they described as 'the E word'. "Clearly we fans were correct about the stadium name," said season-ticket holder Brian Dawes, who signs off his emails with the inscription 'One life, one game, one team, three doubles, an unbeaten season and 1,000+ games at Highbury'. "One would suspect the club will be begging us to lead the way when it comes round to renaming the stadium in 2021. We had to plead for the club insignia to go up on the outside, never mind the inside, and Edelman's excuse that the word 'Arsenal' was not picked out in the seats because it would have been unfair to the sponsors still pisses me off." The fans were fighting a losing battle, however, as all and sundry in the mainstream media adopted the sponsor's nomenclature as soon as the deal was done.

In David Dein's view, the Arsenal supporters' reluctance to accept the *fait accompli* was a misplaced reaction. Experienced in the American ways of sports marketing, he is at pains to point out that naming rights are the norm. But what prevails in the States is the concept of 'league think'. There the leagues created the teams, unlike in Europe where the teams created the leagues. In the USA, the drivers, the big brands, are the NFL, the NBA, MLB and the NHL. The teams are secondary. In fact they are not clubs at all but franchises with the facility to move from one part of the country to another, thousands of miles away at the drop of a financial incentive to the owner. Leagues even create franchises from scratch and sell them to the highest bidder. However important and wealthy the Premier League believes it is, what matters in England is 'club think'. Arsenal, Manchester United and Liverpool will always be more important entities than the league they happen to play in and as such they must work to protect their core business values, namely football. In that sense, selling off naming rights is equivalent to selling a crown jewel to another party with no football connections and makes no sense at all. Most fans would have preferred to see no sponsorship involved. Undoubtedly they felt they were better custodians of the club's heritage and tradition than the board and therefore possibly even better businessmen too.

The stadium represented a fundamental component of the physical and emotional attributes that went together to make up, in marketing parlance, the Arsenal brand. Brands build business. And they are endemic in football: from Arsenal to Aston Villa to Accrington Stanley, there are international brands, national brands and local brands. On every level they are the purest and most powerful form of consumer loyalty because a football fan is different from a customer. Of course customers have strong preferences for a particular product or service but it doesn't preclude for example a Sainsbury's shopper using Tesco to take advantage of the week's special offers. Similarly, a good value-for-money offer might well persuade a staunch user of a particular product to switch sides at least for a trial run. The lower the price, the more likely the switch, football excepted. A customer can and will exercise choice, a football fan can't. He or she is stuck with their club for life. For a true fan not a day passes without thinking of the object of their affection, its past, present and future. At times fans may hate the board and hurl abuse at the team but there is an umbilical cord that joins them to the club for life. And an integral part of the club is its ground.

As a precious asset, the optimum value to be derived from

a stadium goes beyond its role in producing matchday income. Would Marks & Spencer allow British Airways to advertise on its shop facia and encroach on its brand values? And what about the sponsor's own and sometimes extraneous values that they bring with them? Over the years, Arsenal to their credit rejected substantial inducements from gaming and alcohol companies to put their names on the shirts. But Emirates had theirs on Chelsea's as recently as 2005. Within a year 'Fly Emirates' had gone out of the blue and into the red. At least it is a highly rated worldwide airline. Further, it offers tie-ups with in-flight entertainment and in its business stronghold of Dubai, an affluent following with the potential to increase merchandising opportunities for its new partner.

Arsène Wenger once stated that he would make Arsenal a bigger club than Manchester United. It is arguable that even if they become more habitual winners of the Premier League than Alex Ferguson's team, because of the omnipotence of the Manchester United brand Arsenal are unlikely ever to overtake them. Whilst Arsenal look like tenants in their own new home – huge Emirates logos and slogans in Arabic fighting with the Arsenal paraphernalia for attention – United can proudly claim that Old Trafford is the 'theatre of dreams' and as such contributes a pure and powerful message to the United experience.

Of course it could be argued that when you are running a business the extra income generated by the selling of your naming rights could be used in the way the fans want most: to improve the quality of the team and the chances of success on the pitch. What could Arsène Wenger do with an extra £42 million in his transfer war chest? If only! But the Emirates payments for the ground's name will be used to reduce Arsenal's swingeing debt, or rather the interest on it. However, if Arsenal had not been so ambitious they would not have built such a magnificent stadium. They could still have had a 60,000-capacity home without incurring the crippling costs, capping the manager's transfer funds and possibly inhibiting their future through the naming rights deal restricting the commercial potential of their brand.

Alternatively a compromise might have been to include 'Highbury' in the new stadium's name. After all, Highbury was not the official name of the old place (whose address was The Arsenal Stadium, Avenell Road, N5) and this would strengthen the links with a glorious history. Thus any sponsor who joined the party would have had to accept their role as a junior partner, gaining a prefix rather than the name itself: 'The Emirates Highbury Stadium' would perhaps bring in less cash but would certainly be a brand attribute with greater vigour and integrity. The Oval cricket ground used to be the Foster's Oval. It is now the Brit Oval (the sponsor being Brit Insurance) but it is still The Oval and is referred to as such by Surrey members and other cricket fans alike. To use a football metaphor, form is temporary but class is permanent: sponsors may come and go – Emirates airlines are only signed up for 15 years – but Highbury could have been for ever.

To have such an asset as Highbury – the brand not the stadium – and willingly discard it indicates just how important the need to secure the loan was. Either that or even someone like Ken Friar, who started as a post boy and ended up 40 years later as managing director steeped in the history and tradition of his place of work, did not fully appreciate what the club might be foregoing. It is therefore ironic that Friar, even after the Emirates had opened its doors, is fond of recalling that "Highbury was always known as the home of football." Friar explained that this status bestowed on Highbury by the club itself coloured the club's attitude and behaviour. "We believed that we were all one big family and as such we treated our opponents as honoured guests and welcomed them into our home. We even used to go so far as to paint flowers in our opponents' colours if we couldn't actually buy them, in order to welcome them into the boardroom." It was actions like this that set the club apart from their peers. 'Arsenal are alright' is the general view of directors at other Premier League clubs, a sharp contrast to the widely held view of some of their London rivals. The pre-Abramovich Chelsea was dismissed by a northern club as "fur coat and no knickers", while Tottenham were warned by one southern club that "they would not be pushed around by a bunch of north London yobbos". Unfortunately, though, at the modern Arsenal some of the tradition and standards have seemingly been left behind, to the dismay of many.

Emirates paid £42 million for 15 years' worth of naming rights, equating to £2.8 million a year. Sponsorship of the shirts accounted for the remaining £48 million. In securing the £260 million loan, the board had to guarantee the banks that they would achieve an income of £2.5 million per annum for these rights. Actually achieving just an extra £300,000 on top of that figure exposed the limit of their ambitions. To sell part of your soul is bad enough, but to a company totally unrelated to your industry, history and tradition compounds the error. And then to cap it all, failing to get value for money could leave the board open to the charge that they lack marketing expertise. Moreover, £48 million for eight years of shirt sponsorship compares poorly with the sum Manchester United obtained from American insurance group AIG in 2006: £56 million over four years leaving Arsenal trailing in their wake to the tune of £8 million a season. And the difference will bite harder with each passing year (compared to the deals of other top clubs, the cost of signing a long-term contract might eventually be as much as £10 million per annum) until 2015 when Arsenal will finally be able to strike a fresh arrangement. By that time United will have enjoyed a further five years of even greater revenues on the assumption that their price goes up once AIG have had their turn adorning the chests of Wayne Rooney and company. Of course there is an irrefutable argument that United have many more supporters, but Ajax Amsterdam are getting more money in 2008/09 from their shirt deal than Arsenal with no guarantee that their sponsor AEGON, a pensions and life assurance company, will get Champions League exposure or very much television coverage outside the club's native Holland. Not to mention Chelsea, Tottenham and Liverpool, all of whom receive more money per year from the companies whose names are on their shirts.

Managing Director Keith Edelman's explanation for signing the Emirates and Nike deals was simply that "the money was an important revenue stream for us to be able to plug into our financial model, and it will assist us in refinancing the current debt we've got." He admitted, "We are taking on a large financial debt but the extra revenue we are generating from the stadium will more than cover that outlay. It is improper for football clubs to take on debt to run their businesses. But we are taking on a debt to build a new fixed asset. If you are getting into debt to do that then it is perfectly OK but if you are getting into debt to buy players and pay wages then it is not OK" (unless of course you are Roman Abramovich). But the debt didn't stop with the stadium. Another £125 million had to be borrowed to fund property developments, chiefly Highbury Square, which unlike the stadium would not generate any revenue till 2009 when, if all goes to plan, the club envisage they may net £100 million profit. Chairman Peter Hill-Wood admitted, "The gamble we are taking is that Arsène continues to work the miracles that he's worked for the past seven years or so. The team has got to try and get into the Champions League. We budget for that."

Arsenal's was a business plan involving hundreds of millions of pounds reliant on the miracles of a middle-aged man, contractually committed to the club for a mere 15 further months. And the primary miracle required was annual qualification for the UEFA's blue riband competition on comparatively modest expenditure on player transfers for a leading Premier League outfit. Alex Ferguson, on the other hand, had no such restrictions. But in another way the two rivals shared the same burden. To gain possession of United, the Glazers took the most profitable football club in the world and plunged it into debt. And the operation can only be sustained by continued success on the field. Arsenal had gone into debt to secure its future, United as a consequence of a change of ownership. The long-term advantage of Arsenal's position is already apparent as the stadium has enabled it to challenge United in terms of net assets. However, the anticipated enormous growth in Arsenal's matchday income would only start to eat away at the debilitating interest charges if, as an American might put it, the fans got 'more bang for their buck' in terms of entertainment. The board banked on the manager to ensure 'house full' notices irrespective of trophies won, a far cry from the days of *'One-nil to the Arsenal'* and an indication of the dramatic change in image brought about by Wenger.

Edelman's statement about financial models and revenue streams was not the terminology of a fan, but the new managing director was not employed to curry favour amidst the rank and file, despite personal protestations to the contrary. He never connected with the supporters in the natural way that David Dein did, because he simply could not relate to their own experiences as long-time followers of the team. The introduction of a new club crest in 2002 (devised primarily to sidestep an ongoing legal case concerned with copyright infringement of previous versions) said it all to the fans. The way the design was conceived displayed a lack of appreciation of the history and tradition such symbols and logos conveyed. When it was first presented to the fans, paraded around Highbury, it was roundly booed by all four sides of the ground. So the fact that their new stadium would be known by the name of an airline was seen by the fans as just the most salient example of the board failing to take into account their views.

The Arsenal supporters' disquiet would have been more pronounced if they had realised that Arsène Wenger was receiving inadequate funds to keep his team at the same competitive level, and that lean times – in terms of trophies – were unavoidable. The manager had his budget, but a substantial portion of his transfer spending would have to be funded by his own aptitude to get good prices for the players going out the door. And on this level, the income raised from the sale of the academy-developed youngsters who failed to hold down a first-team spot became almost as important as the higher sums picked up for the likes of Patrick Vieira and Thierry Henry when the manager considered they were expendable. Wenger's skill in the transfer market had become a necessity rather than the agreeable bonus of his earlier days. Together with unearthing talent – the "diamonds in the dust" as David Dein fondly calls the manager's best discoveries – this was now the only way Wenger could keep up with his peers. His judgment on new prospects – and who he could afford to dispense with – assumed an unnatural importance, and begged the question of what would have happened if the great talent scout had decided to go before the new stadium was built. Certainly, the board proceeded and still do on the assumption that the manager will be around for the foreseeable future. "We certainly don't have a plan B," said Peter Hill-Wood. "So I don't think about it [Wenger leaving]. The only thing I do think about from time to time is who on earth we would have if we didn't have him. Then I put it out of my mind because I can't think of an alternative."

One of the reasons that Wenger chose to dispense with experience and gamble on youth as the club moved closer to a new life at the new stadium can now be seen as the art of the possible. The practice of only awarding one year contracts to those who had passed their 30th birthday was as much to do with their high wages and dwindling sell-on value as the conviction that their performance would inevitably decline. Far better in every way to put most of your eggs in a young basket. Despite the constraints, as the Ashburton Grove plans fell into place Wenger was upbeat. "I tell you there are half a dozen who have a chance [to establish themselves in the first team]. Really promising players. It thrills me, for one simple reason. It's that I feel that I came here and I've helped this club to . . . not only to win. I would like to [think that I have taken it] through an era where we have put the club at a different level. For the training ground, for the new stadium, for the youth set-up which has become international and of course if we can win everything with the top team it's fantastic. But to think that nothing major can happen to this club now gives me an easier sleep. If the club gets into financial trouble, I can guarantee you it will not be relegated with the players we have."

CHAPTER NINE
UP AND RUNNING

Whatever people were calling the new residence, the funding was in place and Arsenal's new home slowly took shape over a two-and-half-year period. The nightmare of unpredictable costs that had blighted the construction of Wembley was avoided when the board negotiated a fixed-price contract which meant that Sir Robert McAlpine would bear the expense of any unforeseen problems, with hefty financial penalties to be incurred on late delivery. Of course the price was only fixed if Arsenal didn't fall prey to the usual temptation of clients radically changing their minds during the construction process. That this didn't occur is testimony to the clarity of forward thinking by the directors at the planning stage. In fact, the stadium was handed over two weeks early in July 2006, allowing the club to stage three preliminary events to gain the necessary local authority safety certificate ahead of the first competitive fixture.

"To design and deliver such a beautiful stadium on such a restricted site, with different ground levels, railway lines and countless other obstacles in the way – well, to be honest I can't think of a more challenging stadium development in the modern era," commented Simon Inglis, stadium expert and author of the seminal work *Football Grounds of Britain*. "Herbert Chapman and his contemporaries set a very high standard during the 1930s. Now Arsenal has done it again at the start of the new century. The Emirates really is a cut above any other club stadium in the Premiership, as was Highbury after 1936. When I watched my first match in the new stadium, my main impression was that I was now, for the first time – with respect to the City of Manchester Stadium – in Britain's first truly 21st-century stadium. It felt to me as if I was at a World Cup, in another country."

The reason for such critical acclaim is that first and foremost, all the criteria for a state-of-the-art stadium are in place. Wherever you sit the sight lines are excellent and the roomy, padded seats make other stadiums feel constricted and *passé* and thankfully do not spell out a sponsor's name. Unfortunately, though, like most clubs in the Premier League, Arsenal have yielded to the temptation of installing an LED system, an animated electronic advertising medium replacing the traditional perimeter boards (which UEFA later forced the club to resurrect for the Champions League). An intrusive eyesore to fans at the ground and television viewers alike, how ironic then that it is directly in the line of vision of the best seats in the house.

The concourses are broad, well lit and amply stocked with refreshment areas, from the ubiquitous fast food facilities all the way to waitress service in the Diamond Club passing by the bars and restaurants at the Club Level on the way. "We expect," says Simon Inglis, "experienced stadium architects like HOK Sport to get the basics right. But it is rare to find a client in the football world to go the extra mile on fixtures and fittings." (Unlike other football stadiums, public areas and works of art – including two cannons and the spelling out of 'ARSENAL' in huge concrete letters – add another dimension.)

Just as Herbert Chapman left his imprint off the pitch, so will Wenger. Apart from the cups and championships the former acquired, he was the catalyst behind changing the name of the Gillespie Road Underground station to Arsenal and promoted the idea of stadiums with roofs and floodlight football. Wenger will leave behind a first-class training centre at London Colney, the Emirates pitch (having been heavily involved in the process that determined its dimensions and the quality of the playing surface) and other areas where he was directly involved at the design stage such as the dressing rooms and treatment areas that will be a boon for future generations. Notably, the horseshoe format of the home dressing room has been specifically designed to allow the manager to dominate the room, unlike the traditional rectangular changing areas with seats on all four sides, where it is possible for players to avoid his eye. On first seeing it, Alan Smith was surprised: "The dressing room is just so plain, with the slatted wooden benches and the lockers. There's no sign there that it's an Arsenal dressing room and I think Arsène asked for it to be that way." Of course he did. Nothing to distract the focus of his players. Whatever Arsène wanted, Arsène got. And he was insistent that there would be no short-cuts to compromise optimum matchday preparations. So ample space was also given over for a massage and treatment area, a gym, a hydrotherapy pool, showers and baths, and a wide warm-up area leading to a tunnel some four times the width of Highbury's tight squeeze. The overall impression is of functional comfort, in contrast to the antiquated conditions of the past. By comparison, whilst not ramshackle, the opposition dressing room gives the impression that it had nowhere near the same care and attention lavished on it.

Not that the stadium is perfect. Based on the model HOK employed for Benfica's *Estadio da Luz* (Stadium of Light) constructed for the Euro 2004 Championships, in contrast to Highbury's traditional British rectangular shape with four distinct stands and open corners, the contours form a closed oval. Due to the height restriction imposed by the local authority, the only way to reach the required capacity of 60,000 was to seat a large number of the fans much further away from the action than they had been used to. To make matters worse, the North Bank bond holders had been prioritised and could opt for places alongside the pitch ahead of those who had sat in the equivalent spot at Highbury. Thus, many long-term supporters from the East and West Upper tiers found themselves several rows further back than they would have wanted (on top of the greater distance from the action for everyone).

Quite simply, the intimacy of the old amphitheatre was now just a memory, the relationship between the performers and the audience changed for ever, an inevitable consequence of the move upmarket. Gone was the intimidatory feel of the home fans breathing down the necks of the opposing team. Any hostility towards opponents would have to be created by the noise provided by the extra number of home supporters. In an attempt to re-create the big night atmosphere at Anfield and Celtic Park, the club decided to find an 'anthem' to produce the same effect as *'You'll Never Walk Alone'*. They chose Elvis Presley's *'The Wonder of You'*, a decision that had hardcore supporters squirming in embarrassment, although familiarity has started to encourage some scarf waving when it is played as the teams wait in the tunnel.

It is unlikely that Arsène Wenger had a great deal of input into this aspect of the stadium design, although he would probably have been in favour of creating more space between the touchline and the stands to allow for his substitutes to warm up properly and lessen the likelihood of injuries that might be caused by chasing a ball running out of play and crashing into advertising hoardings. But if Arsène prefers to watch from the poor viewpoint of the technical area because he can't stand the separation from his players, how does he think the fans feel, with their heroes that much further out of reach?

The change in atmosphere aside, the crowning glory of the Emirates is that the sheer scale of the arena creates a striking impression. Perhaps this reflects its unusual setting. Suddenly, emerging out of the capital city's concrete jungle, Simon Inglis's matchless 21st-century stadium rises like a phoenix out of the ashes of an area whose heyday had long passed. Normally you would expect to find a similar structure alongside a major thoroughfare and approach it through soulless walkways. Continental in conception, the location is both traditionally and contemporaneously British in character. Surrounded by terraced houses, cheek by jowl with luxury apartments in the process of construction (some courtesy of Arsenal, the property company) and serviced by multicultural supermarkets and takeaways, the stadium exemplifies football's place in the community in today's urban London. Unfortunately, despite the 60,000 capacity it is still not possible to roll up on matchday and buy a ticket. Only season-ticket holders and members have the right of entry and there are thousands waiting to join them (although locals and owners of one of the newly built Highbury Square flats had the opportunity to jump up the priority list).

For the fortunate thousands able to get in from the start there were four categories of membership: platinum (for those who had bought season tickets in the expensive Club Level middle tier), gold (ordinary season-ticket holders), silver (members who were given the first opportunity to purchase individual match tickets on a game-by-game basis) and red (who could buy any remaining match tickets once the silver membership's four-week preferential period had elapsed). There were 9,000 platinum members, 36,000 gold, 22,000 silver and 80,000 red (the red category – the final one on the registered fan food chain – is the only one open to newcomers). In the event that a fixture fails to sell out, only then would non-members get their chance. However, there seemed little likelihood of this ever happening if the experience of the first season was anything to go by and one suspects that only a sustained lack of success will see non-members ever attending in any great numbers. With over 100,000 silver and red members paying £26 and £25 a season respectively just to have the opportunity to buy tickets, the system suited the club just fine.

Naturally the Emirates had teething problems, not least the difficulty of getting away after the final whistle. From the first games, as the clock wound down an expanse of red seats started to become part of the scenery as thousands headed for the exits early in the hope of beating the crush in the streets outside. Although the local council had expected Holloway Road and Drayton Park stations to be upgraded, Transport for London decided that the cost of £70 million was not justified for fewer than 30 matchdays a year, which put excessive pressure on the Arsenal, Finsbury Park and Highbury & Islington stations. Local authority parking restrictions had made it a chore to travel to matches by car, so the by-product for those who did not live within walking distance were inevitable post-match queues to get on the available trains, a situation exacerbated with the authorities themselves on a learning curve, refining their own crowd-control arrangements match by match. "The bottom line," as Mark Woodward, who travels from Felixstowe by road and rail put it after the first few weeks, "is that different people have different journeys to make, and with no upgrade in the transport infrastructure, coupled with the 20,000 increase in attendance, people are still adjusting to the new realities and the number leaving early has increased." A few months were needed for the club, police and local authorities to adjust to the new environment. By the time the Emirates opened for a second season, they had all mostly got to grips with the situation, although old habits died hard for many who had become accustomed to beating the full-time exodus.

Inside the stadium there were new experiences to come to terms with too. Gone were the cramped conditions of the old ground, so that there were not only more ways to spend money on food and drink but it could be consumed in a far more agreeable environment, not least on the upper tier concourses which afforded spectacular vistas of London on all sides. The view from the Upper East side also encompassed Highbury, which brought home the remarkable feat of moving just round the corner. Or at least it did, until the flats in Drayton Park were built and most of the old stadium demolished.

In spite of the increase in the number of outlets, with the amount of additional customers many would vacate their seats after 30 minutes to beat the half-time rush, and those who did wait until the interval would find themselves at the back of the queue and unable to return until the second half was already underway. At times it felt less like being at a football match and more like an NFL or baseball game, where spectators seem permanently on the move in and out of their seats regardless of what is occurring on the field of play. Further, because of the larger seats, to let someone by everyone was forced to stand up, thereby blocking the view for up to four rows behind them. It was not surprising then that many long-term season-ticket holders bemoaned the change from Highbury, exasperated by the new breed of so-called fans who seemed to care more about their stomachs and journeys home than supporting the team they had paid so much to see.

Of course, compared to season-ticket holders and ordinary members, on a *per capita* basis there were more important revenue streams coming from different levels of

VIPs. One of the main reasons that the directors were desperate to move was the lack of availability for premium seats at Highbury – either for affluent individuals or the corporate market. Where the new arena undoubtedly did not disappoint from the start was in bringing in much more revenue than Highbury ever did. The middle tier of the Emirates has over 9,000 premium seats – 7,000 going to Club Level members paying between £2,500 and £4,750 for their season tickets and 2,000 in 150 hospitality boxes, prices for which range from £65,000 to £150,000 a year (which was probably the cost of a couple of weeks' salary to at least two of the boxholders, Thierry Henry and Dennis Bergkamp). These prices applied for the first two years of the stadium's life so will inevitably increase from the start of the 2008/09 season.

The ring of boxes is broken on the west side behind the directors' box, with the Diamond Club. For a joining membership fee of £25,000, the 84 members (and membership to this elite was by invitation only) were entitled to purchase two season tickets at an annual cost of £12,500 each, which include one of the matchday parking spots in the bowels of the stadium, safe from the attentions of Islington Council's traffic wardens. The area behind the seats has been transformed into a setting exemplifying corporate opulence to a standard unmatched by any other football ground. The marble floor, inlaid wood carvings commemorating past achievements, display cabinets with gleaming trophies, classic photos, repro Highbury clock, leather upholstery and glass tables all combine to give a most luxurious art deco feel to the enclave where the privileged members can enjoy complementary food and drink to a standard worthy of a Michelin star before, during or after the match. "Whilst I can never envisage myself hurling abuse at a ref whilst being enveloped in one of the plush leather armchairs," says Brian Dawes, who had the opportunity to wander around the Diamond Club on a non-matchday, "it is somehow comforting to know that we've got such a place in our very own stadium, even if the whole concept gives a big two fingers to the hardcore fans supping over-priced beer on the bland lower-tier concourse."

Directly below the Diamond Club lies the directors' matchday area. It is a world away from the antiquated Highbury boardroom which had to double up as a reception area and could only provide a buffet, a space so confined that there was no way you could avoid the opposing directors and their guests. Now there is no need to fraternise with directors of clubs with which relations are more strained. With a room which can comfortably accommodate 120 people there are allocated tables in the style of a wedding reception (and indeed there is little to suggest that the room is anything more than a spot for an exclusive upmarket do), so there is no need for Peter Hill-Wood to dine alongside Peter Kenyon if he doesn't want to. As in the Diamond Club, the wine flows whilst a sumptuous three-course meal is consumed, with guests often having to make the choice between the dessert course and the kick-off. As on the concourse, why rush when you can polish off the coffee and brandy and see the start on the plasma screens liberally distributed around the room? But of course, you really should go outside eventually and although the directors and their fellow VIPs are naturally located in the best seats imaginable (both in terms of view and comfort) a concession has been made to try to get them on the same wavelength as the fans by not putting in any heating, so on the coldest days they have to make do with a warming Arsenal blanket. (The accoutrements of the old boardroom have been transported across to decorate the new one situated in the turquoise building above the North Bank Bridge known as Highbury House, providing a link with the past, albeit tonally out of keeping with the new surroundings.)

The Club Level members' seats are on the same level as the directors' box, and their perks include free drinks at half time, which invariably sees the entire middle ring almost completely vacated after 45 minutes. As there is no control over the actual amount that can be drunk during the interval, some supporters will commandeer as many as three pints of pre-poured lager to down during the 15 minutes. As beverages have to be consumed on the concourse behind the seats, there are unsurprisingly still a large number of empty places when the second half resumes (reminiscent of the resumption of play after the lunch interval at a Lord's or Oval international cricket match), with many opting to remain on the comfortable concourse to watch the game on monitors while they polish off their drinks. But 10 minutes of a football match is a comparatively greater slice of missed action than half an hour of a day's cricket. If so many are happy to watch a significant part of the action on television, it begs the question as to why they don't opt for the comfort of their own homes on the numerous occasions that Emirates games are broadcast live. Certainly, due to the sheer numbers of thirsty punters involved service is understandably slow, but the thought of missing even a minute with a fantastic view of habitually exhilarating football is a concept that mystifies many in the 'cheap' seats. As one of the minority who put football first, Club Level season-ticket holder Stuart Singer shares their dismay. "I also imagine that this display of apparent indifference must be a major wind-up for those who would give their right arm for such a privileged perspective," he stated. "Considering Club Level's prominent position, surely the players must also be aware of all the empty seats. This can hardly inspire them to sweat blood for the Arsenal cause."

Alan Smith concurred that the behaviour "worries everybody. It's that feeling of theatre isn't it? You want to feel that all the fans are dying for the second half to get underway and they're right behind you. As a player, there's nothing worse than seeing empty seats and then, although you're concentrating on the game, you get this perception of people slowly drifting in. I think it does affect players." The moral appears to be that if you invite in corporate money, you invite in corporate ways. There is no doubt that many in the Club Level are not die-hard Arsenal fans, and some might not even be particularly interested in sport. But a seat at the Emirates is one of the hottest tickets in town.

Corporate hospitality has been prioritised, and has undoubtedly affected the atmosphere, but financially the middle tier is a necessity, with the average premium category season-ticket holder contributing three or four times as much to the club coffers as the standard attendees in the lower and upper tiers. Moreover, when the boxes and Diamond Club are added to the Club Level season tickets the income from the three categories exceeds that of Highbury: fewer than 10,000 people producing an annual matchday turnover of over £35 million. So the 50,000 ordinary fans provide additional revenue (approximately £55 million a year) to that which was ever received before the move from Highbury. In one fell swoop the Emirates went head-to-head with Old Trafford as the biggest revenue-generating club football stadiums in the world – London prices and brand values allowing the club to offset the larger capacities in, for example, Madrid and Milan. Arsenal FC earns a cool £3 million-plus every matchday; a staggering 100% increase over Highbury, overhauling broadcasting as the chief revenue source. Even allowing for whopping interest payments and a substantial rise in operational costs, it would be surprising if the club does not end up with a substantial annual net profit as long as they continue to fill the stadium.

Despite the exorbitant pricing policy and with only the 2005 FA Cup to show for the previous two years' efforts, the entire middle tier with its large number of prestige seats was sold out for the opening season. It clearly demonstrated the club's earning potential and underlined the sheer amount of lost income from the latter years at Highbury. Yet the key question was whether people were paying for the novelty value or was repeat custom likely. And would there be others willing to replace them if they dropped out?

Initially, the premium products had been offered on a four-year basis with a built-in sweetener guaranteeing protection against possible price increases. However, with a less-than-anticipated take-up the board were forced to review their policy and offer both boxes and seats on one-year terms. The corporate market, though, is fickle. With Wembley a substantial competitor for the entertainment pound, whether companies will continue to give Arsenal their custom may well in the short term be dependent on Arsène Wenger continuing to produce immodest results from modest spending.

Due to the heady mix of success, stars and entertainment, Highbury had proved resistant to any drop-off in attendances, despite hefty annual rises in ticket prices. However, the Emirates' pricing policy is a quantum leap from anything that had previously been experienced, particularly by the irregular supporter. 15,000 tickets, of which 3,000 are allocated to the away fans, are made available on a match-by-match basis. Of the remaining 12,000, the majority are in the more expensive upper tier (most of the cheaper lower tier having been snapped up by season-ticket holders). For the first two seasons' Grade B matches against less attractive opponents, upstairs prices ranged from £38 to £66, whilst for Grade A fixtures (five of the most in-demand league games and selected cup ties) the same tickets started at £55 and went all the way to £94. In 2004 Peter Hill-Wood described these prices as "awful. And they're not going to come down a lot. We're going to try and keep the prices at a level where the lower priced seats – £30, it's still a lot of money – are going to be very comparable with what they are at Highbury." In 2008, he was forced to take a more pragmatic stance. "Entertainment's an expensive business. But we've got a lot of people on the waiting list wanting tickets [over 40,000] so presumably we haven't priced ourselves out of the market." What tends to happen when silver members come to book is that all of the cheaper seats sell out quite quickly. So when, a month later, these tickets go on sale to the red members, the beggars at the bottom of the pile can't be choosers despite the often astronomical costs of the remaining tickets.

There are signs that as time goes on, more Grade B matches might have to go on general sale as the novelty factor wears off, whilst heaven forbid if it was coupled with a run of failure and the board might have to contemplate a less-than-capacity crowd. However, given the choice, they would probably prefer a 50,000 crowd paying top dollar than to lower the cost of entry to try to ensure a sell-out and run the risk of less net income. Managing Director Keith Edelman stated at a shareholders' Extraordinary General Meeting in July 2006 (to approve the refinancing of the club's loan) that an average attendance of 22,000 was required for the club to break even and cover its interest charges. Asked at the AGM three months later to clarify whether this meant 9,000 middle tier supporters and 13,000 from the other tiers, Edelman denied he had never given any minimum figure, and said that anyway 32,000 was the break-even number, spread evenly over the three tiers. He was dismissive of the notion that such a scenario would ever seriously require testing, saying it was merely a model that the banks required, but ultimately an irrelevance as he could not envisage ever getting such a low attendance. And if the current practice of always recording an attendance of 60,000 despite the obviously paid-for but empty seats persists, you can follow his thought process.

The stadium's first ever matchday (22nd July 2006) was

the third and final trial run, a testimonial match for Dennis Bergkamp, with a capacity limit of 55,000. Arsène Wenger kicked a giant inflatable football towards the north end of the stadium. Supported by guide ropes, it should have entered the goal. However, the manager missed the target as a gust of wind took it onto the crossbar. It was as far off target as the board's promise that the manager could buy any player he wanted. The figures looked good on paper, but in terms of ready cash, Arsenal had none. The shortfall was down to having received and spent on the stadium the revenue from Nike, the Emirates and the corporate box and season tickets. Club Level renewals would soon be brought forward as interest payments on the two initial loans of £210 million and £50 million were due. These were subsequently renegotiated on a 25-year term but still left the club with annual interest payments of £18 million together with almost half as much again for the property loans. In 2008, at a traumatic time for the lending market, the stadium interest payments (at around 10% of total turnover) look like a smart piece of business. Additionally, deals like the one which brought Theo Walcott to the club have been negotiated so that the transfer fees are paid in instalments, and many millions can be outstanding at any time. A good portion of the cash balance has to remain untouched to cover those payments, which customarily kick in after a certain number of appearances.

As the curtain rose on the 2007/08 season, despite playing to capacity crowds in the brave new world of the Emirates, in one sense, nothing had changed. Arsenal were still relying on their manager to buck the odds, a phenomenon by now taken for granted. But the grandeur of the surroundings merely disguised the reality that the man at the centre of it all was finding his task increasingly difficult.

CHAPTER TEN
ACCESS NO AREAS

An hour and a half or so before matches at Highbury, Arsenal's players used to disembark from their coach having consumed their pre-match meal at their Chelsea Harbour hotel and made the short journey across town. Parked up outside the main entrance on Avenell Road, their few steps between the coach and the marble hall were invariably witnessed by hordes of fans patiently waiting behind crash barriers. For young children especially, it was a thrill to be so close to their heroes. They could shout encouragement and receive nods and waves of acknowledgement in response. At the Emirates the team coach, with its blacked out windows, arrives at the entrance in Hornsey Road. On a dull day it may just be possible to make out the silhouettes of the passengers before the electronic gate opens to admit the vehicle into the bowels of the stadium. It stops directly outside the players' entrance and the dressing room is reached without a supporter in sight. The 'Unbeatables' of 2004 have metamorphosised into the 'Untouchables' of today.

With the move to their new home, an estrangement has grown between the fans and the players. The physical distance between the two groups and the disparity between the outrageous sums paid to these athletes and the earnings of the working man ensure there is far less empathy with the personalities who pull on the shirts. The days when Charlie George – who supported the team as a kid from the North Bank – would proudly wear the Arsenal shirt, providing a tangible bond between crowd and performer, belong to a bygone age.

Sadly, Arsène Wenger prefers it this way, with any distraction on matchdays avoided. In his single-mindedness he has – whilst forging a new identity for Arsenal – allowed something of the bond that binds the supporters to the club to slacken. Wenger often reflects on the special atmosphere at English grounds. "The first time I arrived in the UK," he recalls, "I saw a match at Anfield [Liverpool against Manchester United] and I got a terrible shock. I had no idea football could create such passion." Yet he is unwittingly undermining the communal feeling between spectators and performers by maintaining a policy of protecting the squad from any diversion. Of course he is not intending to drive a wedge between the two parties but with his desire for total control when his players are on duty he has perhaps neglected the value of good PR. Perhaps while the fans continue to stream through the turnstiles, the consequences of a loosening of the chains of loyalty can be put aside for the moment.

Thursday 20th July 2006 saw what the club termed a Members' Day at the Emirates. It was the second of the three scheduled trial runs ahead of the first competitive fixture. At no cost, although limited in numbers through advance booking, several thousand fans were invited to watch the players go through a training session on the virgin pitch. However, due to the stipulations of the safety certificate, only the upper tiers were being utilised, thereby segregating the supporters from their favourites. (Two open training sessions had been held at Highbury where fans had also been restricted to the upper tiers.) Further, as the timing was less than three weeks after the World Cup finals had ended in Germany, only four of the 16 Arsenal representatives who had been at the tournament (new signing Tomas Rosicky, Kolo Toure, Emmanuel Eboue and Emmanuel Adebayor) managed to make it onto the pitch and they exercised apart from their colleagues, who comprised principally reserve and youth team players, some of whom had not even set foot in the stadium before and could not find the players' entrance. Two had had to be admitted via the Armoury, the club's new flagship store, where Managing Director Keith Edelman, despite not recognising the youngsters, had ushered them in after the security staff had brought the problem to his attention. In fairness to Edelman, the duo were not known by any of the fans queuing to get into the shop either, and so it was no surprise that what grabbed the attention once inside was the environment rather than anything that was happening on the pitch.

The session concluded with a somewhat feeble attempt to kick giveaway footballs into the upper tier where the fans were gathered. Given the manager's distaste for the tactic of gaining territory with scant regard for possession, it was fitting that most of his charges were unable to get the appropriate amount of 'welly' and that most of the balls fell well short of their target and came back down to rest in the lower-tier seats. Although it meant most of the supporters went home disappointedly empty-handed, the failure to reach the target could be said to embody the difference between Arsenal of 2006 and the 'Row Z' clearances that were a habitual feature of the George Graham era. Nevertheless it was poor PR. The 'special' day compared unfavourably with the way other clubs act. At Stamford Bridge and White Hart Lane of all places, supporters are not only downstairs, but the players spend time at pitchside signing autographs and posing for photos. On subsequent members' days at the Emirates, the lower tiers were opened so that at least the public could get closer to the action. But there was no interaction. Even on a December Monday when the first-team players merely warmed down from their weekend exertions before sitting in the centre circle watching the second stringers do the serious stuff with a Carling Cup game on the horizon, there was no attempt to stroll over towards the fans. They were of course merely following the manager's orders. There was to be no fraternising. This was a straightforward routine session that just happened to be transposed from London Colney and was to be treated as such with no regard for the onlookers.

If training is a rehearsal to be undertaken seriously at all times, then the training ground is Wenger's workplace and the pitches the tools of his trade. As a perfectionist in the art of preparation he must therefore have been horrified with the dismal quality of the conditions he was forced to work in on his arrival. Arsenal didn't even possess their own training centre. Rented from University College, London, it was a far cry from the well appointed Monaco training ground at La Turbie in the hills above Nice which Wenger was accustomed to; and his eighteen months at Grampus 8 had given him no cause for complaint.

The manager was so keen to upgrade Arsenal's facilities that the players joked about an 'Arson Wenger' being responsible for the fire that destroyed the out of date changing rooms. When questioned by Remi Garde, one of his first signings in London, in an interview for French television to celebrate his decade of service at Highbury, the former utility player asked, with his tongue firmly in his cheek, "Do you remember that you set fire to the place in order to get a new one built?" "I can assure you today," replied the accused, "that it was a true accident. That it burnt down was certainly a stroke of luck as it helped accelerate the building of a new centre and the development of the club." The unspoken thought was that Wenger could now build his secret empire, away from prying eyes with outsiders only tolerated as and when necessary.

GETTY IMAGES

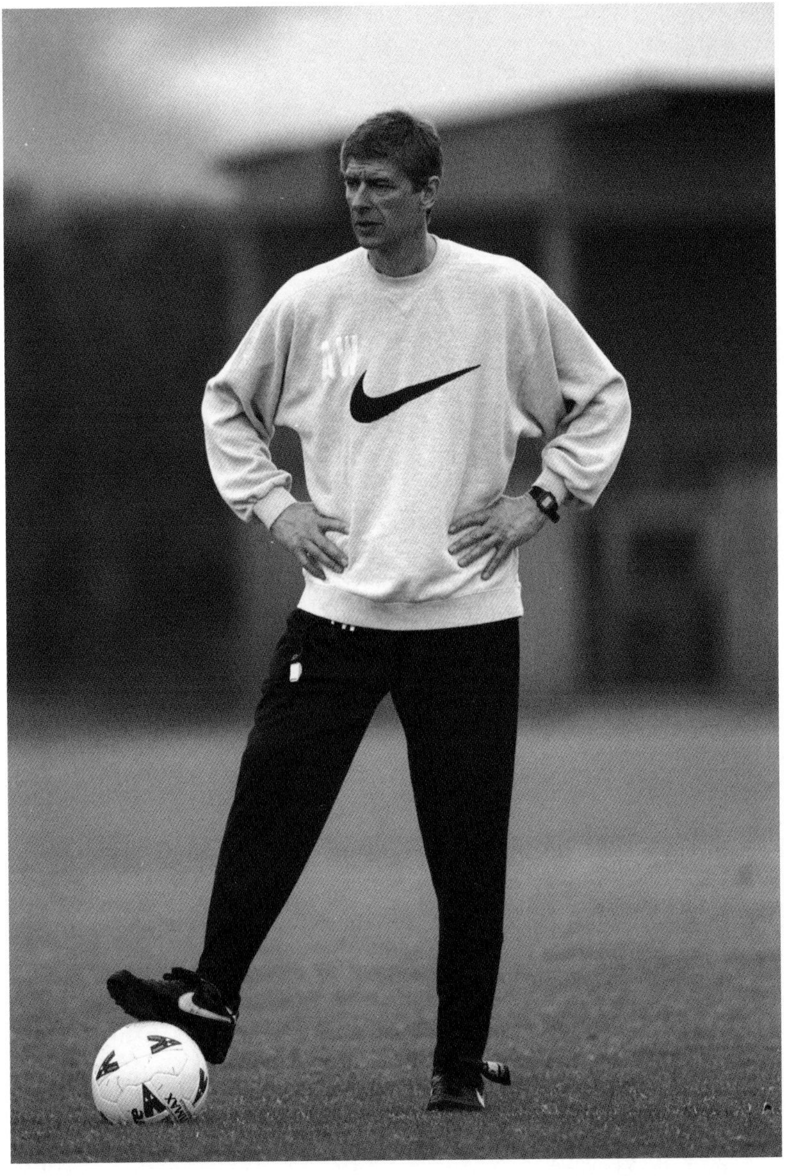

⇧ Where he loves to be: The manager on the training ground.

GETTY IMAGES

⇐ Dennis Bergkamp: Arsenal's first true international superstar.

⇓ The boss and Tony Adams, his Captain Courageous.

GETTY IMAGES

ACTION IMAGES

⇑ Arsène Wenger and David Dein: The dynamic duo who oversaw the club's conversion from also-rans to prize winners.

⇓ Pires , Vieira and Henry: The Three Musketeers.

GETTY IMAGES

GETTY IMAGES

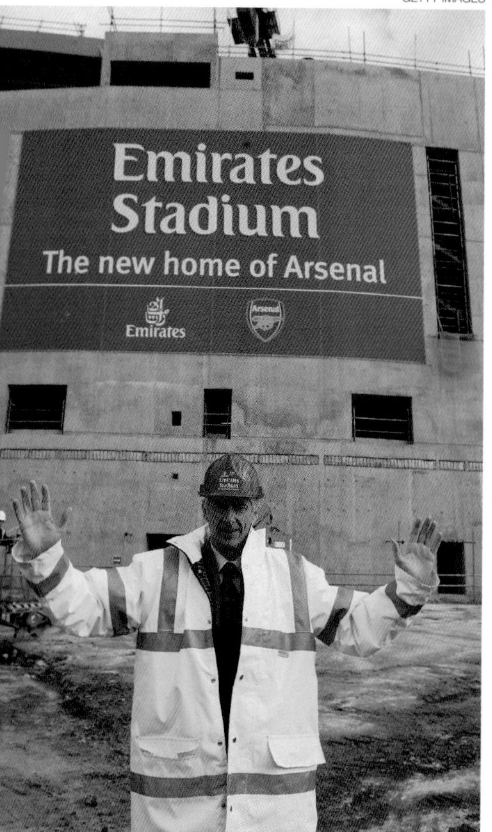

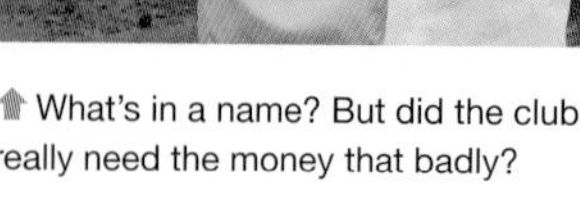
What's in a name? But did the club really need the money that badly?

GETTY IMAGES

The Emirates today: "Britain's first truly 21st century stadium".

⬆ Directors Ken Friar, Peter Hill-Wood and David Dein: Over a century of service to Arsenal.

➡ Former managing director Keith Edelman: Helped navigate the ship through choppy financial waters.

ACTION IMAGES

MIRRORPIX

⇦ Danny Fiszman: Arsenal's masterbuilder.

GETTY IMAGES

⇨ Stan Kroenke: American sports entrepreneur and key Arsenal shareholder.

⇩ Alisher Usmanov of Red and White Holdings.

ACTION IMAGES

ACTION IMAGES

⇦ The new man from the USA, CEO Ivan Gazidis.

GETTY IMAGES

⬆ A team that plays together, wins together.

He had another immediate stroke of luck with the exceptionally generous gift by Real Madrid of £23 million in exchange for Nicolas Anelka's services in 1999. There was never any question exactly where the money was going and the builders went to work straight away. Opened later the same year by Arsenal fan and then Minister of Sport, Kate Hoey, the technician now had his priceless laboratory.

First and foremost there are ten full-sized pitches that would grace any Premier League ground, two of which are specially heated to 17°C so that no session ever needs to be postponed even in the coldest of temperatures. Each pitch is used for no more than five consecutive days before being left for ten to recuperate. The pitches are complemented by a gym, a hydrotherapy pool and medical centre, a first-class restaurant, changing rooms and offices. Ironically, the sumptuous centre is sited literally a stone's throw from the old training ground but it is light years away in terms of its conception and self-sufficiency.

With the complex being designed to accommodate the entire squad of first team, reserves and youths, and to simplify the tasks of the coaches and the players at the different levels, according to David Dein, Arsène, "was involved [in the design] down to the last teacup". Not that there would be much need for this type of crockery, as the traditional heavily sugared workman's tea beloved by British players was now strictly off the menu. Nutritionists and chefs joined an array of medical and fitness specialists to produce a variety of healthy-eating choices that are supervised by Wenger himself.

However, whereas the players needs are prioritised – they also have the use of private, spacious and comfortable changing rooms – the manager's own office is just big enough to meet his basic needs. When one visitor commented on the lack of luxury, Wenger quipped, "I have another one at the stadium and that is modest as well." In 2003, he said, "I know only three places in London – my house, Highbury and the training ground." And it is at the training ground that he spends most of his working hours. Left to his own devices, he puts in long shifts in a small ground-floor space with a prosaic view of the car park with photos of, in his own words, his "inspirational captains", Adams and Vieira, on the walls (Henry is due to join them). The room is divided into two, with a large desk and a three-seat sofa the key items in each section. "The couch is for negotiation and the desk for the agreement [of deals]", explains Wenger.

He also has a third office at his Totteridge home, even smaller than the other two, although this one is mostly used by his wife and daughter when they are on the computer. The only football item on display is a framed Arsenal shirt signed by the players with the inscription 'Arsène 50', a gift on that auspicious birthday. From the outside, the only visible clue as to the identity of the owner of the pleasant, though by no means the most imposing house in the road, was a discreet 'Support the Arsenal' exhortation on an upstairs bedroom window. However, as soon as this information got into the public domain, the sticker was hastily removed.

There is a different tempo to home life that provides Wenger with the opportunity to escape the frustrations and tensions of a high-pressure job that is carried out in the unforgiving glare of the media spotlight. Gone during the most intense of moments is the calm aura that he was able to display whilst still relatively fresh from his time in Japan and the equanimity he had adopted there. Now his body language reveals a man all too wrapped up in the stress of delivering results and the high expectations his success has induced. But not once he gets home. The presence of his daughter, 11-year-old Léa, who cares little for the vagaries of her *Papa*'s vocation, provides a healthy counterbalance that allows him to relax and enjoy his time off. As a diversion he might read a historical biography and take up the challenge of getting a ball on target. A basketball hoop is set up in the garden and is frequently used to improve his shooting and help him unwind. However, a giant television screen is the focal point of the living area and invariably tuned into Canal+, Sky Sports or Setanta, revealing that football is not only the man's trade but his passion as well. The hours spent in front of it are tolerated by an understanding family who accept that he is incapable of ever totally switching off.

Less than 24 hours after the callous Champions League quarter-final elimination by Liverpool in 2008, although one of the lowest points in the manager's career, he appeared outwardly untroubled as he relaxed in the bosom of his family, despite admitting, when asked how he was going to pick the players up for a championship-deciding encounter at Old Trafford in four days' time, "I have no idea." That was tomorrow's work and tomorrow could wait. His wife Annie plays no small part in creating a tranquil home environment and despite the wealth they enjoy, there is no live-in help. Relations often come to stay and the Wengers prefer to live without any extraneous intrusion.

Annie Wenger is a charming and attractive woman who epitomises French chic. She was the perfect adjunct to her husband when she was invited by the directors to unveil a specially commissioned bust of him at the 2007 AGM. Commemorating his immense contribution to Arsenal, the sculpture symbolically reprised that of Arsenal's other managerial legend Herbert Chapman, which famously stared out from the entrance hall at Highbury. Wenger was genuinely surprised to see his wife perform the ceremony to rapturous applause. Later she won over the shareholders as she chatted to them over refreshments after the formalities of the meeting were over, whilst her husband posed for photos and signed countless autographs as is the custom at the AGM.

Back at home, the Wengers take in two newspapers, *The Daily Mail* and *L'Equipe*. The former was originally ordered on the recommendation of David Dein when the Wengers first set up home in London, for no other reason than being a halfway house, neither red top nor broadsheet, and more often than not goes unread. Not so the French daily sports paper *L'Equipe*, despite being delivered a day late. Consequently any major controversies concerning the club are read about from a French perspective, though the primary reason is to keep up with football in his native country. He is also a regular reader of *L'Express*, the French weekly news magazine. Although he quite enjoys jousting with the media at his weekly press conferences, he neither knows nor cares what they have to say about him except in so far as he is resigned to the fact that whatever he says is only fodder for opportunistic headlines.

Consciously or not, he has brought much of the bad PR upon himself. "Yes – I am a bad loser," he says. "I've heard that. I think even my wife would agree with you that I'm a bad loser. But I try to be fair. For example when we lost 4–0 at Manchester United [in the FA Cup in February 2008], I had nothing to say. When we lost after the 49th [unbeaten] match, I didn't agree with the way things happened. And what is difficult now in the modern game is that you cannot express a number of opinions, as only one opinion will be taken out and the whole headlines will be made on this one opinion. So for example at Wigan [in March 2008] we didn't win. I said we didn't fight very well for every ball, we didn't take our chances, we lacked a little bit of spark and the pitch was atrocious. What came out was only that the pitch was atrocious and that I am a whinger because we didn't win the game. But I tried to give some credit to Wigan but that never came out. And what is terrible for me is that you come to a position where you cannot make any fair statement any more. Because only what interests people will be taken out of your statement [by the media]."

When David Dein was still around, he and the press office would brief Wenger in full when deemed necessary. Unlike his former colleague, Dein devours everything the fourth estate has to offer so nothing ever passed his eagle eye and often an erring scribe was taken to task for any perceived misdemeanours. In his view, so far as Arsenal's good name was concerned life is too short not to carry grudges. When *Newsnight* questioned the propriety of Arsenal's relationship with Belgian club Beveren, Dein took the investigation as a personal affront against the club's way of doing things, forgetting perhaps the opportunistic signings of Anelka and Fabregas. The BBC Sports department were consequently given the cold shoulder, not that they had anything to do with what *Newsnight* got up to. In his own mind, the vice-chairman had been hung out to dry too often for comfort and his blanket wariness of the media was transmitted to the press office who picked up their cue from him.

With a keen sense of their own importance, the Arsenal press office see themselves as self-appointed vigilantes for the club's cause. Wherever possible, criticism is not tolerated and the poor unfortunate purveyor of unacceptable comment or even a journalist who has not applied for accreditation in the accepted way will find their position undermined. Those who go a step further and dare to criticise the press office itself soon find that it is a sure way to become the recipient of a banning order. Complaints to UEFA have not softened their attitude. Only the football correspondents of the major national newspapers appear beyond the reach of their rough justice. Even a favourite son is not beyond retribution. When Alan Smith in his role as a Sky pundit ventured to suggest that it takes two to tango in the Old Trafford fracas of 2003, his next assignment for the club magazine was promptly cancelled and he remained *persona non grata* for some months. In the view of many fans, this was just desserts. "He was towing the Sky line and not being objective," said one, "therefore a double crime."

As the director ultimately responsible for the public face of the club, David Dein would often take up the cudgels at the request of the press office for the perceived injustices Arsenal had suffered. But he was loath to get involved when fielding complaints about their behaviour. On one occasion he was phoned by the head of the press office regarding a story that was about to break which alleged that one of the club's forwards had hit his girlfriend. In an effort to play down the situation Dein asked rhetorically, "What do you expect me to do? He's a striker isn't he?" Similarly Wenger will often turn a blind eye to petty injustices, not because of any unfeeling on his behalf but because they are a distraction from the job in hand. He admitted, "David does my dirty work [dealing with agents] for me." It also suits his purpose for the press office to manage events even if he suspects they might be carried out with a heavy hand. But heaven help them if they intrude on team matters.

Wenger, as always, is most interested on what happens on the pitch. On occasion that he catches a glimpse of himself on the touchline his own behaviour can astound him. When watching Arsenal games on television, he may catch sight of an agitated figure on the touchline and stare at his antics in disbelief. At difficult times he makes a conscious effort not to let stress undermine him. However, he does not always succeed. "I'm usually calm," he says, "but I am concerned that, with calm people like me, when I lose my temper it may quickly become extreme." In one of the rare instances of this actually happening, it was a member of the press office who was the recipient of an astonishing amount of vitriol after an unnecessary distraction compounded a poor performance in a key Champions League away match earlier in the evening. Wenger is always keen to get home as quickly as possible after a match, and was therefore furious that the whole party had to wait for one player to finish an interview arranged with the local media.

Wenger's press conferences on the day before a match are held at the training centre. They used to take place in a room adjacent to the players' dining area, but with contact inevitable as both parties went about their duties, the risk of fraternisation was more than the press office was prepared to countenance. So the media gatherings now take place in a separate building across the car park, where there is no danger of stumbling across a player. In fairness to the press office, it is hard work getting the stars to do anything that the manager does not personally give permission for. Interviews are often tied up with personal sponsorship obligations, but it is hard work to persuade players to sacrifice time for the club's own media, such as the official magazine and Arsenal TV, launched in 2008. The players are even more elusive when it comes to what are described as 'commercial and community' duties. The standard Premier League contract stipulates that tasks involving club services (such as signing sessions in the club shop) or promoting relevant campaigns (for example visiting schools to endorse the Kick Racism Out of Football initiative) should be undertaken for at least four hours a month. But in common with a lot of other clubs Arsenal do not rigorously enforce this clause. They are lucky to get four hours a season from some of them. So when the Supporters Services Centre located within the All Arsenal store under the Highbury House building was officially opened in the presence of a collection of invited supporters, the ceremonial ribbon was cut by 1980s captain Kenny Sansom and the club's reserve right back Justin Hoyte. The stars have, it seems, got better things to do than meet their public. Paid extravagantly, they profess their love for the club and the fans and kiss the badge to demonstrate allegiance, but their words and gestures can ultimately be seen as insincere when they are actually asked to give something back that their agents and their consciences have ensured they are not obliged to.

When the club arrange their annual end-of-season dinner to raise funds for the year's nominated charity – in 2008, the local Treehouse school for autistic children – tickets are sold at premium prices, with the attendance of Arsène Wenger and the first-team squad the main attraction. With the guarantee of a personal greeting on arrival from Wenger and being joined for an after dinner chat by one of the squad, individual places can cost up to an astonishing £2,000. And yet the staff responsible for organising the event are afflicted by the perennial fear that the players may not bother to turn up. Only a few are known for being generous with their time – Gilberto, Gaël Clichy and Theo Walcott amongst them – a sad state of affairs and further evidence of an ever-growing chasm between those who 'represent' the club and those who pay to keep it going.

The situation is exacerbated by regarding the media – the conduit between the players and the fans – as tolerated rather than encouraged. They are certainly put in their physical place at the Emirates by the incorporating of the press box into the lower tier, towards the corner flag. At Highbury, the press had plum positions at the front of the East Upper Stand, next to the directors' box. The view at the Emirates is far inferior, but if a number of the expensive seats upstairs do not have to be sacrificed for the hacks, all the better. Before the Premier League, the press were regarded as fans with typewriters. Now tolerated in the main as a necessary evil, no club building a new stadium or even refurbishing an old one is ever going to allocate them the best seats in the house. However, UEFA and FIFA, at major international tournaments, wherever possible, ensure they are placed adjacent to the VIP seats.

At the end of Arsenal matches, the press office comes into its own. A jobsworth's paradise, having watched alongside the newspaper reporters, they have a clear idea of any controversial issues from the evidence of their own eyes and the television monitors, and thus the likely line of questioning to be taken in the post-match player interviews. Being 'on message' is key, and woe betide any player who says anything controversial or even interesting. As employees, the players toe the company line for fear of being stitched up, an anxiety indoctrinated into them during their media training sessions held as part of their education once they have signed pro forms aged 16 – a justified anxiety perhaps, given that a voracious football media with pages and airtime to fill often look to spin a story or even invent one. Senior staffers such as Thierry Henry marked the youngsters' cards for them.

UEFA and Premier League regulations insist that the players depart through the 'mixed zone' where the waiting media try to accost them for a sound bite. Unfortunately, the rules stop short of insisting that the players actually speak and most choose not to, particularly after a poor result. Even those who deign to utter their thoughts do so with a member of the press office hanging over their shoulder to steer queries away from unwelcome territory. There is no avoiding the cameras though, unless your manager feels that the BBC has exceeded their remit and should be ostracised as Alex Ferguson has notably done, starting a trend amongst fellow managers with thin skins. Sky and Setanta pay the piper millions more and usually get their choice of post-match interviewees.

After the final whistle, especially if events have not turned out as planned, emotions can run high. Certainly, comments are made which are regretted in hindsight. It was surprising that Arsène Wenger should have fallen foul of the strict Arsenal protocol in the aftermath of the match at Birmingham which began his woes in the run-in of the 2007/08 Premier League campaign. Striker Eduardo had suffered a broken leg from a challenge by Martin Taylor, who received a red card and the automatic three-match ban that went with it. "The tackle was horrendous and this guy should never play football again," Wenger told the BBC after the match. The press office would have briefed any players the broadcaster requested to be non-committal about the incident, but the last person they were going to instruct was the man most responsible for the image of the club. The manager subsequently felt his reaction to have been excessive and issued a retraction later that day.

Another bane of the press office is the close relationships some foreign players have with their native media. Copy approval for many written media interviews is demanded as a matter of course, but if players talk to journalists of their own accord, the worst they can fear is a slap on the wrist. Not something that will cause the likes of Jens Lehmann and William Gallas much trepidation, so they often use their compatriots to get a message across that would never get through the normal British channels.

So when Eduardo, broken leg in plaster, was quoted from his hospital bed by the Brazilian newspaper *O Globo* as saying "To go in like he [Martin Taylor] did, it had to be with malicious intention", the story was quickly picked up by news agencies and circulated in English. The press office were not happy, and a reproduction of the story on the Sky Sports News website was later withdrawn. Whether or not Eduardo had actually been interviewed over the telephone within 24 hours of the injury is questionable, although it is interesting that Arsenal's own official website carried the remainder of the interview, evidently having deemed the less controversial part of it to be credible enough for reproduction.

Arsène Wenger is of course a law unto himself and will speak to whoever he chooses. So he has direct contact on a regular basis with a couple of favoured French writers on

L'Equipe and *France Football* (as well as being retained by France's main commercial channel TF1 as a pundit providing regular comments for the weekly news programme *Telefoot* and for the live broadcasts of the national team's games). As a courtesy, they inform the press office that they have spoken with the boss. The information tends to be grudgingly received, probably because there is nothing they can do to prevent it, despite the fact that the French journalists are unlikely to fall into the category of writers who would opportunistically exploit their access.

In elevating Arsenal into the club it has become, Arsène Wenger has encouraged a culture of separatism. The notion of control permeates the organisation. The manager has reason to ensure his players are controlled in what they can eat and drink and how they train, but the idea extends to other areas that cocoon them. There is little exposure to the paying public or the media, except in situations that are heavily supervised. The culture of the club is very protective, very inward-looking. There may be surprise and spontaneity on the field, but elsewhere there is none and the club should be confident enough to allow the human touch to proliferate without fear of a backlash.

With the apprehension over terrorism, players are advised not to do lifestyle pieces and interviews carried out under the copy approval arrangement often have mentions of players' religious beliefs removed. You wonder whether, had Brazilian superstar Kaka ended up in north London, his 'I belong to Jesus' vest under his shirt would have had the postscript 'but the press office would rather you didn't know'.

The notion of the Milan player plying his trade at Arsenal is not so fanciful, as Brazil was not unchartered territory for Arsène Wenger in less busy times. "It's my big regret now that I cannot travel," he reveals. "I like to travel to watch players and find people. I found Silvinho and Edu on my travels. I knew Kolo Toure since he was 16. I helped create the Kolo Toure school [in the Ivory Coast]." (And there are other more specific regrets. Claude Makelele and Petr Cech are two notable examples of star quality that Wenger was aware of when they played in France, but who he allowed to slip away.)

As other managers had their eyes opened by Wenger's groundbreaking voyages and followed in his footsteps, so Arsenal had to put together a more structured operation to ward off the increasing intrusion into what once was virgin territory for other British clubs. Nowadays the scouting network does the travelling for him while he sits at home in Totteridge and does the best he can. Kaka had already been snapped up but occasionally television will give him the chance to catch sight of a potential signing his scouting team have been reporting on. He would certainly have had ample opportunity to verify the good reports on José Antonio Reyes and Bacary Sagna ahead of the decision to bring them to north London. However, the number of potential purchases watched *chez* Wenger that have simply fallen outside the available budget is a moot point.

Yet it was one that David Dein was all too concerned about. "Arsène has to sell before he can buy," he said before the January 2007 transfer window. The perspective back in 2004 was that the stadium was going to make that situation obsolete. "What I want is to put this club on a level where we have a 60,000-seater stadium and if the manager or the board takes the right decision we can compete with everybody in the world," said Wenger at the time. "At the moment, I am sitting here – if Milan or Man United or Real Madrid is after the same player, I say thank you very much, I'll go somewhere else. And I want one day that the manager – if it's me or somebody else – can say, 'OK, how much is it? I can compete.' And that gives you a guarantee, but at the moment if we are wrong in the buys, we cannot compete. If you get one or two buys wrong, you are dead. With the biggest clubs it is different. They can say, 'OK, this year we were wrong. We'll put in £50 million again and we will be right next time.'"

By March 2007 it seemed as if nothing had changed. The team were out of the Premiership title race, still adapting to a life of careful husbandry at the home that was supposed to ensure that they were able to vie with their free-spending rivals. However, the club simply had too much money tied up in property development, particularly Highbury Square. And until all the money was in from the sale of the flats there would have to be economic sacrifices in the short term, a situation many fans, David Dein among them, were having trouble getting to grips with. Now was the time for the man of action who had seen off Terry Neill and Don Howe to return with a vengeance. If Arsène needed £50 million he should damn well have it and in the vice-chairman's view that is exactly what he did need and he was going to ensure that he got it.

CHAPTER ELEVEN
YESTERDAY'S MEN

At the end of January 2007, Arsenal entertained Tottenham in the second leg of a Carling Cup semi-final. In the light of Arsène Wenger's policy of using the competition to blood young players and provide match practice for his second-stringers, the home club wanted to reduce prices as they had in previous rounds. However, their opponents were entitled to 45 per cent of the gate receipts and they insisted grade A fixture admission charges should be levied. The stand-off was only resolved with the intervention of the Football League, and a compromise reached whereby Arsenal agreed to apply their grade B rates, which ranged from £32 to £66 apart from the concessions in the family enclosure.

The Carling Cup was not included as one of the games which gave admittance to the 36,000 standard season tickets, so a huge number of upper and lower tier seats were available to see the reserves of a team who had failed to challenge in the Premier League. Surely it would be a tough sell. Remarkably, an attendance figure of 59,872 was posted. It was positive proof that Arsenal's expensive new home could continue its phenomenal financial contribution even under extenuating circumstances.

Watching from the directors' box, David Dein must have experienced some very mixed emotions. It was a triumph to get so many people through the doors and, moreover, the team qualified for yet another cup final trip to Cardiff by defeating the full-strength line-up of their neighbours after extra time. But how did he feel, in the light of his dispute with his fellow board members about the financial hazards of Ashburton Grove, now that it appeared set for a prosperous future? His friend down in the technical area was still being forced to buck the odds. In Dein's view it was all well and good looking to the future when extravagant spending would be possible, but Arsène Wenger might not be around by then and he himself was certainly no spring chicken. He fervently believed that his colleagues were complacent. He felt strongly that the winning of trophies was too far down their list of priorities. He felt that they were concentrating too much on the building of apartments rather than the building of a football team.

Arsenal had their stadium, but not much money in the bank. They needed cash to compete and they needed it now. Unfortunately it didn't appear that the board, four of whom featured on the *Sunday Times* Rich List with an estimated combined wealth of £500 million, were going to reach into their own pockets to buy a Ronaldo or a Kaka, so it was down to him to find someone who would. Keith Edelman's emphasis on the balance sheets meant he was not the football man Arsenal needed at the helm as far as David Dein was concerned, and for him there was one far more suitable and obvious candidate for the role: the rather dapper character he sees on a daily basis in his bathroom mirror when shaving.

Less than a fortnight after the semi-final against Tottenham, the club announced a partnership with Major League Soccer team the Colorado Rapids, with the aim of "building the Arsenal brand in the US; helping to improve the quality of football at MLS team Colorado Rapids and supporting grassroots football in the US". Really? There must have been other and better marketing opportunities available. Were there thousands of Arsenal fans in the States that a link-up with a team from Denver was going to exploit?

However, although he didn't initiate the association, David Dein immediately saw how it might be better used back home. Stan Kroenke, the proprietor of Colorado Rapids, is a sports mogul who either owned outright or had significant stakes in five other US sports franchises, including the St Louis Rams of the NFL and the Denver Nuggets of the NBA. He was well-heeled, and his wife even more so, being related to the founder of the Wal-Mart retail chain. With the new Sky, Setanta and overseas television deals coming on stream Dein, mindful that his club needed more financial muscle, encouraged Kroenke that investment in a top Premier League club, specifically Arsenal, would be a profitable exercise. Unwittingly, Arsenal's biggest shareholder then gave Kroenke the chance to dip his toe in the water.

Recently moved to Switzerland, Danny Fiszman disposed of 659 shares in March 2007. It was subsequently assumed that he did this in order to test his tax status with the UK revenue. The sale took his portion below the 25 per cent which hitherto gave him a measure of control over any special resolutions the club might wish to propose. (He later admitted to a group of shareholders that he wouldn't have sold the shares if he'd known what was to follow and advised one of them who had a single share, "Hang onto it. Every one is vital now.") At the time, the board owned 60 per cent of the club so Fiszman's falling below the 25 per cent mark was not regarded as a risk. The buyer of the shares, who acted through a third party, was Stan Kroenke. The entrepreneur's next acquisition a month on was far more substantial. In 2004 two of the main ITV companies, Granada and Carlton, merged and the new company (confusingly now called ITV) was looking to unload its 9.99 per cent stake in Arsenal as part of its policy of selling off its non-core assets. 50 per cent of the ownership of Arsenal Broadband went with the deal. One of the conditions of the agreement was that ITV could dispose of its holding as and when it liked without any obligation to Arsenal. A total price of £65 million was agreed with Kroenke, the shares element being valued at £42.3 million, which was believed to be at the top end of the market. With other smaller purchases, Kroenke soon owned 12 per cent of Arsenal Holdings plc.

At about the same time, 152 shares belonging to Peter Hill-Wood that had been registered in Ken Friar's name in the early 1980s were transferred back to the chairman. It was a tidying-up exercise, but the timing, together with Fiszman's sale, fuelled speculation that the board was preparing for a takeover. Certainly, Dein and Kroenke's holdings combined outweighed that of Fiszman's and if Lady Nina Bracewell-Smith's 16 per cent could be added to the pot then the 43 per cent stake they would then control could precipitate a change of ownership.

To this end, Lady Nina must have seemed a likely ally to the vice-chairman. If that was the case, Dein was mistaken. The daughter of an Indian diplomat, she met her future husband Sir Charles Bracewell-Smith while working at the Park Lane Hotel, which her husband part-owned with his cousins, the Carrs, also Arsenal directors. After marrying him in 1996, she was invited onto the board of the hotel. Over the next eight years, due to the gradual decline of her husband's health, the Arsenal shares registered in his name and others held in trust for him by the Carrs were gradually transferred into her name, eventually giving her sole ownership of 16 per cent of the club by 2004.

Geoff Klass is a mutual friend of Lady Nina and David Dein. In 2005, he was considering whether to dispose of his four per cent shareholding in Arsenal (he subsequently sold half of it) and suggested to Lady Nina that if she was ever of like mind, as a businessman he could get a better deal for both of them if they acted in concert. Chinese whispers then spun the proposal into a tale that Klass wanted to acquire her stake and in so doing was acting as a proxy for Dein. Putting two and two together and maybe making a lot more than four, it struck the board that having such a large shareholder on the inside could only be an asset to them. In April 2005 she was invited to become a non-executive director.

Lady Nina's loyalty to her family's 80-year history with Arsenal and her fellow directors was tested when Dein suggested, in the interests of the club's future, that there might be a better home for her shares. Dein certainly underestimated the pleasure Lady Nina got from her new role and her empathy with the direction the board felt the club should be going in. Talking about the episode in February 2008 she said, "He [Dein] spoke to Kroenke on his own initiative and Kroenke is a businessman with a different agenda. The board are fans." In her view, by trying to get Kroenke on board, David Dein was going against his own repeated response to the suggestion that there should be a fan's representative on its board – "An Arsenal fan, who do you think we [the Directors] are then?". Now, in Lady Nina's view, he was attempting to bring in a stranger "who might use the club for profit". She relayed her discussion with Dein to her colleagues who felt that his manoeuvring could no longer be tolerated. A special board meeting was convened and a decision reached to give David Dein his cards. Peter Hill-Wood confirmed that "the vote was 100 per cent unanimous". A letter informing Dein that he was no longer a director of Arsenal Football Club, signed by all of the other board members, was handed to him at the club's Highbury House offices by the chairman on Wednesday 18th April 2007, the morning after Arsenal had beaten Manchester City at home as the season wound down. "Chips Keswick was with me," Hill-Wood explained. "If you have a potential confrontation it's better to have two people present than one." Sir Chips Keswick was one of two non-executive directors appointed to the board in November 2005, Lord Harris of Peckham being the other.

On the decision of one woman, "inexperienced with regard to football politics" according to Dein, but whose heart was indisputably in the right place, Arsenal Football Club remained on the same course it had been following since Danny Fiszman became the major shareholder in 1996. Whether it was the right one was open to debate.

Dein's fate had been determined by a sequence of events no one could have predicted when he was instrumental in bringing Arsène Wenger to the club in 1996. The on-field success enabled the board to contemplate moving way upmarket, and in doing so the specialist financial acumen required saw Dein shunted aside. If he had still been in charge, the Emirates would probably never have come about. Now, as the board could envisage 60,000 filing in at least 20 times a season, they justifiably felt their bold choice had been fully vindicated. But in Dein's eyes, investment was needed to complete the picture. What price a wonderful new stadium if there wasn't a wonderful new team playing in it who could send all their rivals packing? No prophet in his own land, he had felt compelled to take tremendous personal gambles to try to achieve his objective. And the prospect of returning to a greater position of influence than he had enjoyed since Keith Edelman's arrival would have been no disincentive.

Dein was not helped in his relationship with his fellow directors by the involvement of his son Darren in club-related business. Initially working for agent Jerome Anderson, Darren went on to represent several Arsenal players, including Thierry Henry. The other directors warned his father about the potential conflict of interest, a notion denied by the vice-chairman. Yet their fears would not have been allayed when the chairman spotted Darren Dein at the hotel when the board struck their agreement with Emirates in early 2004. "I was surprised that he was hovering about the hotel when we had this secret meeting," recalls Peter Hill-Wood, "which obviously wasn't as secret as we thought it was. I had no idea that he was anywhere near it [the naming rights negotiation]. But I think he must have had some involvement." It probably didn't help his father's cause.

David Dein's exit was unceremonious. Choosing not to sign a contractual letter of dismissal, the vice-chairman was forced to clear his desk and leave behind the company perks such as his mobile phone and any monetary settlement. As far as the board were concerned, he was now *persona non grata*. Dein said his dismissal felt "like a family bereavement. Initially there is shock, then the grieving." By the time Arsenal played at home again on 29th April, the nameplate below Dein's seat in the directors' box had been removed, and the seats he and wife Barbara had traditionally occupied were filled by others. For a few days he lay low until the paparazzi gave up camping outside his Totteridge home for pictures or comments, deluding them into believing that he had gone abroad when in reality he simply hadn't left the house.

In negotiating with Kroenke, David Dein would have felt he was acting in Arsenal's best interests but he was certainly acting on his own initiative. Chairman Peter Hill-Wood justified his dismissive rejection of the American ("We don't want his sort and we don't want his money") by saying "I didn't know what he wanted to do. I had absolutely no idea. I defend the integrity of Arsenal Football Club. We're going to have some unknown American buying control? I didn't think that was good and I still don't think it's good."

To put it mildly, Arsène Wenger was not happy at losing his pal and closest ally on the board. However, by the time Hill-Wood went to see him at the training ground the next morning, he had – after discussing the situation with Dein – decided to stay. Nevetheless, asked how Wenger took the news of his friend's sacking, Hill-Wood recalls, "Not very well. I didn't expect him to. I know perfectly well he's friendly with David and still is." (Indeed, the two remain in constant touch and have occasionally been spotted together with their wives enjoying a meal in a local restaurant.) The chairman believes the manager wanted to stay because "he enjoys what he's doing". Ken Friar was detailed to take over Dein's work on contract and transfer negotiations and prepared himself for a busy summer ahead.

Some months after his departure, Dein was "still feeling the pain". Anger had replaced grief as the predominant emotion. He felt that he was the victim of a personal vendetta. "They [the board] were jealous of my profile." And he could have added influence at the top tables. When he was replaced by Keith Edelman as Arsenal's representative on G14, the members were disappointed to lose such a knowledgeable administrator. The Arsenal board, Dein felt, were out of touch and not acting in the club's best interests. He cited a regional Premier League meeting at which no Arsenal representative had bothered to attend. Additionally, no-one took the plane to Switzerland for UEFA Club Forum meetings at which a number of other English clubs were present. Even Peter Kenyon of Chelsea, his long-time adversary, expressed astonishment at what he took to be Arsenal's new non-interventionist policy.

Admitting sorely missing "the buzz of being in the inner circle" (with club, country, UEFA and FIFA) Dein began to carve out a new role for himself as a speaker on the football conference circuit, his opinions on the state of the game still carrying enough gravitas for him to be much in demand. He was also sought after by his former competitors who, having enjoyed jousting with him across boardrooms and Premier

League meetings, felt his experience would be an invaluable asset to their clubs. However as a one-club man, whilst flattered by the offers, he rejected top management roles at Newcastle, Everton and Barcelona.

He was determined to keep his own counsel. He recalled the dignified way the actress Koo Stark back in the 1980s refused all temptation and pressure to kiss and tell about her escapade with Prince Andrew. He was going to keep his powder dry until the opportunity arose to respond to what he called his "brutal sacking". In the meantime, he contented himself with justifying what Stan Kroenke could have brought to the party. "All the very wealthy football investors I've met are in it for the sport," he claims. "They want some fun out of it. They're not looking for a return on their investment. OK, they don't want to lose anything, they have put in good money, but, invariably, it represents only a very small part of their overall wealth. It is a passion investment. They could put the money in the bank but that would be boring." It was a view that wouldn't be shared by everyone at Old Trafford.

Despite Dein's exit, the Kroenke story wouldn't go away and the furore was such that Peter Hill-Wood wrote to all shareholders reassuring them about the board's resolve to resist any takeover. And, exceptionally, the reclusive Danny Fiszman went public for the first time anyone could remember, agreeing to an interview for Sky Sports News. He was adamant that the club was not for sale. "We are open to anything that will improve the club but it's going to be very, very difficult to explain to me and to the rest of board how you can actually make substantial investment – which would be another £400 million, £500 million, £600 million – and not expect a return for that. If it's just an eight to 10 per cent return, you're talking about £50 million or so. That's got to come out of the club, otherwise there's no point making a purchase. I don't know how they're going to be able to improve the finances of the club at that sort of amount." And anyway as long as the directors remained united, a takeover would be impossible. "The board has 45.5 per cent of the shares. We also obviously have friends which takes us over 50 per cent. They [Kroenke/Dein] can mount a hostile bid but they're never going to gain control. The future of the club is in the hands of the board." To prevent further speculation, this stance was confirmed by the entire board signing a lockdown agreement for 12 months, which meant they could not sell any shares until April 2008 at the earliest.

Around this time the Arsenal Supporters' Trust (AST) emerged as a key opinion-former on the ownership issue. Formed in 2003 to bring together the smaller shareholders under one umbrella, the AST's board represented its members in discussions with the Arsenal board and other significant shareholders. Comprising a number of highly qualified professionals from the banking, legal and PR industries, they could talk to the directors on equal terms about the minutiae of Arsenal's business and quickly won the respect of all those who dealt with them. They discovered that following the share issue to Granada in 2005, one authorised share was left unissued due to a mathematical error. Dubbed the 'orphan share', the AST ran a successful campaign to persuade the club to donate the share to them for safekeeping. They also secured the club's backing (and promised financial assistance) to start up a sharesave scheme to allow supporters to contribute towards the eventual purchase of shares in the club. When the AST launched its own website, they contacted the club to have a link posted on arsenal.com. The result was an immediate placing at the very top of the list of Fanzone entries on the site's homepage, even above links to the club's own pages for its recognised roster of supporters' clubs and the Junior Gunners. There was no doubt they were the board's favoured sons in the fan fraternity (which included the Arsenal

Independent Supporters' Association (AISA) and REDaction). Further, the media recognised them as a reliable source on how the rank and file viewed proceedings. Prepared to talk to all parties, the AST kept in touch with David Dein, cognizant of his considerable stake, and kept an open mind as to the benefits of greater involvement from Stan Kroenke (but were always consistent in saying they would not support a debt-laden or hostile takeover).

Publicly, Kroenke never commented on his association with Dein. He had probably expected him to obtain Lady Nina's shareholding in the light of paying top dollar for ITV's 9.99 per cent. After that failed, short of selling up himself, all he could do was to bide his time and ensure his investment was in safe hands. Visiting the UK in October 2007 on the occasion of an NFL match at Wembley between the New York Giants and the Miami Dolphins, 'Silent Stan' (as he is known due to his public reticence) was asked about his relationship with the Arsenal board. "It's a partnership at the moment," he responded. "Everybody has a tendency to speed up but actually these things take a lot of time and a lot of effort and many years to develop. We tend to look in the long term. If you are an investor in a sports team and you don't look long term you are probably not a good investor. This is a strategic investment for us." He sounded a lot more cautious than the type of big spender David Dein had in mind.

Presumably Dein had also come to this conclusion and on 30th August 2007 he emerged from his Totteridge bunker and announced, at a specially convened press conference, that he had sold his shares to Red and White Holdings Ltd, a company specifically formed to acquire shares in Arsenal by Moscow-based billionaire Alisher Usmanov and his right-hand man Farhad Moshiri. Part of the deal, which paid Dein the handsome sum of £75 million for his shares, was that he was installed as the new company's chairman. Presumably if Usmanov was ultimately successful in securing control of Arsenal, Dein would be back in the saddle again.

A statement issued at the press conference to announce the purchase of the former vice-chairman's shares indicated that Red and White Holdings intended "to approach the board of Arsenal in the near future to discuss its ideas, to understand the future direction of Arsenal and to explore areas of potential cooperation." It followed up with the assertion (reiterating Dein's long-held conviction) that "Red and White believes that in order to remain competitive at the top level of the game, Arsenal will require access to significant funding." The speculation that Red and White were interested in a takeover was supported by Farhad Moshiri commenting that "we look forward to increasing our stake". And there was no hanging about as, within a month, they had raised their stake from Dein's 14 per cent to 23 per cent, putting themselves well on the way to overtaking Danny Fiszman as the largest shareholder. Immediately the share price rocketed to £10,000 as Red and White bought out some prominent smaller shareholders such as the hedge fund Lansdowne Holdings and Birol Nadir, son of the Polly Peck tycoon Asil Nadir.

Dein now felt able to return to watch his team from the comfort of Usmanov's box. He had retained his paid-for season tickets in the Club and upper levels and made them available to friends and family but for the first time in years there was no reserved parking space. He had to leave his car in a school car park and walk the few hundred yards to the ground, rather than use the parking space under the stadium reserved for the boxholder.

However, mixing with the hoi polloi showed Dein he had a lot of personal support. Walking from his parked car to the stadium for the Saturday afternoon game against Birmingham in January 2008 he passed the Tollington pub on the Hornsey

Road, which had fans packed outside in a pavement terrace area. A friend who was accompanying him, anticipating potential ill feeling, dropped back a couple of paces. Over his shoulder Dein shouted to him, "You think they're going to throw their beer over me, don't you?" "Yep," replied his friend who was dumbfounded to find that they greeted him like a long lost son. Lads leaned over the railing to shake his hand. "When are you coming back?" they asked. "I'm here, aren't I?" he responded. Outside the stadium he was stopped for photos and autographs, asked the same question and gave the same answer. In spite of some negative press in internet blogs and fanzines and a large banner created by the REDaction group to relay the message that Usmanov was not wanted, there were no catcalls and abuse for Dein, nothing in fact to warrant him needing the kind of minders a Russian magnate wouldn't dream of leaving the house without.

Arsène Wenger was circumspect about the predatory share-buying of the company that had installed his friend as chairman, adamant that he had no intention of getting involved in the boardroom politics of the ownership issue. However, he did admit, "I'm concerned with the intent of people coming in", although he distanced himself by stating, "What is happening up there [in the boardroom] is nothing to do with me. I'm not a shareholder and I don't want to be involved in a strategic struggle for shares because, basically, it's not my problem. Self-sufficiency should be any club's target. You cannot have a policy at the club that, every year, somebody puts £50 million or £100 million in. Prices are rising but will people continue to pump in £40 million, £50 million or £100 million every year without any natural resources or dividends paid back? I'm not convinced. You have to work with a club's natural resources."

The manager with the degree in economics had previously expressed a distaste for the exorbitant spending that other clubs practised, and Dein's reasoning behind bringing Usmanov to the party was not going to change that view. "Am I concerned that major foreign investment might affect the way we work here?" said Wenger. "Yes. There are many ways to work in the game. You can say you don't want any youth development at all and I'll respect that. If there are good players on the market, you go for them. But we've gone for a different solution and that's what we want to continue to do. We go this way. I feel we are strong enough to compete and that's what I want to show." Defiantly, he emphasised, "If I wanted to buy a player today I have money available, it's not a problem." The company books, however, suggested that in fact he didn't quite have a blank chequebook.

Wenger's transfer and wages budget was later described by Ken Friar as being a case not so much of the manager saying "I need this much" but more asking "How much have I got?" Was it significant that Theo Walcott did not appear for the first team between joining from Southampton in January 2006 and the end of that season, before being selected for England's World Cup squad? Although he made the bench on occasion, the suspicion was that if he'd actually trod the turf in Arsenal colours, an immediate further instalment on his transfer fee to his former club would have been activated. At a time when every penny was being counted, perhaps the decision was taken to give him first-team experience purely from the perspective of a non-playing substitute.

Now Wenger was in a situation where he could concentrate on developing younger players without any internal pressure to buy more established names. There was simply no choice. So he accepted it willingly, and got on with the job he loved. It was certainly a different position to the one Dein had taken up on his behalf. However, Wenger had been content to work without any cash and then when given some, he didn't necessarily spend it. Nevertheless, Dein's position was that he needed "bags more", and quickly. Not so long ago Dein and Wenger were, in Dein's words, "a team". Peter Hill-Wood had been asked "Have you ever known David Dein to disagree with Arsène Wenger?" "Never", he shot back. Perhaps Dein felt he had been given the licence to act as Wenger's *agent provocateur*. More likely, as with so many self-made millionaire businessmen, Dein trusted his own judgment implicitly and found it difficult to veer away from his predetermined course of action.

If the situation regarding Stan Kroenke a few short months earlier had been unnerving, then the new threat to their position had the board reaching for their tin hats as shares were being hoovered up by Red and White at a rate of knots. Contrary to the view of many who regarded David Dein as no longer having any influence, the former vice-chairman believed he held an even stronger hand than hitherto. He could now wield Red and White's shareholding which was much larger than his former stake. There were even mischievous rumours that, to demonstrate his resurrection, he might turn up at the club's AGM in October 2007, although they proved inaccurate. It was just as well, as he would not have enjoyed hearing the board give the strongest indication yet that they would be around for the long haul with the announcement of an extension to their 'lockdown agreement', which was greeted by spontaneous applause from the large gathering of several hundred shareholders (more than anyone can ever remember seeing at an AGM). Under the new agreement, none of the directors' shares could be sold until 2009, and even then, only to family members or fellow directors. In 2010, if there is unanimous agreement, then shares can be disposed of, but failing this, no one can sell until 2012. Keith Edelman later triumphantly claimed the pact made the board "bulletproof". The edict sent a message out that the status quo would remain. (By 2010, the Highbury Square residential development is due to be complete, a decent chunk of the outstanding debt should have been paid off and the future should look much rosier. The value of the club might actually be greatly enhanced and the board members might be able to cash in if there is any inclination to sell.)

Despite the backslapping, there were still unresolved issues regarding the future. The Hill-Wood and Bracewell-Smith families may have had three generations on the board over the years but none of the offspring of the current directors are being groomed for succession. Despite Danny Fiszman, the board's major shareholder, having five grown-up children, there is currently no sign that any of them are ever likely to be involved in establishing a third Arsenal family dynasty. Further, with the majority of the board in their seventies, their ownership of the club could soon be subject to last wills and testaments, worth tens of millions of pounds in the cases of Danny Fiszman and Lady Nina. Peter Hill-Wood revealed that discussions had taken place about the years ahead. Asked whether the board might bring in someone who would be around in 20 years' time, Hill-Wood replied, "When you say the board is not youthful, they are very experienced." When put to him that this was not necessarily true in terms of marketing or television rights, he responded, "But do we realise that the world is changing? Indeed we do. If the perfect answer is a 40-year-old from Google or something, we'd be very happy. We're not excluding them but we certainly look at it and we all know that we're unfortunately getting older." Equally unfortunately, inaction was speaking so much louder than wishful thinking. However, the growing relationship with the AST indicated that the directors were beginning to widen their horizons.

The board donated use of the Diamond Club suite for the AST's annual Christmas drinks do, held in conjunction with AISA. Four of the directors – Danny Fiszman, Keith Edelman,

Ken Friar and Sir Chips Keswick – attended. Obviously there was no compulsion to do so, but a board meeting had been held at Highbury House earlier, so it was convenient for some of those attending to pop along and show their faces. The first drinks were on the AST, but Danny Fiszman appeared somewhat taken aback at being asked for £3 when he subsequently ordered a Coke at the bar. Possibly never having had to buy a drink at the stadium before, his grasp on the club's finances may not have extended to the mundane matters that affect the rank-and-file. When questioned about the events of recent months off the field, Fiszman responded, pointing towards the pitch, "I haven't given up six years of my life to make this happen only to walk away from it now."

Fiszman spoke of the stress of being responsible for the well-being of the club, in that so many people cared so deeply about it and thus were reliant on him "to get the stadium right without endangering the club. It's one thing if by failing you suffer yourself," he explained, "but it's different when there are so many people relying on you." If the remarks were reassuring, the motive may not have been entirely without self-interest, but it suited all concerned to take it at face value for the time being. Fiszman told senior members of the AST he would in future be spending more time on club matters, having understandably taken something of a back seat after the extraordinary commitment he had displayed in getting the stadium up and running. Despite the message, some observers still believe he might contemplate selling up when the time is right as long as it does not entail the Red and White Holdings chairman replacing him.

There was no danger of that happening in the short term as financially the club looked to have turned a corner, the Emirates effect having been responsible for catapaulting it into the top strata of the football money league. After the first season in the new stadium, the club announced a 34 per cent increase in their football turnover, up to £177 million, over half from matchday revenue (season tickets, corporate hospitality, through the turnstiles, catering and dining and programmes) – twice that of Highbury. They were now the fifth largest club in the world in terms of footballing revenue, although when their property activities were included, their turnover exceeded £200 million and saw them climb above Barcelona and Chelsea, with only Manchester United and Real Madrid ahead of them in June 2007. The US business magazine *Forbes* rated the club as the third most valuable in world football, worth £600 million albeit with debts of 43 per cent of this valuation.

Arsenal are now indisputably a mega-club. And this status was attained in spite of Wenger funding much of his buying by selling first, the very situation that David Dein could not live with. Not only that, but he has been such a shrewd seller (with Dein's assistance) that he actually contributed handsomely to the bottom line. A profit of £18.5 million was made on player sales in 2006/07, excluding the Thierry Henry transfer fee which fell into the following year's accounts. Peter Hill-Wood revealed that in the summer of 2007 Wenger had told him, when transfer matters were discussed, "You're going to have to be brave this year. I've got every confidence in our young players. There's nobody I want and I'm not going to buy just to impress everybody."

In March 2008 the chairman was asked, "Has there ever been a notion at the club that Arsène has a bit too much power?"

"Never crossed my mind," he replied. "But I'm probably a reasonably self-confident person. And therefore, I'm very happy for the manager to manage and he's a much broader person than many football managers. And therefore he has a bit more leeway because if he started doing things that the board didn't like . . ."

"Has he ever done anything . . . ?", his questioner interrupted.

"No. I think his contribution, not only with the team but with the development of the training ground, the stadium and everything else, has been extremely positive."

If the chairman's thoughts on Stan Kroenke were initially unwelcoming, by early 2008 the American had been superseded in the suspicion stakes by Usmanov. "He is certainly not an open book," said Peter Hill-Wood. "I would not want him to be the owner of the club." Taking heed of the message, Usmanov responded, "What we heard about David Dein and the board at the outset of our Arsenal adventure and what we can see now are two different pictures. But we won't be hostage to any hostility that exists between him and the board." So, taking Peter Hill-Wood at his word ("I will avoid it [getting involved with Dein] if I can help it") the conclusion must be that the only way Red and White will gain a presence in the Highbury House boardroom is by jettisoning its chairman or as a consequence of a hostile takeover. As far as Peter Hill-Wood and the rest of the board are concerned, David Dein had long since been airbrushed out of the picture. At the AGM, it took an unexpected interjection from the floor to remind the board that "without David Dein there would have been no Arsène Wenger", and that it was a shame, despite the acrimonious divorce, that they couldn't bring themselves to acknowledge his contribution. To his credit, the chairman concurred and apologised for the omission.

Peter Hill-Wood and Keith Edelman did meet with Farhad Moshiri, but the ties with Kroenke were the ones the board chose to strengthen. How ironic, Dein must have thought when he found out. His overtures to Kroenke contributing to his own downfall, now Hill-Wood and Kroenke are breaking bread together. In April 2008, Kroenke was in London and spent time meeting directors, sitting next to Keith Edelman for the duration of a rather uninspiring Premier League home draw with Liverpool. Edelman chatted sporadically during the game to his guest. 'Silent Stan' lived up to his nickname and for the most part patiently listened. It was the penultimate match that Edelman would view from the directors' box.

Just as suddenly as David Dein's departure just over a year earlier, on 1st May 2008, Edelman was gone. The man who had replaced the former vice-chairman as the day-to-day decision-maker at the club joined him in having his name-plate removed from under his seat in the directors' box, despite leaving with a 12-month 'consultancy' agreement. The abrupt nature of his parting, hinting at a dramatic turn of events, was evidenced by people turning up for appointments with him on the day of his dismissal. The exact reasons for the decision remain a secret, although speculation circulated that the Highbury Square development may have been a particular problem. There were newspaper stories stating that the board had already been actively seeking to install a more football-orientated managing director. Certainly, it was an unusual state of affairs that saw "the number cruncher" go just a month before the financial year end. Edelman's final sighting at Arsenal came the following week when spotted by a couple of shareholders who had just attended a question-and-answer session with the manager. They saw him on the way from Arsenal Underground station heading for Highbury House, presumably to collect his effects, uncharacteristically dressed in jeans and a casual shirt. He was almost unrecognisable without his usual working attire of suit and tie. For once he had the appearance of a football man, which he never really was. That he should suffer the same fate as Dein – unquestionably a football man through and through – was a rich irony as the two men never hit it off from day one.

A petty incident symbolises their mutual distaste for one another. There was a particular parking space that was best placed to enter the Clock End reception area at the old Highbury Stadium. It was commandeered by Dein before Edelman's appointment by the club. Edelman, who used to arrive for work earlier than Dein, took to parking in his spot. The vice-chairman did not take kindly to being trumped in the car park as well as marginalised in the boardroom. One evening, on leaving later than Edelman, he placed a traffic cone across the empty place to reserve it for himself the following day. When Edelman arrived, without a moment's hesitation he drove straight over the cone, indifferent to any possible damage to the undercarriage of his expensive vehicle and went upstairs to his office. One can only wonder if anyone ever put Dein fully in the picture.

Edelman tried to get onside with the supporters by talking the talk, citing Robert Pires as his favourite Arsenal player. (Surely it was just a happy coincidence that Pires had reserved an apartment at Highbury Square.) But he never convinced. When the club made moves to trademark the word 'Gooner' – a term adopted by the fans themselves in the mid-1970s after being labelled as such by Tottenham supporters – the managing director explained that as far as he was concerned "we [Arsenal] own it [the word]". His reasoning presumably was that without the club, the term wouldn't exist. It indicated how, despite his efforts, his sentiments were different to those of the supporters. Following David Dein, Edelman was named as his successor as the president of the Arsenal Ladies football team. But unlike his predecessor, he didn't attend many of their matches. One of his final moves was to tell Vic Akers he might be replaced as the coach of the Ladies, bewildering after they had won 29 major trophies in 17 seasons under his stewardship, peaking with a victorious UEFA Cup campaign in 2007. According to Dein, still keeping tabs on his former charges, Akers was heartbroken, but Edelman thought it would be better to have a female coach. On the Managing Director's departure Akers, a popular figure at the club, was informed that he would be allowed to continue in the role after all.

Edelman would not have come top of a popularity poll amongst the staff, but the tough decisions required to keep the club running smoothly within a tight budget at a time of huge change weren't going to win him that particular contest. More importantly though, he was able to extend the 14-year, £260 million, loan on the stadium at a cheaper fixed-interest rate over 25 years. Under the terms of the deal, the club had to make a one-off payment of £21 million to buy out the original commitment but the annual interest repayments fell from £32 million to £20 million (less than half that of Manchester United). With £3 million-plus coming into the coffers with every home matchday, it was a far more manageable amount. The restructuring proved to be a smart piece of business as, a year on, a crisis in the US sub-prime market made borrowing a far more difficult and expensive business. In fairness to Edelman, he was ultimately a beneficiary and then a victim of the changing economic environment that first facilitated the successful refinancing of the new stadium debt but then led to concerns that for the club to develop Highbury Square themselves might not have made such sound economic sense in the light of the credit crunch that came along. By perhaps second guessing fiscal trends he might have made himself a hostage to fortune and, although his departure left the club with a short-term vacancy, he had fundamentally achieved what he had been brought in to do: secure the financing of the stadium and thereby underwrite the future of the club.

So, barely two years after the opening of the Emirates, two nameplates had already been removed from the spanking new directors' box. Ken Friar, who was doing David Dein's job, now had to step into Edelman's shoes *pro tem* as acting managing director. Friar had become the boardroom equivalent of a reliable utility player, an Arsenal man to the core.

But he was no replacement for Dein. Four weeks after Edelman had been given his cards, Danny Fiszman announced that the club were searching for a chief financial officer and a chief executive officer to replace the position of managing director. "The CEO will work with the manager, negotiate player purchases, sales and wage contracts," he explained. Until the appointment was made, Wenger resumed his travels to procure new talent when time permitted now that Dein was no longer available to make such sorties. But perhaps the club had already paid the price: the Brazilian wonderkid Alexandre Pato and France's Frank Ribery might have ended up in north London instead of Milan and Munich in the summer of 2007 if Dein had still been around. There can be little doubt he would have been dutifully scouring the globe on Wenger's behalf.

By the conclusion of the 2007/08 season, Red and White Holdings Ltd was still in the market for Arsenal shares. There weren't many available, but at a reduced going rate of £7,500 each due to the lockdown agreement it was not surprising there wasn't much buying and selling going on. It was a slow journey towards the cherished 25 per cent that would allow Usmanov to block any special resolutions the board might require an EGM for. But without one of the significant shareholders selling up or Usmanov offering ever-spiralling amounts to those with smaller holdings, he will find it difficult to reach the 30 per cent that would oblige him to make a compulsory bid for the company, a bid that would not succeed anyway, as long as the directors stayed true to their extended lockdown agreement.

However, the fear that a good number of the prospective purchasers who had put 10 per cent down on Highbury Square apartments might cut and run in the light of plummeting property prices means Arsenal's garden is suddenly far from rosy. The board know they are treading financial water until the Highbury Square revenue starts coming in. It is a tortuous wait, but they've made it most of the way, albeit with some casualties. Crucially, Wenger is still at the helm, the team are contenders again and the stadium continues to put up sold out notices. Now, the directors look forward to a new era when they can concentrate on being a football club once again.

CHAPTER TWELVE

TWO STEPS FORWARD AND A HUGE ONE BACK

The original cover of Arsenal's *2007/08 Handbook* featured a photograph of three players standing proudly together, arms crossed. Gilberto was in the middle, slightly in front of William Gallas and Kolo Toure. All three were displaying the captain's armband. By the time the publication went to press, the photo had been swapped for one of the giant club crests that adorn the exterior of the Emirates Stadium. The arms crossed picture had been taken at a time when the somewhat fanciful notion of sharing the captaincy was doing the rounds. Wenger evidently felt was that there was no obvious choice to replace the departed Thierry Henry, although Gilberto had been his deputy the previous season. All three had a justifiable claim to being the chosen one.

The captaincy had become a thorny issue ever since the departure of Patrick Vieira. Wenger had been fortunate to inherit Tony Adams, and by the time of Adams's retirement, Vieira had worn the armband on enough occasions to make the transition seamless. In the summer of 2005, when Wenger decided it was time for Vieira to move on, Thierry Henry had two years remaining on his contract. With no obvious alternative, it was a difficult for the manager not to make his star striker the skipper. To have overlooked him would have been deemed a snub to a sensitive soul that could have strained relations.

Meriting pride of place, Henry undeniably contributed some inspired performances in the Champions League campaign that culminated in a return to his Parisian roots in May 2006. However, in a below-par performance in that final he missed gilt-edged chances to score, perhaps a consequence of the added responsibility weighing him down. Did his position as captain influence his choice to stay with the club at a critical period in its history? Whether his decision was an act of selflessness or not (albeit one with enormous financial rewards when his £100,000 plus weekly wage was combined with the upfront payment of his entire loyalty bonus), it cut little ice once the manager decided that the chief benefit of the contract renewal was the fact that he would not be forced to dispose of the player for less than his market value.

How would the club cope without Thierry Henry after his move to Barcelona in 2007? Of more immediate concern, who should succeed him as captain? Arsène Wenger had elevated Arsenal to the top level in world football – huge stadium, sell-out crowds, phenomenal income – and yet he did not have an obvious leader in the ranks. The three-way experiment was never put to the test as Gilberto was absent leading Brazil in the *Copa America* in June and July, and as a consequence missed out on the pre-season preparation enjoyed by colleagues. In the warm-up matches Gallas and Toure each took turns with the armband, although when tournaments – the inaugural Emirates Cup at home and in Amsterdam at Ajax's ArenA stadium – were won, Gallas collected the trophies. Three days before the first Premier League fixture against Fulham, Wenger announced that Gallas had got the nod ahead of the other contenders, explaining, "Centre back is always the best position to lead on the pitch and it is Gallas who has more experience at the back." An interesting thought process, but one he discounted two years earlier when Sol Campbell could have filled the role given to a centre forward.

The decision to select Gallas raised a few eyebrows, as the player had been with the club for less than a year. However, there was no question that he detested losing and his CV included a World Cup Final and two Premier League titles, although the manner of his exit from Chelsea hinted that accusations of a quixotic nature might be justified. Additionally he had already earned a reputation for being outspoken, bypassing the censorious mechanism of the Arsenal press office by giving interviews in his native tongue to the French press. No diplomat he. A view amongst some fans was that he was such a moaner that he must have been given the captaincy to encourage him to choose his words more carefully.

Gilberto's *Copa America* duties had ended with a yellow card in the semi-final in early July but Arsène Wenger wasn't about to rush him back into the fray. The Brazil captain was given three and a half weeks off, during which time he learnt he had been overlooked. The manager explained his absence: "It will take two or three weeks to get him ready. If we don't do that he will suffer during rest of the season." He suffered anyway, as the impressive form of his stand-in Mathieu Flamini ensured he never regained a regular starting spot.

Despite the apparent upheaval, the team enjoyed the kind of dream start – eight wins and a solitary draw from the first nine games – that no one had seen coming, except possibly Arsène Wenger. He told a friend, "I am confident that we can challenge; the question is whether the youngsters can last a season." With Henry no longer around and a perceived lack of improvement in the squad, a top-four place – according to the pre-season previews in the media – was seriously in doubt. During the summer, Wenger had recruited right back Bacary Sagna from Auxerre, striker Eduardo from Croatia Zagreb and midfielder Lassana Diarra from Chelsea. Only Sagna started matches as a matter of course, and immediately looked like an inspired purchase, improving the team both defensively and going forward and suffering none of the usual inhibitions in adapting to a new environment.

It would be a bit melodramatic to say that the pattern of the entire season was set during the very first game, but that is how some supporters saw it. Behind at home to Fulham, and finding it difficult to break through the massed ranks of their opponents, two very late goals turned a potentially humiliating defeat into a springboard for the weeks ahead, even if there were some early hiccups, such as individual errors by Jens Lehmann that resulted in Manuel Almunia replacing him as the first-choice goalkeeper. The team were now scoring many more goals from midfield than hitherto; their possession was more incisive, less prone to over-elaboration. The consistent selection of the mobile Emmanuel Adebayor added variety to the build-up, and with his height and that of substitute Nicklas Bendtner they became more effective at set pieces, particularly when the ball was crossed into the area. It was an aspect of their approach where Wenger's Arsenal had often come up short, epitomised by the relatively low number of headed goals notched by the recently departed club record scorer. It had seemed at times as if the emphasis on possession meant that the team were under orders to forego the aerial option, and the quality of free kicks and corners resulted in poor returns compared to other leading teams.

There was improvement in other respects too. The team became less prone to succumbing to the rumbustious style of opponents like Bolton which in recent seasons they had found difficult to combat. Firstly, the zip of the passing and movement was working so well that more often than not opponents weren't able to get close enough to disrupt the fluidity of the play with crude challenges. Secondly, the resilience of the side took a turn for the better with the presence of Mathieu Flamini alongside Cesc Fàbregas. With his sleeves rolled up and his combative approach he reminded older fans of Peter Storey from the 1970/71 double team. Much more of a battler than Gilberto, when the going got rough he could give as good as Arsenal got. Now into the final year of his contract, Wenger had actually given Flamini the option of leaving during the summer due to an anticipated lack of first-team opportunities, but the player elected to stay and fight for his place and both parties were glad that he did. Not that Cesc Fabregas was a shrinking violet. Still only 20, he began to show a steely side to his instinctive imagination and passing skill. Further, his finishing became far more incisive, so that his efforts were rewarded far more frequently than his meagre return of four goals the season before.

With Flamini and Fabregas prepared to battle in midfield, the team actually comprised a more robust spine from defence to attack, and it was on this basis that the logic of making William Gallas the captain made some kind of sense. He may have missed his on-field arguments with Jens Lehmann, but at least with the more amenable Almunia in goal, he could concentrate his aggression on the opposition. And in attack, Robin van Persie did not lack the ability to get beneath the skin of opponents, with a streak of aggression he shared with his illustrious predecessor Dennis Bergkamp, an attribute not uncommon in mercurial Dutch forwards.

Progress in the Champions League was equally positive, with the qualifying round against Sparta Prague handled comfortably. A kind group stage draw then matched Arsenal with Sevilla, Steaua Bucharest and Sparta's neighbours Slavia. They started like a train with nine points from the first three matches, including a 7–0 demolition of Slavia. However, as good as qualified, in the concluding three fixtures Wenger then fielded weaker selections with the result that they ended the group in second place, inviting a tougher draw in the last

16 and foregoing results bonuses of €900,000 (approximately £700,000 given the exchange rate at the time) through dropped points.

But there is always a cloud somewhere on the horizon, and early on it took the form of uncertainty over Arsène Wenger's future. His contract only lasted until the end of the season and, as usual, he seemed in no rush to sign a new one. And if he went he could be followed by an exodus of the talent he had developed. It was not as if the board had any kind of succession plan in place. How would Arsenal compete then? With money? Not for a while yet. Stability was desperately needed. "We're talking and usually when we talk, there's always a positive outcome," Wenger said when pressed on the matter at the start of the season. "What I think when I'm negotiating the deal is whether I have the freedom to work the way I want to," he added. "I always had that with David Dein and, since David has gone, I still have it. That is, for me, the most important thing." In truth, Wenger had already made up his mind. As long ago as April, he and Annie had settled on their daughter Léa's secondary school. It was only David Dein's exit that rocked the boat but with the aid of his friend's encouragement the turbulence soon passed.

And so the Frenchman, only a month into the campaign, signed on for a further three years' tour of foreign duty. "Since the beginning of the season something has been happening in this team," he enthused when the news was announced. "They fight for each other, they have a great togetherness and love for the game. I have a responsibility to the players to help turn our potential into prizes."

On occasion, the team's play was so adroit and flexible as to warrant the plaudits of being the arch exponents of 'Total Football'; the standard filtered down to the Carling Cup second-stringers, whose difficult ties against first-choice Premier League line-ups were successfully negotiated and the club progressed to the semi-final for the fourth time in five seasons. Players who were not able to break into the starting line-up at the weekends performed in an equally dominant and watchable manner; their versatility was such that they looked at ease whatever part of the pitch they appeared in. After the mostly younger squad members had convincingly accounted for a full-strength Newcastle side, long-time supporter Brian Dawes expressed the view "We don't need to buy another player for ten years!" The kids would go on to defeat a full-strength Blackburn Rovers away, despite being reduced to ten men. Meanwhile, their elders and betters remained undefeated and top of the league, two points clear of their free-spending rivals behind in the chasing pack. Arsenal were not only contenders for the title once again, as time progressed they became the bookies' favourites.

The way the team were playing and the results achieved appeared a total vindication of the manager's methods. On limited resources, he had produced a group of artists and artisans, the sum total of whom was more than the contributing parts. How else can you explain the creation of a world-class team with obvious individual deficiencies (Almunia, Senderos and Eboue being salient examples). Wenger had compiled his side as a balanced unit so that even the absence of a key component did not disrupt the strategy, Gallas and Rosicky both being out of action for some of the early fixtures.

A measure of the progress made was gauged when Arsenal travelled to Anfield at the end of October. In March, they had sunk to a humiliating 4–1 defeat there. A few months on, and Liverpool manager Rafa Benitez, despite overseeing the only other unbeaten top-flight team, opted to prioritise defence and set up a counter-attacking gameplan, regardless of home advantage. "Maybe Liverpool were a little bit afraid of us," opined William Gallas in the aftermath of the 1–1 draw.

Robin van Persie succumbed again to injury after scoring

five goals in seven appearances. It was fortunate then that his first-choice partner Emmanuel Adebayor had an even better strike rate, with six goals. The failure of Togo to qualify for the African Cup of Nations was an unexpected bonus, as Van Persie did not reappear regularly until mid-March (earlier attempts to return him to the fray merely aggravated his ailments). However, the squad did lose Kolo Toure, Emmanuel Eboue and Alexandre Song to the competition for a few weeks in January and February. As Adebayor's rich vein of form continued, he often found himself playing as a lone striker, although occasionally Eduardo was drafted in to partner him.

With the team topping the table despite a first league defeat in December away to Middlesbrough, Wenger was faced with the dilemma of whether to strengthen his hand in the January transfer window. He told an acquaintance in December, "I am the happiest I have ever been with the team. This group of players has the potential to be the best I've ever worked with." He was most pleased with the development of Mathieu Flamini and, as a result, his final summer signing Lassana Diarra found himself in the unlikely position of being selected for his country, but unable to displace his then uncapped compatriot in Arsenal's eleven. Together with Gilberto, Abou Diaby and Denilson, the manager had a surfeit of midfield cover, which may have influenced his decision to sell Diarra to Portsmouth for a profit of £3 million. All the same, he was a talented and versatile player who could fill in at full back and anywhere across the midfield. To have picked up a French international so cheaply was a bargain, especially when Chelsea, of all clubs, could afford to hang on to him even if they had no intention of utilising his talents except in an emergency.

However, as Wenger later reflected, "I came to the conclusion that Diarra could not cope with the fact that he was behind the other players in midfield. If he had been able to be patient he would have got his chance. He wasn't capable of that." Matters came to a head when Diarra was reluctant to play in an FA Cup tie at Burnley. This eventually turned out to be a stroke of luck for him, Portsmouth ultimately winning the competition for the first time in 69 years and Diarra, a key element in his new team, feted as a hero, However, true to form, his start at Fratton Park was hardly auspicious. He announced that he would be using his new club as a stepping stone to greater things. "The people at Portsmouth know I will not spend my life at this club," he said. "If I shine, if a really big club wants me, I know already that everything will go well." How to win friends and influence people. The surprising conclusion from the episode was that Arsène Wenger brought in someone who rocked the boat to such an extent that he was forced to move him on at the first available opportunity.

With or without the Diarra money, there was a lot of cash in the kitty to strengthen the squad for the remainder of the season. Figures released by the club in 2008 revealed a cash balance of £69 million at the end of November 2007, of which £25 million was available to the manager for spending on new players and their wages. It remained unused. Wenger subsequently explained, "You have to keep the balance right between having competition and having too many players. The squad did not look light at any time." However, at the conclusion of the season he admitted that his statistics had shown that his team had conceded more goals from long balls played into his central defence than any of his main rivals. "We gave more goals on direct balls, in the air, through the middle, and most of the time on second balls." With hindsight, he might have taken a chance on Jonathan Woodgate from Middlesbrough, the 28-year-old England defender reputedly interested in joining the club, but who ultimately signed for Tottenham for a fee of £8 million.

Up front there was no need for reinforcements. Eduardo was given a run in the team after Christmas and did so well he was actually rested in the two Carling Cup semi-final clashes with Tottenham to preserve him for the league. His goal-poaching was badly missed as Spurs recorded victory over their neighbours in the second leg for the first time since the turn of the millennium. According to David Dein, "Arsène has a remarkable ability to communicate in a foreign language." Brevity was Wenger's forte as he summed up his response to that Spurs defeat to a friend. "The defence . . . mamma mia!" (More inventive was his use of the word the French had coined, 'footballistic', turning it into an English adverb to describe the talent of the then 16-year-old Fàbregas. After impressing in the 2003/04 Carling Cup, his manager enthused, "Footballistically, he's ready for the first team.") Nevertheless, Wenger could argue that the Carling Cup run had served its purpose as Lukasz Fabianski, Alexandre Song, Armand Traore, Denilson and others experienced first-team action.

Following three successive victories consolidating their position at the top of the table, four days before they were due to face Milan in the Champions League, Arsenal had to negotiate an FA Cup fifth-round away trip to Manchester United, their closest challengers in the Premier League. Would the manager stick with the first team or twist with rotation? Perhaps when the club's official website announced the application details for tickets, they should have reminded the thousands of paying punters intending to make the long trip north of Arsène Wenger's words from the previous March: "The FA Cup is a competition we love but [in 2006] when we went out early, we reached the final of the Champions League. [In 2007] we had two replays in the FA Cup, one just before the PSV Champions League tie and one right in between that and the next [leg]. We had already given a lot, playing 17 games in December and January. Also, we had no possibility to rotate the side because we had many injuries and then suspensions. So I think it was a mistake on my part. When we drew Blackburn at home we didn't think we would go to a replay. When you have 60,000 fans in your own stadium you can never say you will sacrifice the game. But the replay? Perhaps I should have sacrificed it."

Sacrifice: the concept in Wenger's interpretation of deliberately giving something up in order to gain an advantage. By the time that the Old Trafford match kicked off, he knew that the next two scheduled FA Cup weekends could ensure league fixtures for his team if they were eliminated, with their opponents (Wigan and Liverpool) both already knocked out. If the road to Wembley was halted now it might be a blessing in disguise; midweeks could be the sole preserve of Champions League commitments, with domestic encounters in the Premier League limited to weekends. He couldn't have planned it better if he tried, although maybe this idea was picked up by his players. In losing 4–0, once the first goal had been conceded most of them didn't appear to try very hard at all. It was one of the most lacklustre displays the fans had ever witnessed from a Wenger team.

The fact that Wenger had rested a few players provided little comfort or mitigation, as Alex Ferguson had done likewise. Four regulars returned for the visit of Champions League holders AC Milan. Milan might have been group-stage winners, but in failing to top their own quartet Arsenal had become the runners-up none of the big boys fancied. Milan, content to return home with a clean sheet, showed limited attacking ambition. For Arsenal the 0–0 result would only be seen as a good one if they could avoid defeat in the return leg, but on the night the abiding feeling was one of what might have been had Emmanuel Adebayor not headed against the crossbar with the goal gaping in second-half injury time.

However, according to the manager's rationale – less commitments, improving odds – the outlook in the Premier League remained optimistic. Wenger's Arsenal teams had historically performed at their best domestically after the turn of the year. When league points were dropped, it was often in the first months of the season with the onset of winter bringing with it an air of vulnerability. So the two humiliating cup exits to Tottenham and Manchester United could be brushed aside as long as the ends ultimately justified the means. The pursuit of the Premier League crown was certainly on track, with a sequence of wins that showed the absent African internationals were not missed. The Adebayor/ Eduardo partnership was developing nicely so that the loss of Robin van Persie was not unduly felt. With 12 fixtures of the 38 outstanding, Arsenal led their nearest rivals by five points, having suffered a solitary defeat. So on the weekend of the Carling Cup Final, it would not have been unrealistic to envisage an eight-point lead with a victory at Birmingham. For instead of a training session in preparation for a trip to Wembley, Arsenal had a commitment at St Andrew's on Saturday lunchtime due to its selection for live transmission on Sky.

In fact, Arsenal should have been sitting on an even bigger lead at the top of the table as they travelled to the Midlands. But in one of their most insipid performances of the season six weeks earlier, they had been held to a draw at home by Birmingham. So with the visiting fans anticipating retribution and three points, the St Andrew's ground put on a three-act tragedy that took everyone by surprise. First and most distressing was the broken leg suffered by Eduardo as a result of a late challenge by opposition skipper Martin Taylor. Sky told their viewers it was "so horrific we do not want to show you that again". While several minutes elapsed as Eduardo was treated and then taken on a stretcher to a waiting ambulance, his teammates were visibly distraught.

Taylor was given a straight red card, and so despite losing Eduardo Arsenal still had 87 minutes to play with a man advantage. However, they were so shaken by the traumatic incident that the half-time score was 1–0 to the ten men. At least it gave Arsenal 15 minutes to compose themselves, and it seemed like business as usual when Theo Walcott put them ahead with a brace before the second half was even ten minutes old. Birmingham were like a boxer on the ropes, awaiting the final blow that would end the contest, a strike that would give the visitors their desired eight-point lead over the chasing pack. Although Arsenal created some excellent opportunities and had a cast-iron penalty claim waved away, the knockout punch was never delivered. As injury time ticked down, Gaël Clichy allowed the ball to run across him in his own penalty area rather than hoof it clear. He failed to see Stuart Parnaby closing in to steal possession, but recovered by dispossessing him in the box.

Unfortunately, in making the challenge he also gave Paranaby the opportunity to fall over his outstretched leg and the referee to award a penalty. The spot kick would be effectively the last action of the game, although if it was saved, there would be time for a shot on the rebound before referee Mike Dean blew his final whistle, so Arsenal's players needed to be poised on the edge of the area to pounce on any loose ball.

But not William Gallas. It was all too much for the captain. He'd spent the previous week comforting Sagna over the tragic death of his brother, seen Eduardo's harrowing injury and now an act of defensive naivety that looked as if it would result in the dropping of two precious points against opponents who were struggling at the other end of the table. He stood on the halfway line looking on in evident fury from afar. His action, or rather lack of it, effectively reducing his own side to ten men, didn't ultimately affect events as the penalty was converted for a 2–2 draw, but his lack of preparation for any parry by Manuel Almunia would have made Gallas a poor boy scout. His response to the penalty being converted was to kick the advertising boards near the dugouts, for which he earned a yellow card. After a restart that lasted just a few seconds, Gallas then sat down on the pitch and stayed there. When everyone else had left the field Arsène Wenger walked over to his captain who eventually got to his feet and poured out his frustrations to his manager, who just listened.

In the space of moments, Wenger's decision to award him the armband came back to haunt him. Then, Wenger had emphasised, "He has to set an example everywhere, not just on the pitch but off it as well." Gallas had said all the right things, a few weeks before proclaiming, "Mentally, I think we are ready, but the tough games come now. When we feel tired we have to be strong in our minds, in our bodies." But cometh the hour, where was the man? Gallas's behaviour was more like that of an emotional supporter rather than a responsible and highly paid employee. Arsenal lost a player under horrific circumstances, threw away two points and had their captain go AWOL. William Gallas looked for all the world like his team had just conceded the title, when in fact the table showed them to be six points clear, albeit having played a game more. But what events at Birmingham seemed to do was halt the momentum of the leaders in their tracks, with fate and their own destructive tendencies acting against them in the fixtures that followed. Whether the captain's post-match sit-in was a contribution to the decline or the result of his realisation that his young colleagues were not up to the task is academic. In his role, he should have known better than to behave in such an ignominious fashion.

When the season was over, Wenger reflected, "We could not win the next game [a 1–1 home draw with Aston Villa] and then confidence dropped a little bit. Then every time after that when we were in a situation leading 1–0, we did not have the same drive going forwards, we just wanted to keep the result because we had less confidence. That all started at Birmingham."

March's Premier League programme saw one deception after another for Arsenal. Ahead of the run of fixtures against Birmingham, Villa, Wigan and Middlesbrough, some Gooners were anticipating who the opposition might be when the title was confirmed. But these encounters saw a pitiful return of four points from a possible 12; certainly not the form of champions elect. The players who had shown they had it in them to 'win ugly' in Prague back in August had forgotten how to eke out victory when the chips were down. Arsène Wenger had once more failed to prepare his men to come out fighting and strong leadership on the field was conspicuous by its absence. It was difficult to imagine that Tony Adams or Patrick Vieira would have let control slip away in this manner.

Injuries compounded Wenger's problems. Eduardo was on crutches, whilst Robin van Persie, though finally able to return never regained his early-season sharpness, a converted penalty his only goal in the first eight appearances after his mid-March comeback. The disappearance of Tomas Rosicky had the fans renaming him 'Rosicknote', as he did not feature again after the end of January, with the medical team apparently unable to explain why his hamstring injury was the cause of such a prolonged absence. Wenger was mystified. "It is not a serious injury but a strange one; he is not making much progress," he said. "It is impossible to say when he will return. It is a frustration for me." So much reliance had been placed on the good form of Emmanuel Adebayor that when his own scoring run hit a lean patch, results suffered.

Wenger was forced to field players – Theo Walcott and Nicklas Bendtner were tried as starters – whose form or readiness for the task in hand was found wanting, hardly a surprise given their youth and inexperience. The fragility of Arsenal's situation was laid bare. The alchemist had accomplished so much with so many non-world-class performers, but now his unit had been breached. While United had Cristiano Ronaldo, Carlos Tévez *et al* and Chelsea a variety of international options, Wenger was forced to run arguably his only world-class star into the ground. The midfield appeared to visibly wilt, and the wisdom of letting Lassana Diarra go was again called into question. The dip in form may not have been purely down to physical reasons, but the decision to depend on younger players, whilst initially providing Wenger's pace and power prerequisites, was shown to be misplaced. Would more experienced professionals have paced themselves better? By the time of the Birmingham game that changed the course of the season, Fàbregas had already made 30 appearances and Flamini 28. At the campaign's conclusion they had registered 45 and 40 respectively. It placed huge demands on two young men still learning their trade. Arsenal were top dogs for the first seven months of the campaign, but the only trophy handed out in February was the one that Wenger conceded to Tottenham by sending out a mix-and-match team at the semi-final stage of the Carling Cup.

Then in the midst of their woes Arsenal faced their most difficult assignment so far. They travelled to Milan needing to avoid defeat to progress to the Champions League quarter-final. At a time when they were producing turgid domestic displays, where exactly did they find the mettle that saw them dethrone the holders of the European Cup in their own back-yard? The goals in the 2–0 victory might have come in the latter stages of the match, but the scoreline accurately reflected their superiority on the night. At times, Wenger's young team ran rings round their illustrious foes, who at the same venue the previous April had made Premier League champions

Manchester United look like continental novices. It was a remarkable triumph, and one of Arsenal's great nights in Europe.

The contrast to domestic disappointment might be explained by the greater self-belief of opponents who consider themselves at least to be the equal if not superior to Arsenal. So there is more of a positive approach by both sides and less concentration by one team to simply deny the other. Greater space is a consequence, which is then expertly exploited by Wenger's men. In an ironic way, it probably gives them a better chance of beating a Barcelona than a Bolton.

So even with major rivals on the horizon, perhaps all was not lost. In the Premier League, visits to Chelsea and Manchester United lay ahead. In the Champions League, the quarter-final draw saw them paired with Liverpool, the second leg at Anfield. The San Siro result was a reminder that Arsenal were capable of beating anyone anywhere, and if they could repeat their away form in the key clashes to come then maybe the season could still be salvaged. The table said that Arsenal had still only suffered a solitary league defeat after 30 matches. If they could keep that statistic going until the end, surely they could still take the title?

CHAPTER THIRTEEN
CLOSE, BUT NO CIGAR

The series of key encounters that would determine the outcome of the 2007/08 season for Arsenal began with a visit to Stamford Bridge. There they faced a Chelsea side who were in the midst of a lengthy undefeated run under José Mourinho's replacement Avram Grant, making them legitimate title challengers alongside Arsenal and Manchester United. Ahead of the clash, Wenger addressed the problems he had faced in recent weeks. "I believe we need to get back to speeding up our passing around the box," he said. "That's where we can be neater and where we can make a difference. We have been too narrow. That's down to the fact that I play Alex Hleb on one flank and he is more comfortable centrally and always comes inside. Therefore if teams defend deep like Middlesbrough did, we can be a bit narrow. We will play wide on Sunday, and Eboue is a natural wide player."

Certainly a lack of width had been an unresolved issue since Thierry Henry last contributed a full season and used the flanks to such devastating effect. Emmanuel Eboue's return in the 27 appearances up to that point was a paltry total of two assists and not a single goal in all competitions. Being forced to rely on a squad member so patently out of form to improve the team's attacking potential exposed how bare Wenger's cupboard was. With Van Persie, Eduardo and

Rosicky all able to play wide, and all absent for so many matches, Wenger had no real alternative than to field players who, under normal circumstances, might have struggled to make the substitutes' bench.

In spite of his limited choice, at least the manager could rely on someone to find a goal from somewhere. But the *'One-nil to the Arsenal'* scenario was a scoreline from another era. The predicament in 2008 was that once ahead, Arsenal's inability to maintain a hard won advantage against their main rivals became their Achilles' heel. Unfortunately it encouraged some feeble gallows humour: Why wouldn't you trust Arsenal to take your dog for a walk? Because they can't hold a lead.

Against Chelsea, the goal they needed to win the game arrived in the 58th minute, courtesy of Bacary Sagna. But if it appeared that the tide might have turned, the sensation was illusory. Moments later, the scorer suffered an ankle injury in an innocuous challenge, and one of Wenger's most consistent and invaluable performers did not appear again for the remainder of the campaign. While Sagna was receiving treatment, Chelsea rang the changes and Nicolas Anelka was brought on to reinforce the attack. Within seconds they were level, the Arsenal defence unsettled and not adapting in time to counter the change in their opponents' formation.

As if the succession of injuries wasn't bad enough, it seemed as if officials' questionable calls always went in favour of the opposition, with scorer Didier Drogba receiving the ball in an offside position in the build-up to the goal just the latest example. Despite the fates conspiring against Arsenal, had the players performed to the level they were capable of against weaker sides such as Birmingham and Middlesbrough their misfortune would only have registered as consolation goals for their opponents. They could then have afforded to come away empty-handed from Stamford Bridge and Old Trafford and still been at the top of the table (instead of in third place) such was their earlier points advantage.

Arsenal were duly defeated by Chelsea, the central defence allowing Drogba a snap shot to register his second goal of the game. According to former Arsenal double-winning captain Frank McLintock, Gallas and Toure would always be vulnerable to opponents such as Drogba, "who disrupts them because they lack a bit of height [both are under six feet tall] and strength. When they come up against a player with sheer physical strength they sometimes get bullied." This was certainly a state of affairs neither McLintock nor Tony Adams would have permitted. When Arsenal had registered a home win against Chelsea earlier in the campaign, Drogba had been absent through injury, undoubtedly a contributory factor in their first victory over their West London rivals since the Ivory Coast international's arrival from Marseille in 2004.

In answer to the criticism that in January he should have bought a centre back, Wenger replied, "I expected Johan Djourou to come back from Birmingham but he was injured. You have to accept in January to find a centre back who can play for Arsenal Football Club at the top of the league is not easy." Well, Liverpool managed it, their improving form from the turn of the year owing much to the arrival of the Czech international Martin Skrtel. According to former player Alan Smith, Jonathan Woodgate was waiting and hoping that Wenger's oft-expressed admiration for him would, in a reverse of the Dennis Bergkamp transfer (when the Dutchman wanted to sign for Arsenal's neighbours) see him land at the other end of Seven Sisters Road. If Wenger was interested, he procrastinated, and Woodgate signed for Tottenham. There was speculation that Woodgate had indeed signed for Arsenal hours before he was announced as a Tottenham player, after the production company responsible for the club's TV channel was notified of an unscheduled press conference. But it was suddenly pulled, prompting a belief that the new signing the conference had been called to announce might have failed the club's very thorough medical. With the experience of Van Persie and Rosicky's frequent unavailability, might it have been that the club simply didn't want to take another chance?

In a question-and-answer session held with shareholders two days after the end of the season, Wenger specified he was in the market for a defender (and a creative midfielder). "We have to rectify how we deal with direct balls," he admitted to the audience. "When a team just goes for long, direct balls against us, we have to improve." The obvious conclusion was that the sought after defender would be a big six-footer who would provide a better option than Philippe Senderos, Johan Djourou and Alexandre Song.

Following the Chelsea defeat Senderos, who had performed admirably against Milan, was given the chance to address the lack of height at the back and with Sagna unavailable Kolo Toure moved to right back. Presumably, Wenger felt Toure to be a better bet in an unfamiliar role than either Eboue or Justin Hoyte, whose defensive qualities he had come to question. Unfortunately, a number of key goals in the final matches of the season were subsequently conceded as a result of attacks down the right side of the defence, with Toure – struggling for form ever since picking up an injury playing for the Ivory Coast in the African Cup of Nations – unconvincing in the position. Sagna proved a huge loss and another case of 'what if?'

Due to the quirk of the fixture list sandwiching the two legs of a Champions League quarter-final around the scheduled Arsenal v Liverpool Premier League match, the two sides faced each other three times in seven days. For the first leg of the European tie Arsenal, the home team, went ahead, only to concede an away goal that left Liverpool far better placed to qualify. There was a bitter taste in Arsenal mouths when Alex Hleb was clearly tugged back by Dirk Kuyt in the penalty area in full view of the referee. Events the following week would compound the sense of injustice.

Despite dropping points left, right and centre, Arsenal were still in with a chance of the title, but a second home draw with Liverpool in succession, both sides resting many of those who had been on European duty, more or less lined up the nails in the coffin of any lingering hopes of overhauling Manchester United and Chelsea. Some felt that Wenger was wrong to prioritise Europe and that he should have fielded his strongest line-up for all three matches against Liverpool. He chose to return to the Toure / Gallas partnership for a final time in the league fixture and lived to regret it as the duo were at fault for Liverpool's goal. The similarity between the two games was reflected in the same scoreline and another decent Arsenal penalty claim being waved away by the referee. The personnel may have changed, but it was a surefire case of *déjà vu* all over again (as the legendary baseball catcher Yogi Berra first declared). One hammer blow after another.

Travelling to Anfield for the deciding leg of the quarter-final, many Gooners were optimistic. To have any chance, Arsenal had to score and in spite of not getting the rub of the green in recent weeks, they could normally be relied upon to do just that. The game was set up perfectly for Wenger's attacking philosophy. They had little to lose by playing positively, a simple case of score or go out, and Liverpool notching one of their own wouldn't actually change that situation. The consequence was a marvellous first half as the visitors handed out a footballing lesson. The goal, with the final brushstroke applied by Abou Diaby, illustrated the interplay, precise passing and speed of movement that is the hallmark of Arsenal football at its peak. Once again, they were ahead in the tie and with the advantage of knowing that they too had scored a vital away goal.

Having seen Gallas and Toure struggle to deal with Peter Crouch three days previously, Wenger had brought back Senderos to partner the captain, with Toure again moved to right back. All had reason to feel personally responsible for subsequent mishaps. Senderos failed to challenge Sami Hyppia at a Liverpool corner and the scores were level. It was a rank loss of concentration that galvanised a side who had looked second best up till then, their improvement given further impetus by yet another injury. This time Mathieu Flamini was the victim, his 42 minutes being his last appearance in an Arsenal shirt (at the end of the season he joined AC Milan as a free agent). No Sagna, no Rosicky, no Eduardo and now no Flamini. Van Persie was still short of full match fitness after a long absence and Flamini's replacement Gilberto a shadow of his former self. The momentum was now with Liverpool and it was no surprise when they took a 69th-minute lead through Fernando Torres.

However, the twists and turns of what was developing into an epic encounter were far from over. Theo Walcott replaced Eboue and created a wonder goal to put Wenger's team ahead in the tie on the away-goals rule. As a Liverpool move broke down on the edge of Arsenal's penalty area, Walcott ran the length of the pitch, outpacing opponents and skipping tackles before delivering a cutback for Adebayor to roll in. Pandemonium broke out amongst the visiting supporters as, with 85 minutes on the clock, the goal looked decisive. Unfortunately, the excitement was contagious, and what followed exposed the team's immaturity. By fair means or foul, any attacks had to be halted to buy time to regain concentration. Patrick Vieira would have ensured they were prepared for any eventuality and stopped any momentum with, if necessary, a foul, the subsequent break in play ensuring the minds of his colleagues were fully focussed on the task in hand. Instead his successors fell to a sucker punch.

Left winger Ryan Babbel collected the ball near the touchline and ran towards the penalty area. Wenger was devastated at what followed. "Kolo didn't touch him. Babel pulled Kolo's shirt because he knew Gallas was blocking his way. He did what most strikers would but he went down because he was going nowhere." It was an expertly engineered example of gamesmanship as initially it even convinced neutrals that Toure had been at fault. The referee was certainly in no doubt, awarding the spot kick and even booking the hapless Toure for good measure. Would Sagna have done better and dispossessed Babel before he was anywhere near the area? Possibly. Toure had rarely been convincing as a full back before his transition to a central defender and did nothing to change that view on his return four years on.

A tale of two penalties. The one denied Hleb in the first leg was far more clear-cut than the one awarded at Anfield (and successfully dispatched by Steven Gerrard). Arsenal were dead and buried. A fourth Liverpool goal in the dying embers of injury time was an academic footnote, although that the scorer was Babel was the final insult.

Arsenal's season was encapsulated in 90 minutes. Playing sublimely to establish a lead and then – with the prize in sight – undone by injury, defensive incompetence, lack of experience and poor luck, they managed to snatch defeat from the jaws of victory. The Arsenal party put Anfield behind them as quickly as they could and after the short flight to Luton, Arsène Wenger arrived home just after midnight. Unable to sleep, he put on the television and played back the nightmare again.

The following day at home, outwardly calm and relaxed, Wenger admitted that he "still hadn't got over it". He was adamant that in the same circumstances he would pick an identical line-up. "Senderos played well against Milan, Gallas and Toure couldn't cope with Crouch and Eboue can't defend well enough. The loss of the right back [Sagna] really hurt us. The decisions had gone against us. I looked at the tape again. The ref had a clear view [of the penalty incident]." Apparently, the official excused his decision by explaining to one of Wenger's colleagues that "he was concentrating on the feet".

Asked how he would pick his players up for Sunday's crucial fixture at Old Trafford, Wenger replied simply, "I don't know". He was reminded that at times like this he had rhetorically asked himself, "Who motivates the motivator?" He agreed that it was all down to him "and in a couple of days there's another match and you have to focus on that". With Annie cooking him "something special for dinner" and Léa doing her homework, he was already looking ahead.

The FA Cup and Premier League trips to Old Trafford topped and tailed the two months that pulled the rug from under Arsenal's season, as defeat to Manchester United in the second visit ended the remotest hope of landing the title. As at Anfield, the team played without fear, took the lead, made United look distinctly second best, but succumbed to a penalty and a set piece, even if the award of the latter – a free kick on the edge of the area, looked harsh. A relieved Alex Ferguson actually had some words of consolation for his opposite number at the final whistle. At least Arsenal's display was in marked contrast to their embarrassing FA Cup debacle. This time, hundreds of the travelling fans chose not to head for the exit at full time and stayed behind to chant *"We love you Arsenal, we do"* for ten solid minutes, by which time the rest of the stadium had emptied. It was a heartfelt endorsement on what Arsène Wenger had accomplished from those who had accompanied him all the way on the tumultuous journey that was Arsenal's 2007/08 season. Arsène had allowed the fans to tap into their dreams. He had inspired loyalty beyond reason and created such a strong bond between himself and the supporters that his mistakes, even at this most sanguine of times were readily forgiven: 'Arsène knows' and 'In Arsène we trust'.

In the end, Arsenal fell four points short of the 2007/08 Premier League champions. Manchester United retained the title on 87 points, with Chelsea runners-up on 85. "I feel we were one game away in this championship," Arsène Wenger reflected. "If we win at Old Trafford, we are champions. It's just one game, and in that game we were 1–0 up and we had two or three chances to score the second goal, so you cannot say we had a bad season." Wenger's point that the final outcome was a close run thing was entirely justified. Further, for the first time since 2004 Arsenal had been in with a genuine chance of adding to their tally of titles.

When Arsenal won the Premiership in 1998, they accumulated five points less than the total posted a decade later in finishing third. But in that time the bar had been raised and a Champions League Final between Manchester United and Chelsea (who had eliminated Arsenal's victors Liverpool in the semis) showed that Premier League prosperity was being reflected both domestically and internationally to ever-increasing effect.

Wenger had tried to win the Premier League and the Champions League but came away empty-handed. By the uncompromising rules of sport, he failed. But for Wenger, victory alone is never enough. So by his criteria – the style in which the team played and the pleasure it gave to millions around the world – it could be said that he won. As always. However, it could be argued that if his view was taken literally, he was providing his players with an alibi when they failed to land a title or a championship: never mind the score, in the boss's eyes they were victorious. But to watch the feverish figure on the touchline towards the end of the season was to realise the fallacy of this view and appreciate just how much Wenger wants to win.

If great teams are measured by their trophy count, there is still a long way to go before his current squad can be awarded this accolade. Never one to rest on his laurels, it was simply a case of asking himself "What's next?" and he already knew the answer. "Same again please, but this time with trophies."

Wenger has managed to get Arsenal dining at the Ritz on a budget that should only buy them breakfast in a greasy spoon. And no one at the top table has ever questioned their right to be there. Clubs like Tottenham, Newcastle, Aston Villa and Everton rack their collective brains and bank balances to find a way of emulating Arsenal since 'Arsène Who?' arrived from Japan in 1996, a time when they all had genuine aspirations of dethroning Manchester United. Yet until the transfusion of Roman Abramovich's millions into Chelsea, Arsenal were the only club to keep the runaway United in check.

The financial constraints Wenger has had to work within expose those critics who censure him as being more short-sighted than the man himself is notoriously supposed to be from the touchline. It was put to him, "You know people say that you don't see things because you choose not to but you're down on the pitch – you can't see from there, can you?" Wenger answered, "Yes, it's true. I can't see. But what is also true – because I have this reputation now – is that I will not come out against my players. But now, even when I am honest, people don't believe me. Because it's true that [by the touchline] you are in a bad position to see everything." Short-sighted or not, on a net spend of £4 million a year in the transfer market, Wenger's vision means he has never failed to get Arsenal into the Champions League after their first qualification in 1998, and has overseen the transformation of the club from the also-rans at the tail end of the George Graham era into a football superpower. In spite of not winning a trophy for three seasons, such is the level of popular support the team enjoy, they continue to sell out a 60,000 seat stadium where the price of admittance does not make for a cheap day out. Over 40,000 are on the waiting list for the opportunity to buy a precious season ticket.

Could any other manager have both maintained the club's much envied status as permanent members of the Premier League's elite and provided quality entertainment while doing so? Could they have put Arsenal into a position where, going to Old Trafford in 2008 with five matches remaining, the title was still in the balance? To put it another way, is there a club anywhere in the world who would hesitate for a second if they had the opportunity to employ Arsène Wenger as their manager?

Arsène Wenger may not be perfect. Yet he has ascended the heights with Arsenal. On several occasions, within sight of the peak, they have fallen short, but without the man from Alsace they'd still be sorting their climbing gear out at base camp. It's a place they are unlikely ever to return to.

CHAPTER FOURTEEN
HIS WAY

The real eye-opener regarding Arsène Wenger's current team is not that they failed to clear the final hurdle at the end of the 2007/08 season, but that they reached it at all with so many non-world-class players in their line-up. Getting the balance of the team right so quickly was a startling achievement by the manager and mitigated the loss of stars – Bergkamp, Vieira, Henry – he could previously call upon who were the fulcrum of his successful past teams. But finding the right balance is a delicate business and when injuries and bad luck piled up, a lack of worldliness was apparent in so many.

To underline the point, how many of the current team would get into the Invincibles side of 2003/04? Sagna certainly, perhaps Fàbregas and Gallas, maybe Clichy and Van Persie. But that's it. Sagna apart there are no undisputed certainties and arguably he owes his selection to Lauren being the weakest link rather than his own world-class status, although that may yet come.

Prioritising invention and trusting that winning is the natural consequence is all very laudable, but winning trophies is also a laudable end in itself and one that has been absent for too long. Pound for pound, Arsène Wenger has probably given his employers more value than any other manager in the history of the English game, but relativity does not win titles. In absolute terms of winning trophies, he has in recent seasons finished behind Ferguson, Mourinho and Benitez. Perhaps George Graham's discredited mantra, "I love one–nil victories", needs to be revisited, at least in spirit. Certainly, Arsène Wenger can point to the plentiful number of goals scored and to the fact that they arrive from all over the place, but how many opportunities did Adebayor squander? And the combined goal haul of Arsenal's midfield in 2007/08 was just over half of the 42 Manchester United's Cristiano Ronaldo managed on his own. Alexander Hleb was not able in three seasons to equal what Robert Pires scored in one. Nevertheless, the quantity would have sufficed if so many hadn't been given away so readily at the other end. Arsenal's lack of aerial dominance at the back exposed a crucial vulnerability. Since when did an uncapped goalkeeper and a less-than-world-class central defensive pairing anchor a championship-winning side?

After paying the penalty for failing to buy in January 2008, Wenger made encouraging noises when speaking at the season's end that he is prepared to deploy more of his budget and pay the price to add quality in key positions. Unfortunately, there was no indication that he was prepared to face up to other deficiencies. Prospects must be given the opportunity to play, to demonstrate the skills learned under his tutelage. The few-and-far-between cup appearances are no substitute for the experience gained in the school of hard knocks that is the Championship. Loans can be beneficial both to the individual and the team. Wenger just has to make sure that he is sending his young players to the right club with the promise of a starting role.

But who will tell Arsène that this should happen? Certainly not Boro Primorac; it's not his job. Nor Pat Rice, more assistant than manager. Unlike Manchester United, Chelsea and Liverpool, where former top bosses are happy to take a supporting role, Arsenal do not have the calibre of back-up. At these clubs, despite his status, the manager does recognise he might be wrong on occasions. "I'm not perfect, me least of all," says Arsène Wenger. But if he had a strong number two, he would have certainly felt that he could delegate more and indulge himself in his love of international talent-spotting. How many more bargains might he have picked up?

However unchallenged on and off the field, it doesn't appear that he will change his way of working. So just as there is no one to tell him that on occasions his selection and tactics might be questionable, there is no one on the board to tell him that he should tackle certain issues which could shape the club's future, the main one being his succession. Wenger's legacy in bricks and mortar – the training ground and the stadium – is an infrastructure that should provide a conducive working environment for whoever follows him. The process of planning for this eventuality should start now. When there was past talk of him leaving, it was accompanied by the fear of how his exit might precipitate a similar reaction from his players. Now the fear is more of leaving a young team bereft of a father figure. The board should insist that one of Wenger's main tasks is to put in place a three-year plan for his succession (his current contract ending in 2011).

Questioned on this very subject, clearly Wenger has given the matter some thought. It was put to him, "As you get nearer to the end of your time in England, you've been here an awfully long time . . ."

"Yes, you want me out!" he interjected.

"No, I don't want you out. I think you're a national treasure!" his interviewer replied. "But then I am biased."

"Listen, as I told you before, I had the feeling to work here that I could push this club into a position where I really feel 'OK, I've accomplished something.' I would like to be proud of the work I've done here and push the club as far as I could and then someone else takes over who's better."

Whoever takes over should do his utmost to persuade Wenger to remain involved. He would surely benefit by welcoming him as a Director of Football whose main task would be to determine the strategy for the playing side and develop a conveyor belt of young players. However, finding talented footballers is not an end in itself for Wenger. Would he be satisfied with turning them over to other people to work with?

For Wenger to stay in a new capacity, the club would have to change its structure radically. However, until the ownership issue is resolved, there is no incentive for the board to initiate the draconian reforms necessary. Of course, in an idealistic world, the club would be well-served if it became a member-owned club as Rogan Taylor is attempting to achieve at Liverpool, based on the Barcelona model (where the 150,000 members – *socios* – vote for their president and management board). The Arsenal Supporters' Trust could have a paramount role in such a situation. They only have the interests of the club at heart – which is not to say the incumbent board don't, but they do not represent the vigour and depth of resources that are available through the Trust and the wider world. Despite the lockdown agreement, the Arsenal board are at the mercy of their own financial proclivities and free market forces. Liverpool, Chelsea and Manchester City are just three examples that illustrate the instability that can occur when a club is bought and sold like any other commercial enterprise. Aston Villa and Middlesbrough just got lucky with the support and financial commitment of their owners.

Similarly, the Arsenal board can be praised for the importance they attach to stability. There has never been as much as a whiff of a suggestion that Wenger's job has ever been under threat. He is one of only four contemporary managers in the top four divisions of English football to have served more than a decade at the same club (along with Crewe's Dario Gradi,

Alex Ferguson and Hereford's Graham Turner). In sticking with obviously talented men, these clubs have experienced peaks and troughs, but recognised that they would not have achieved their respective successes unless they kept faith with the man at the helm. It is a lesson Everton seem to be taking on board with David Moyes. But not Chelsea. Avram Grant's narrow failure to win the club either of the two major prizes in 2008 cost him his post, with Brazil's World Cup winning coach Luiz Felipe Scolari becoming the third astronomically paid manager at Stamford Bridge within 12 months.

"Arsene has a philosophy of how you play the game," says Tony Banfield, admittedly a biased though absolutely credible witness. "He has lived his dream, producing open, fresh, mature, powerful and quick football that is beautiful to watch." At times Arsenal may have fallen agonisingly short, but with the entertainment they have given it would be churlish not to acknowledge their contribution to football folklore. When people talk of Hungary in the 1950s, Holland in the 1970s, Brazil of the 1980s, do they talk about the World Cups they failed to win? Are the teams who actually lifted those trophies talked about with the same fondness and reverence as the vanquished? Only in their own countries. Yet Wenger's Arsenal won trophies as well, and are likely to continue to do so.

The second season at the Emirates was evidence that the club had come through the lean times and were credible contenders again. If a couple of situations had worked out differently, it could easily have been Arsenal in possession of two trophies after the 2008 Champions League final in Moscow. The season before had probably been Wenger's most frustrating, as the growing pains of his 'third' team, the youngest ever, saw their interest in titles and trophies evaporate after early March. However, excited by the potential of his players and the superclub status Arsenal have attained, Wenger signed another contract to see the job through. The refinements continue. So, as Henry, Ljungberg and Lauren move on, Sagna, Eduardo and Diarra join. Two unqualified successes and a quick profit, whilst Adebayor matches Henry's goal return of better times. Despite the expenditure by Premier League clubs on players' wages and transfers continuing to rise inexorably – they comfortably exceeded £1 billion in 2007/08 – Arsenal, along with everyone else (apart from Chelsea) are at the mercy of the Italian and Spanish mega-clubs whose ability to sell their *Serie A* and *La Liga* broadcasting rights individually give them a financial edge. So when Flamini, Hleb and Adebayor are known to be on the wish list of a Milan or a Barcelona, the sound of euros talking might drown out any plea on Arsène Wenger's part. Already the offer of a substantial pay rise wasn't enough to persuade Flamini to re-sign and others tempted by the prospect of a huge salary hike may well follow him out of the club. However, new names will be recruited and become stars. Why should the manager's eye for talent let him down now? The scouting system is in place and young prospects will prefer to join Arsenal, confident that they will receive a good apprenticeship and knowing that if they make the grade, they are likely to see first team action. As if to emphasise the point, in June 2008, 17-year-old Aaron Ramsey was signed from Cardiff City for £5 million. The young midfielder chose north London in preference to Old Trafford.

Despite admitting, "I don't think I will ever work as a manager in France any more," he and Annie would like to return home eventually. He intends to continue working but not as the national team manager. "I've worked so much in my life on a daily basis, that I think I would be lost. If you have a good generation in a country, you can do a good job. If you don't, you can do nothing. With a club, you can find someone in Spain and a player in South Africa that nobody has seen and still make a good team. That is not possible with a country." And if FIFA's President Sepp Blatter has his way it may not be possible any longer with Arsenal. His controversial '6 plus 5' proposal to restrict the number of imports to five in order to enhance the quality of national teams may have received an unequivocal thumbs down from the European Commission, but it has the backing of world football's governing body. If the regulation actually came to pass, would Arsène Wenger feel content to change his priorities and work with players who might have less quality but possess the necessary birth certificate?

In revolutionising Arsenal, the imitation of his methods has raised the general standard throughout the Premier League. In cementing the preference for continental talent at the expense of domestic, an area in which Wenger has led the way, as England's clubs become more popular and successful, the reverse effect has befallen the national team. So it was no huge surprise that as a Euro 2008 pundit for French channel TF1, he would not be analysing the efforts of the country where he plies his trade. Now the Football Association can't even find an English-born coach capable of qualifying the country for a major tournament. He might claim he never looks at his players' passports when quizzed about the limited number of Englishmen in his squad, but if he ever goes to catch a potential signing in the flesh there is every chance he will need his own. It is a policy that has served Wenger well, especially when the price of English players makes Arsenal's imports look like such bargains.

Even if he would not consider managing in his native country again, perhaps his next role could be back home. With Paris Saint-Germain wooing David Dein, and Arsène Wenger equally friendly with the club's new president Charles Villeneuve – who intends only to stay in the post for a couple of years – the future could see the dynamic duo back in harness, one as a CEO and the other as technical director or even president. Some are concerned that Arsenal had better get their act together while there is still time.

But does anyone have justification to question Arsène Wenger's conviction after all this time? "Arsenal is the club of my life," he said when signing his fifth contract in September 2007. "I have been entrusted with complete freedom to implement and execute my plans on what will make the team successful. That means I have a responsibility to the fans to deliver silverware and also a responsibility to the players to help turn our potential into prizes."

He will do it his way. When his work is done he will leave behind a club he has completely reshaped and fundamentally changed the culture of in the way only a select group of men have done in English football's long history. Herbert Chapman, Sir Matt Busby, Bill Nicholson, Bill Shankly, Don Revie and Brian Clough are foremost amongst them. But arguably none of them, apart from perhaps Chapman, can rival the sum total of his achievements. Aside from the physical changes in Arsenal's stadium and training facilities, he has transformed the reputation of the club. The defence was regarded its greatest strength in the titles won by managers from Herbert Chapman through to George Graham. Now, Arsenal are ranked with Real Madrid, Barcelona and Manchester United as entertainers. In being responsible for that change, Arsène Wenger has moved the club dramatically up the popularity stakes as well as the money league, just at a time when economic resources have become a necessity in keeping a team together. He will hand over to his successor a club that is one of the richest and most valuable in the world, with a dwindling and easily manageable debt and expanding revenues. Little wonder that predators lurk at the door. In making Arsenal one of the elite number of superclubs, the existing owners had to gamble on Arsène Wenger continuing to produce the quality of football that has made him the world's most coveted manager. He did not let them down.

"I am not God," he joked with an acquaintance recently. "He has more work than I have!" Maybe so, but Wenger's not known as a "miracle worker" without good reason.

CHAPTER FIFTEEN
STORMY WEATHER

"We think you should leave." To be told by chairman Peter Hill-Wood that her fellow directors would like her to step down was not what Lady Nina Bracewell-Smith expected to hear just a few hours after being unanimously re-elected at the October 2008 Arsenal Holdings Annual General Meeting. In fact the re-election had been a formality under the company's articles of association that had to take place in order that the meeting could progress without any of the shareholders questioning what was going on behind the scenes, but it was in keeping with a day full of surprises.

At the meeting, Lady Nina had sat next to Arsène Wenger and Stan Kroenke. Few shareholders had expected to catch their first sight of their newest director, Kroenke – invited onto the board only a few weeks before – so soon. The name-plates on the top table had also initially included that of the most important shareholder, Danny Fiszman, but it had been hastily removed when it became apparent that he was not going to be in attendance – due, it later transpired, to transport difficulties from his Swiss home. However, several interpreted his absence as a sign that the club was no longer a major priority of his and that he planned to make an exit once he could sell up under the terms of the lockdown agreement in April 2009. (Until then no director could sell their shares and afterwards should they want to sell, first option had to be given to their fellow board members.)

The charade of Lady Nina's re-election to head off any shareholder inquisition was not the day's only irony. The directors had given their blessing – as they had on previous occasions – to the Arsenal Supporters' Trust setting up a stand at the meeting in the hope of attracting more recruits to their cause. To promote their manifesto, the Trust had produced a small volume, *Custodianship at Arsenal*, highlighting the ownership and good governance of the club over many decades. The Hill-Woods were well represented, and after the AGM had finished, coincidentally a bust commissioned by the club of Peter Hill-Wood's father, Sir Denis, was unveiled. The other notable family prominent in the Trust book was the Bracewell-Smiths, with Lady Nina the latest of a long line to serve on the board. Copies had been given to the directors, and it was favourably commented upon by the chairman. What he did not tell the meeting was that the immediate future of the just re-elected Lady Nina meant the publication was going to be somewhat dated within a matter of hours. It was a day that saw one dynasty at Arsenal celebrated, and witnessed another chopped down.

Lady Nina eventually resigned a few weeks later after failing to overturn the decision to force her out. Peter Hill-Wood admitted, "She came into the club because she took over her husband's shares and I fervently wish that she hadn't left in the way that she did, because we tried to persuade her to stay in a capacity which she ultimately refused to do." She had been offered an honorary position, a symbolic role, but nevertheless one that would allow her matchday privileges in the directors' lounge. But of course she would no longer be able to harbour any aspirations of influence or power. "As a director she was not right," revealed Hill-Wood, "but why not stay in a capacity that would allow her to maintain all the other status? But she wouldn't do that." There was a palpable sense of relief amongst the directors after her announcement that she was quitting. "She confused me and upset me considerably because we offered her all sorts of olive branches," admitted Hill-Wood. "I'm a reasonably easy person to get on with and as long as you don't totally upset the apple cart I'm going to go along with it [but] she was not very easy to deal with." What he would not disclose was that one of the main causes of concern was the board's belief that she was becoming too well disposed to Alisher Usmanov's Red and White Holdings company, an unhealthy liaison with a potential predator, but one which Lady Nina vehemently denies. "I had been unfairly treated since the day I entered [the boardroom]," she said. "Danny Fiszman always kept his distance and you got the feeling that if you didn't fall in line you were marginalised."

The invitation to bring Stan Kroenke into the fold was a key tactic in the move to repel a possible takeover by Red and White Holdings. Hitherto persona non grata, Peter Hill-Wood's view of Stan Kroenke had changed somewhat with the passing of time. "Stan Kroenke is absolutely the right kind of shareholder," the chairman reflected after the American entrepreneur had been appointed as a fellow director, "because he's a wealthy man and isn't leveraged up like Russians. He's really dedicated to sport. He's very interested in football and trying to develop it in his country and very realistic about it. He doesn't think it's [Major League Soccer] going to rival the Premier League and he believes in what we are doing at Arsenal. And he's not remotely interested in taking over the club, at least he says so and I've no reason not to believe him." "He owns his own franchises and has a big property portfolio," Ken Friar added. "He knows a great deal about property and so it was felt that he could add to our understanding of both sports and property. He's also involved via his family in retailing, and we're involved in all those areas. We felt that he could bring a lot to the table and he has."

Hill-Wood explained the reasoning behind his outburst – "We don't need his money and don't need his sort" – which he made in the aftermath of Dein's dismissal. "I said it because I had no idea who he [Kroenke] was. I objected to him because David told me he'd never heard of him and very clearly that wasn't correct. I rang him [Dein] up and said, 'I gather this American is going to buy ITV's shares and I thought I'd let you know'. He said 'Oh really? Oh, I heard something was going on'. And I thought 'Uh-oh'. So that really antagonised me and I'd no idea who Stan Kroenke was. When I first met him I said I was extremely sorry about the remarks, [some of] which actually I didn't make. I shouldn't have spoken to the media. They did quote quite a lot of what I said and then embroidered it quite considerably. I said to Stan, 'Look, I'm sorry, I didn't make all the remarks that were quoted but I did make one or two of them, and I withdraw them immediately.' He said, 'Don't worry about it, I'm not worried'." Reflecting on Dein's version regarding his involvement, Hill-Wood said, "I know David had made contact. That was wrong."

With Kroenke on the board it was no longer critical to keep Lady Nina onside as a counterpoint to Red and White Holdings. She understood the harsh reality. "They [the board] didn't like having to take me in, but because of the dismissal of David Dein, I had 15 per cent and they had to put up with it. Now they've got Stan Kroenke they don't need me any more." The chairman was sanguine about the potential dangers of forcing her out. "If her shares were sold, so what?" he pondered. "The position has changed dramatically in the last five or ten years. If some outsider comes in and makes an offer for the club in his wisdom and wants to buy it, that's maybe the end of an era but you can't fight against it unless you own 51 per cent of the thing yourself, so we took a chance [with Stan Kroenke]."

That Lady Nina had Hobson's choice was made clear by the resignation of her cousin Richard Carr from the Arsenal Holdings Board. It indicated that the rest of the board wanted to unanimously vote her off as they had with David Dein some 18 months previously. Carr's decision to step down ensured he would not have to face the embarrassing choice of whether or not to vote against another family member. He remained a director of Arsenal Football Club itself, although with the construction of the stadium and the ramifications of the property development, the power base had shifted away from the football club to Arsenal Holdings plc, the company that oversaw all of the club's activities, football or otherwise.

Whilst at one time Red and White had been buying shares for as much as £10,000 each, the going price had drifted down by about 25 per cent around the time of the 2008 AGM. If Lady Nina had sold to Red and White Holdings, their stake would have exceeded 30 per cent and they would be forced to make a mandatory offer for control at a high price that simply wouldn't reflect the current value of Arsenal. Moreover, in common with a number of Russian billionaires, the extent of Usmanov's fortune had dwindled dramatically as economic problems manifested themselves across the globe. Thus, the threat of a hostile takeover had receded somewhat. In February 2009, Red and White bought just enough shares to take them over the 25 per cent that would allow them to block any extraordinary resolutions the board might propose. The only real menace to the status quo remained Usmanov forming an alliance with Lady Nina with combined shares of 40.9 per cent, an ever-present cloud on the horizon to a board without a majority stake.

For Danny Fiszman, Red and White was synonymous with

David Dein, and hence no love was lost. It was a message that came through loud and clear to those who had paid the former vice-chairman handsomely for his shares. Installing Dein as the chairman of Red and White Holdings, whose sole *raison d'être* was to buy an interest in Arsenal, was presumably a move to court favour amongst the club's supporters, ensure the loyalty of Arsène Wenger and have an experienced administrator at the helm in the event that they gained control. But even if Dein himself remained a soulmate of the manager's and a popular figure amongst many of the fans, that affection did not carry over to Alisher Usmanov and in time Dein's usefulness became questionable. He failed to gain his new enterprise any significant groundswell of support, and was an insurmountable obstacle to them having any meaningful influence or relationship with the existing board. Asked what exactly he did in his role as chairman of Red and White Holdings, Dein always sidestepped the question, although he kept his top-level contacts at FIFA and UEFA, whilst remaining a sought-after figure at football conferences.

In September 2008, David Dein resigned from the company. He denied he had been exploited by Red and White and became expendable when Arsenal refused to deal with him. Privately he explained, "It was my choice. I brought two billionaires [Alisher Usmanov and Stan Kroenke] in. The exercise had run its course. It is no bad thing it has come to an end, I want to retain my independence and call it as I see it." He was now no longer an *habitué* of the Red and White corporate box and had to watch the game from his Club Level seats. (He has four together with several in the upper level, most of which are given away to charity and friends on a match-by-match basis.) Subsequently, Red and White were granted four seats in the directors' box and a table in the directors' dining room at the Emirates. It was a clear signal that with Dein out of the way, relations had begun to thaw.

But it was too late for Lady Nina. The lockdown agreement was the equivalent of a marriage and the suspicion amongst the board was that Lady Nina might have been playing away. She claims that she was frozen out after committing the apparent minor misdemeanor of visiting the Red and White box at the Emirates at half time during one match. The invite came from Usmanov's partner, Farhad Moshiri, whom Lady Nina asserts only wanted to introduce her to his sister. Her downfall was in the timing. If the meeting had occurred after Dein's departure from Red and White or in the directors' lounge then perhaps there would have been no repercussions. The final Bracewell-Smith to serve as a director at Arsenal had left with a bitter taste. "Dismissing a director is taking matters to an extreme," she said. "And the timing was callous [half an hour after the directors' lunch following the AGM]. People shouldn't behave like that to a woman."

What seems likely is that Lady Nina not only wanted to have more input reflecting the size of her shareholding, but she found herself increasingly at odds with the board's decisions. She conceded that there was "one particular aspect [that may have caused friction]. I didn't accept the plurality of the shareholding." She certainly felt that she had as much to contribute as her elderly colleagues. In a telephone conversation her friend Geoffrey Klass suggested to her that she employed the wrong tactics. Klass gently rebuked her. "You should have kept quiet, gone with the flow and realised how lucky you were. I was jealous of you," he said. "You were a director of a fantastic football club. They wouldn't even let me sit in the directors' box." (When he had a substantial shareholding – four per cent – Klass had asked for a seat in the box and was politely refused.) Irritated, she exclaimed "You think so little of me," and promptly put the phone down on him.

Though in hindsight Lady Nina feels "I could have been a bit more proactive", her abiding feeling remains one of injustice. "They [the board] wanted to remove me; they had other plans up their sleeve," she said. One of these was the appointment, after a long drawn out interview process, of Keith Edelman's successor. The two leading candidates were Arsenal season ticket holder Paul Donovan, then CEO of Vodafone, and the Celtic CEO Peter Lawwell, who significantly had experience in property development. Lawwell was considered the favourite, but he decided to remain in his current post. Someone who knows Lawwell commented that, "as an ambitious man who had served his time at Celtic, perhaps he wasn't reassured regarding the stability of the situation he was going to inherit." Rather than then appoint Donovan, it was decided to continue the search.

So septuagenarian Ken Friar had to hold the fort a bit longer, taking on the duties of two vital positions at a time he should have been enjoying his well-earned retirement. Wenger himself later admitted, "It [was] important for the club to get someone because we always relied on Ken, who had to do absolutely everything and that's too much for one man." With his tenure as acting MD lasting only a matter of months, Friar certainly wasn't going to make any major long-term decisions and as a result the club marked time. All the right things were said about supporting Arsène Wenger, but the manager was working a lot harder than he had to when David Dein was around: any weeks without a midweek fixture were often filled by an overseas recruitment trip. (After "the most disappointing week" of his Arsenal tenure – humbled by Manchester United in the Champions League semi-final and having the heaviest home loss inflicted on them in 20 years by Chelsea in the Premier League – he couldn't wait to get on a plane to France with next season's reinforcements top of his agenda.)

In fairness though the club had offered to draft in a replacement under the guise of 'director of football' during the summer after Dein's exit. "David used to do that before he left us," Friar said (Dein would represent the manager, often relieving him of the travel, trials and tribulations invariably involved in transfer deals). He went on to explain how things worked subsequently. "When he left I was asked by the board if I would take on that role, which I did. Arsène would identify the player – and that always has to be the way. The manager has got to identify the player. Depending on who he was and where the player is etc, generally speaking, either Arsène or I would make a call. It's horses for courses. If the club was Blackburn Rovers or Manchester United it would be me that made the call. If it was Lyon or a team that he knows the people there, he would make that call. Then the appointment would be made, and they would come in. Generally speaking, the meeting would take place at London Colney and there would be Arsène and myself and the manager or chairman of the other club getting things moving. Sometimes it involved more than one meeting. Once we've got the terms agreed in principle, then we get the player and the agent and it might mean us going abroad, which we've done, or them coming here." (Both Gilles Grimandi, Wenger's top man in France, and Nicky Hammond, who occupied the position at Reading, were mooted for the role of director of football. It seems that Grimandi was reluctant to commit himself as a result of the uncertainty of Wenger's own long-term future. And so the situation was allowed to drift.)

"Arsène takes too much on himself," a friend opined to David Dein.

"As I said at the time when I left," Dein responded, "the landscape is changing. Manchester City, Aston Villa, Everton and Tottenham are not going to stand still, to say nothing of Manchester United, Chelsea and Liverpool and with the tax situation changes, costs are just going to get higher as players' salaries will not go down."

"So you're repeating your mantra," said his friend, "to get a winning team, you need more money and lots of it? But Arsène wouldn't spend the money even if he had it."

"He's never had the luxury," Dein replied and questioning the board's ambition asked, "Is it strong enough to compete with the likes of Barcelona and Milan? Compared to Manchester United, we [Arsenal] are in the Stone Age. Have they [the directors] ever said, 'Arsène, don't have a conscience over the cost. We've gone past that stage now. We've got to be brave and bold in the market. Just tell us, how much do you need to win the Champions League?'"

Maybe not, but evolution if not revolution was definitely the direction the Board wanted to follow.

The antiquated fixtures and fittings of the boardroom at the old Highbury Stadium may have been moved piece by piece a few hundred yards west to the Highbury House building (including the 1970s green leather chairs in the boardroom which look *passé* in contrast to Ken Friar's wonderful historic desk handed down from Herbert Chapman through successive managers and club secretaries) yet the relocated boardroom could have usefully employed a more contemporary item, namely a revolving door. Since the move, three directors have been effectively booted out, with Richard Carr demoted, to be replaced by the end of 2008 with two fresh faces from the USA.

The idea that the board would eventually view an American billionaire as a potential bedrock of the club must have seemed a very fanciful notion in the summer of 2007, but with Alisher Usmanov a constant presence, Stan Kroenke gradually came to represent a much safer option. His approval rating was also helped by an endorsement from the Arsenal Supporters' Trust, who held meetings with Kroenke and his key men in both London and Denver, as part of their objective to maintain relations with all of the club's major shareholders in their mission to influence its ownership and governance. Even so, it was a surprise when Kroenke mingled with members of the Trust at their 2008 Christmas drinks gathering in the stadium's Diamond Club. The function was arranged for the same day as a board meeting, to encourage directors to come along. Even so, few anticipated Kroenke would be in the country to attend the meeting, never mind the social gathering held by the Trust, which he did in the company of Danny Fiszman.

It was soon apparent that the two men had formed a good relationship (though Fiszman the consummate professional had concealed his estrangement from David Dein for some time, putting on a show of corporate unity in public which even fooled some of his colleagues). If Fiszman, in keeping with his reserved nature, was slightly guarded, Kroenke was open and effusive. The appointment of the club's new CEO Ivan Gazidis, previously Deputy Commissioner of MLS, had recently been announced. Gazidis would start work in the New Year, and there was a strong belief that Kroenke had been instrumental in bringing him to the club. "I had nothing to do with it," he told his Trust inquisitors as he supped a beer, "If my fellow team owners [in the USA] thought that they'd be very upset with me, but he [Gazidis] is a good man." And Gazidis himself confirmed the correct protocol had been observed. "Stan Kroenke was not involved in my appointment to this job," he corroborated. "I was very specific that I didn't want him informed until the decision was made." A fortunate coincidence, then, given Kroenke's divided loyalties and the high regard with which Gazidis was held back in the States.

The man who took the job was born in South Africa (unlike Danny Fiszman who is often categorised erroneously as South African by the media, when in fact he spent his early years in Antwerp before growing up in Willesden Green in north London where he learnt to love Arsenal) and raised in England.

He played football competently enough to gain a blue for Oxford University as a right winger ("I had speed and very little else," he claims) and even played at Wembley Stadium in the Varsity Match against Cambridge in the mid-1980s. He qualified as a lawyer, and worked for a couple of years in the USA before he was headhunted for a job to help develop a fledgling league born in the aftermath of the 1994 World Cup. The first Arsenal match he attended after the announcement of his appointment was the 1-0 home victory over Wigan in December 2008, a sterile encounter best remembered for substitute Emmanuel Eboue being booed off, his performance so dire he had to be substituted himself. A month later after a similarly insipid 1-0 victory against Bolton (who, according to their chairman, came "expecting to get beaten by 2 or 3-0 and were pleasantly surprised to get within 15 minutes of the end at 0-0"), when it was suggested to Ivan Gazidis that things were sticky on and off the field, he discounted the notion. "I'm certain that's not the case," he told a guest in the boardroom, "otherwise I wouldn't be here."

Unlike his predecessor, Keith Edelman, Gazidis was someone who could be termed a football man as well as a businessman. Peter Hill-Wood admitted it was important to start looking to the future in the boardroom: "He [Gazidis] is 45 years old, the younger generation – which is better than being 70-something years old. We are looking to recruit younger people at the top." But there was so much more than his age that must have commended Gazidis. "In October I was approached by the Arsenal board and asked if I would be interested in this position," he recalled. "The moment I realised that this was a real possibility something just took over me, and I knew it would be a once-in-a-lifetime chance. It was a purely emotional decision and not a rational decision at all. The decision was driven by the fact that I love watching Arsenal play. There is something about the purity of the way that Arsenal try to play the game that appealed to me. There is something about this club. It's a set of values, traditions, continuity, excellence but not just looking backwards, also a real vision for the future." Straight away he got to grips with the key issues. "Our fundamental questions are: Are we operating as efficiently and as well as we can? Are we choosing the right players? Are we spending the money in the right way? Are we generating as much money as we can as a business to fund our player acquisitions? And within those parameters you can have a very interesting debate about whether we are being as efficient as possible. This club operates on the self-sustaining model."

With Gazidis's experience of marketing in Major League Soccer, he should undoubtedly add something to the club's commercial operation, an area that badly needs some attention, as Hill-Wood conceded. "On the commercial side we're lacking and we've got a lot of catching up to do with Manchester United, Barcelona, Real, even Liverpool and maybe Chelsea. There is a lot that we can develop and a lot of things which are probably alien to my background but I'm hopefully realistic enough to realise that I'm going to have to forget that we're not a little old football club in north London. Ivan's going to help develop the club in every aspect of our business, which is now much more than a football club, it's all the commercial activities. It's a big brand." And it needs a different calibre of person to service it. "I'm just looking for very, very smart people," says Gazidis, "who are able to help in the development of a business plan, a strategic plan for how we manage our playing pool amongst other things. There aren't many clubs that have a fully developed business plan."

Gazidis subsequently detailed his way of working. "I'm very systematic in the way that I do things," he explained. "My focus over the first five months has been one of evaluation. Less on communication of vision, direction and plans so far, more focused on the needs of the club where the club can benefit from additions and adjustments. The focus has been relatively small and inward looking, [about] the changes we need to go through as an organisation so that we can take the next step. And the next step is the big step we have to take, which is to move beyond the Emirates and look at where the club is really going over the next five to ten years and deeply understand which strategies we are going to be adopting and which steps need to be taken in order for those strategies to be successful. To do that requires us to take a little bit of a step back from some of the activity that we're involved in and to come up with a business plan for the club."

The CEO was certainly aware of the crucial importance of the paying public (who were taken for granted by some of his peers who had been around much longer) and readily met with the various supporters' groups within a few weeks of his arrival – the Arsenal Supporters' Trust, REDaction (a pressure group formed to improve the atmosphere at matches) and the Arsenal Independent Supporters' Association. He immediately tuned into their language. In his very first interview, he talked about the role of the board in terms of its custodianship of the club – using the kind of terminology that could have been scripted for him by the Supporters' Trust. "I do think the fan/club relationship is key," he emphasised later. "I think that fans have the right to express their opinions in the stadium. Obviously as a club you hope it's supportive and I do think in general fans understand, particularly with a group of young players who we have right now and that if they've got fragile confidence, maybe you're exacerbating the problem rather than helping it by expressing dissatisfaction. Nevertheless, I also accept that fans will feel at some point that this is where they exercise their voice and that's absolutely right."

He apparently took heed of critical comments regarding

the lack of Arsenal identity at the stadium – something both Keith Edelman and Ken Friar had promised to do something about with little to show in the way of change except for the decoration of a concrete ring between the upper tier and the executive boxes which celebrated the years of the club's trophy wins. "One of the things I'd really like to do," Gazidis said, "is to move away from the architectural vision that we have of our stadium. I think in terms of what it is, it can be more Arsenal. It can be made more into a home. I don't think it will ever be Highbury, you can't recapture that history, but I do think it can become its own place and its own home." Asked whether the selling of the naming rights made this process more difficult, he replied diplomatically, "I'm very happy with Emirates as a sponsor."

Hitherto, it had only been the nagging of Antony Spencer, the land agent who found Arsenal the site for their new home, that pressured the board on 'Arsenalisation'. Disappointed that the stadium was going to carry a sponsor's name, Spencer at least achieved a small concession and ensured a link remained with the historic home, albeit in the name of the company office block, Highbury House. Danny Fiszman on the other hand had wanted to create a completely new era, his focus on the present and the future. Spencer recalled, "He was adamant that the old clock from the Clock End at Highbury was not going to be sited anywhere inside the new stadium." Finally, after some fan representation, it was mounted on the rear of one of the scoreboards and is visible from the approach along the south, or 'Clock End' bridge. But inside there was very little – a photograph or two – to suggest the team had ever played at Highbury. Even the naming of the sections of the grounds broke from the obvious nomenclature. No longer did fans enter the East, West, North or South sides of the stadium, but different quadrants. Using colour coding to facilitate different access routes to the Emirates, most ignore it and arrive via Gillespie Road much as they did when attending matches at Highbury.

Peter Hill-Wood explained the reason for the need to bring in a different type of personality at the helm. "Keith [Edelman] did a very good job for us, but to take us forward in the future he wasn't necessarily the right person," he reflected. "It was the decision of the board collectively. Not me personally, we basically all agreed in the end, but I supported Keith as much as anybody. But we felt we needed a change. He'd done a good job and it was time for him to move on." The club offered him a seven-figure retainer for 'consultancy work' for a year after his departure, although the former managing director has not been spotted at the club since the day he collected his personal effects, giving rise to some fanciful conspiracy theories.

One of Edelman's major projects – to turn the old stadium into the Highbury Square residential apartments – has flattered to deceive. In the view of many, too much time and effort was taken up on property rather than football. Worse, it gradually became apparent that the huge surplus – profits of £100 million were initially bandied about – was wishful thinking as the economy faltered. "Keith had a quick mind," recalls Antony Spencer, "but sometimes too quick for his own good. He wanted to do things his way." A case in point was one part of the development which became a sticking point because Edelman wanted to break with precedent and go about it in a different fashion. He was so adamant it had to be done his way that it took the intervention of Danny Fiszman to return to the tried and trusted policy.

Danny Fiszman had put his heart and soul into making the Emirates a reality, and was second only to Arsène Wenger in transforming Arsenal from the underperforming football club it had been before his arrival. Peter Hill-Wood concurred, "I can't describe the effort and time that Danny put in. It was seven years overall and we'd never have done it without him, and he's not a man with a big ego." And Ken Friar adds his own compliments. "Danny is one of the best things that ever happened to the club," he believes, "and a very genuine Arsenal supporter. He's very intelligent, gets on well with people, is a good negotiator, and he's been a big, big benefit to us. He's not one of those who wants to be upfront everywhere and not a man wanting to be on committees."

Testament to Fiszman's unassuming nature was a conversation he had with an acquaintance as they entered the directors' box together.

"What a terrific sight," said the acquaintance, surveying a full stadium with the teams about to kick off.

"Not bad, is it?" was the understated reply.

"You should stay around and enjoy it."

"I intend to," said Fiszman pointedly.

"Well as long as you do, Arsenal will be in good hands."

"That's sweet of you to say so," said Fiszman.

But even if he was in for the long term, he decided now was a good time to share the burden and divvy up his stake. How much the uncertainty regarding the large shareholding on the outside played any part in the decision of Fiszman to transfer, in the spring of 2009, a third of his shares to Stan Kroenke is not known, but the outcome unquestionably pointed to a future in which the American would play a more active role, if only to safeguard his multi-million pound investment. After paying £42.5 million – the shares were valued at £8,500 each – in one fell swoop Kroenke became the largest shareholder on the board with a 20 per cent stake. The arrangement over the transferred shares was rather an odd one, as no money changed hands even though Kroenke now had the voting rights attached to them, and became the director with the most shares. Effectively, Kroenke owed Fiszman £42.5 million (Kroenke probably could have afforded to pay Fiszman immediately but perhaps he was accommodating the seller with regard to tax implications at the end of the financial year).

Curiously the new power shift reflected the arrangement that Fiszman had with David Dein during the 1990s, although then the boot was on the other foot. Over time, Fiszman had filtered money through to Dein for shares they initially joint-owned, and thereby built up his stake. If the shares transferred in 2009 were totally under Kroenke's control, the indications are that Fiszman has total confidence in his colleague, stating that his "greater involvement will be in the best interests of everyone involved in the club". It was a view backed up by Gazidis: "This is somebody [Kroenke] that shares the same philosophy as the [other members of the] current Board," although he hinted that change might be in the air when he added, "and will be influential as we go forward".

But only if Danny Fiszman permits it? Previously, despite owning only a quarter of the club, the pride of place held by the stadium project presented Fiszman with a whip hand, which on occasion he deployed resolutely. After Geoffrey Klass had been instrumental in bringing in Antony Spencer and Fiszman understood the prospects for the site, Klass was brusquely told "Thank you Geoffrey, but you are no longer involved," presumably because of his friendship with David Dein. Dein's opposition to Ashburton Grove was an irreducible black mark in Fiszman's book, and apparently so was Lady Nina's wish for more involvement (from day one she felt she had never been made welcome, tolerated rather than embraced). So it augured well for the stability of the club that at this point in 2009 the two directors with the largest shareholding appeared to be acting in tandem regarding how the club should be run.

Pointedly, before the deal with Fiszman, Kroenke had been picking up odd shares on the open market (which he belatedly disclosed, presumably initially unaware that the Stock Exchange had to be informed). At the time there was uncertainty as to whether he had ambitions to strengthen his hand in the hope of one day taking control himself or that he felt the club represented a good investment which he could recoup with interest in the event of a future takeover bid. The reasoning became much clearer in April, a month after the exchange with Fiszman, when it was announced that Kroenke had bought out the Carr family's shares at between £8,500 and £10,500 per share, the higher price reflecting the inherent power attached to them. The purchase from a combination of Richard Carr, Lady Sarah Phipps-Bagge and Clive Carr raised the American's share of the club to 28.3 per cent. As with the transfer of shares from Fiszman, no money actually changed hands at the time. Kroenke and Fiszman now had an amalgamated holding of over 44 per cent, so that even if Alisher Usmanov's Red and White Holdings attempted to combine with the other disaffected shareholder, Lady Nina Bracewell-Smith, they could now only muster 41 per cent. The prospect of overthrowing the board was killed stone dead by the deal. The Carrs had shown fidelity to the existing hierarchy, leaving Lady Nina and Usmanov – even if they did want to combine forces – effectively powerless in spite of the size of their respective holdings.

Kroenke and Fiszman had cleverly managed the situation whereby they could ensure the board retained control without either man being forced to make a mandatory takeover bid that a 30 per cent stake would entail. The takeover panel at the Stock Exchange were asked to investigate the notion that the pair were acting in concert to the detriment of other shareholders and should be forced to bid for the entire company, with the payoff that both Usmanov and Lady Nina would then be able to cash in their chips at £10,500 a share (the highest price paid for a share in the previous 12 months, which any takeover buyer would be obliged to pay under Stock Exchange rules). By reason of acquiring the Carrs' shares, Kroenke became the main man at the club and there was speculation amongst knowledgeable outsiders that this was the intended outcome ever since talks began about inviting him onto the board. Although no one would confess to such Machiavellian planning, the pieces of the jigsaw fell into place and completed a picture (with the happy co-incidence of Ivan Gazidis as the new CEO) that left two very substantial shareholders – Alisher Usmanov and Lady Nina Bracewell-Smith – on the outside looking in.

Having originally been welcomed to the inner sanctum so that the powers that be could keep an eye on her, if the intention all along was for Kroenke to control a dominant stake, Lady Nina had become expendable, as long as the cooperation of the Carr family was maintained. Richard Carr's departure from the board when Lady Nina was forced out may have led her to believe he was unhappy with events and would remain loyal to her. Anything but. On learning the Carrs had sold out, she felt betrayed. "I had no idea they were going to do this," she revealed. "And they've still got all their seats in the directors' box, whilst I have nothing." The Carrs played the game and played it well, both cashing in and retaining their matchday privileges. If Lady Nina had accepted that she was fighting a battle she could not win, then she too could have remained a luminary.

The bottom line is that she was never taken credibly as a director but was endured as long as it suited. She was justified though in her acrimonious feelings. She had remained faithful to the Carrs and the board by refusing to sell to both Kroenke and Usmanov. Two years after rejecting the American, the tables were turned and no loyalty had been shown in return. Once her stake was the key to who held power. Now it only had a cash value. She felt she had been "deserted" by her husband's family, who sold out to make Stan Kroenke the key man at Arsenal.

Danny Fiszman's own position remained unbreachable. The 16 per cent he retained ensured he would remain as influential as he needed to be. He had replaced Lady Nina in holding the key to power, as his alliance with Kroenke determined the club's future. The only way Kroenke could act without Fiszman's blessing was to make a takeover bid himself. Why bother if the two men were comfortable with each other? The irony was that Fiszman was effectively handing the reins over to a man who had been brought into the fold by David Dein. So much had changed in two years.

Kroenke may have been encouraged in his actions by the interim accounts for the six months to 30th November 2008 that the club had released a few weeks before the transfer of a third of Fiszman's shares. They demonstrated a sustained growth in a difficult climate even though most of the revenue had been attained before the recession really began to bite. Turnover increased by 10 per cent to over £98 million as a result of more matchdays and higher ticket prices for season 2008/09 and higher broadcast fees including a beneficial €/£ exchange rate on Champions League income. Football operating profits (before debt service costs) also rose as Arsène Wenger's expertise in player trading again proved very profitable. Sales of Alex Hleb to Barcelona and Justin Hoyte to Middlesbrough as well as sell-on fees for players who had previously left the club and been subsequently transferred again, such as David Bentley who moved from Blackburn to Tottenham, netted Arsenal several million pounds.

Football costs – primarily the players' salaries – are exorbitant, perhaps surprisingly so considering the ages of so many in the first team squad, although with a wages-to-turnover ratio of around 50 per cent (way below the Premier League average of 62 per cent) are perfectly manageable as long as

Arsenal continue to play before a sell-out crowd and qualify for the Champions League (the penalty for failing to do so could amount to as much as £40 million from lost broadcast and matchday revenue) as they have done for the past 11 years. The demand for season tickets and premium seats (boxes, Diamond Club and Club Level) will be severely tested prior to the 2009/10 season, despite renewal prices being the same as 12 months ago, after another year without a trophy. Any fall-off from the premium sector (box holders and Club Level season ticket holders) will be particularly painful as it rivals the Champions League as a revenue stream. Now the veracity of the waiting lists – over 40,000 for ordinary season tickets according to the club in 2008 – will be exposed.

Rather than loan out a quarter of the playing staff with a short-term cost saving as a result, perhaps it should be trimmed permanently. Certainly UEFA feels it is unreasonable to have over 50 players on the books, when 25 can cope with a season-long Champions League campaign. Because of the squad size and with player wages rising faster than club income (wages in the Premier League exceeded £1 billion for the first time in 2007/08), it is revealing that the bill is now 50 per cent higher than the last time Arsenal won a trophy. And then Arsenal had the quality of the likes of Henry, Vieira, Pires, Campbell, Bergkamp and Ljungberg in the ranks.

Whilst not reflecting what David Dein termed "the black hole that is Highbury Square", Dein's assertion that the club 'should have stuck to what they know' (ie football matters), whilst made with the benefit of hindsight, rings true. The construction of the Highbury Square apartments continued apace and in the autumn of 2008 over 90 per cent were ready for completion to buyers who had already parted with deposits of 10 per cent. However, the mortgage market had collapsed. Many were unable to find a lender in order to complete their purchase and some were actually pulling out and forfeiting their deposits rather than completing, so dramatically had the housing market changed. By the end of November 2008, 595 of the 680 units had been sold, but only 186 were fully paid up. Arsenal had a £140 million loan taken out to construct the flats, due for repayment by April 2010. At least any future building costs were covered so each completed sale went towards reducing the outstanding debt. Unfortunately, they just weren't happening quickly enough.

So naturally the club sought to extend their credit facility. However, the cost of buying some breathing space and time for the property market to recover would be further interest charges, putting extra pressure on the manager and players to achieve success. The bottom line was that around a further 340 of the 409 pre-sold units would need to be completed before any profit would be seen. And there wasn't much interest in the 85 that were still unreserved at the asking prices. Anyone who could actually manage to find a mortgage might be better off buying one of the myriad other properties in the area that appeared to offer better value.

Peter Hill-Wood could not foresee a prosperous outcome to the situation, admitting, "I said a year ago if we made a profit from the property side it would be a bonus. Many people I suspect will find that some of their financial projections have not quite worked out in the way they thought they would and we're certainly one of those." He continued, "The property side would be much more fun if it was working well. It's annoying. It's a wonderful development and it'll sell like crazy one day, but we're in 2009. It's tough and we're selling a few flats. It would have been very nice to have extra profit there but we're not going to have that. It's not something that impacts on the running of the football club at all which we've stressed many times." But generating extra cash for the football club now appears a distant proposition. Certainly the chairman's statement of 2008 that a revenue of circa £350 million (and a profit of perhaps £100 million) could be expected now appears wildly optimistic. "Sitting here today if we had sold the whole bloody thing three or four years ago and taken a one-off payment of X million that would look very clever. When we decided not to do that we looked at all the downsides other than the current downside – which has taken not only us but everybody else by surprise."

The conversion of the club's old home into funding a nest egg had been eagerly anticipated by Arsène Wenger. Talking about the debts Arsenal were facing in 2007, he said, "I believe that we will see the difference after the end of the 2008/09 season. We will have much greater resources at our disposal.' As the economy suffered, David Dein fervently believed Highbury Square was having a more adverse effect than Wenger himself would ever admit and believed money was being taken out of the football budget for property. "Arsène had £18 million to spend on players in the summer of 2008. By January, that had dwindled to £12 million, due to the property," he confided to a friend. "We need quality reinforcements, but where is the money going to come from? The cupboard is bare and Arsène is running out of hats and rabbits."

Having deleted any mention of Ashburton Grove from all of the club's communications, how ironic that the property development company (Ashburton Properties) should be named after the street where their new stadium was constructed, although it had been wiped off the face of the earth. Further, at the same time it was airbrushed out of Arsenal's recent history, in much the same way as a certain David Dein. Dein remained in constant contact with Wenger, even after his departure from Red and White effectively made him just another Arsenal fan, albeit a very wealthy one. But he had no right to feelings of resentment as his own role in bringing about the dilemmas the club now had to face up to (which ultimately affected his friend Arsène Wenger) could not be denied.

CHAPTER SIXTEEN
WINTER OF DISCONTENT

May 1999. John Sienkiewicz, a charismatic civil servant who established the London Development Unit, part of the newly created Government Office for London, leaned across the table in the Highbury boardroom and in front of Danny Fiszman and Ken Friar thumped it to make his point to the representatives of Islington Borough Council. The council, and the football club, had become obsessed with the idea of Finsbury Park as a site for the new stadium. Sienkiewicz told the club that "they were being taken for a walk in the park" and that the only way forward was Ashburton Grove. All the same, it took the Arsenal board months to come to the same conclusion – they flirted with other sites including the Millennium Dome – that regeneration in the form of social housing and a new waste transfer station would be the sacrifice they would have to make if they wanted a new home.

In 1998, Antony Spencer had first brought his scheme for Ashburton Grove to David Dein's attention through their mutual friend, Geoffrey Klass. As Arsenal belatedly signed on a year later and Spencer was given the green light, Dein became an obstacle with his insistence that Arsenal consider other options, by which he meant Wembley. In so doing, Dein took his eye off the ball and as the Ashburton Grove project proceeded, Danny Fiszman became the main man.

So much so that Spencer was instructed not to keep Dein in the loop.

It was a monumental achievement to be up and running within six years. Yet if David Dein had introduced Spencer to Fiszman at the time the land agent requested and the directors had realised sooner that their best home from home was on their doorstep, then the stadium might have been completed a year earlier (before the economic downturn with all its implications for Highbury Square) and far more money could have been available to strengthen the playing staff.

Dein baulked at the whopping costs of the club building their own new home. His attempts to save money and thereby increase the playing budget (in line with his 'get a winning team' maxim) were undoubtedly laudable taking the short-term view but Danny Fiszman reasoned differently, and wanted to set the club up for a century of prosperity rather than just the remainder of his own days. To Fiszman it was worth the heartache and immediate financial pain. And with Arsène Wenger at the helm, the club had the ideal man to ensure that the effects of the lack of ready cash could be minimised.

Keith Edelman arrived in May 2000 and David Dein was now well and truly sidelined, his mandate purely playing matters. He was forced to take a back seat on the new stadium project. Although by late 2001 he had hopped on the bandwagon and excitedly relayed the news that Islington Council had granted planning permission to Arsène Wenger from outside Upper Street's Union Chapel where the decision had been taken. "Arsène? We've got it!" he exclaimed into his mobile phone.

Summer 2008. David Dein had passed into history, but his gripe lingered on. The club continued to receive more money for outgoing transfers than they spent on acquisitions, at a time when pivotal players had departed and there were palpable faults that cried out for attention – weakness in the air at the back, lack of combativeness in midfield, an absence of leaders à la Tony Adams or Patrick Vieira, an international class goalkeeper and real depth in the squad.

Mathieu Flamini, out of contract, took advantage of his status to join AC Milan in the summer of 2008. "I really thought he was going to stay," Wenger later admitted, but his faith was misplaced. The French international, understandably, sought to improve his pay but if Arsenal had agreed to his financial demands, it would have set a precedent that would have had unfortunate financial repercussions. Peter Hill-Wood describes the situation as "slightly annoying. If you look back he had one good year for us, his last season. Prior to that, he wasn't that great. So when he decided he wanted to go (on the basis of one excellent season), we didn't cede to his requests, but we regret it all the same." Certainly Flamini ended up materially better off, but as he spent the majority of his debut season in Italy on the bench, his career stagnated. "I don't think he's been a great star," reflects the chairman.

As early as September 2007, Wenger had stated, "My priority will be to keep the players I already have. If the club only becomes a place to go to and a place to leave, then the club won't go very far." By the end of the season, his view had not wavered, despite the failure, albeit a narrow one, to capture a trophy. And yet, he could not hang on to Flamini nor Alexander Hleb. Despite their different backgrounds, the two were good friends along with fellow midfielders Cesc Fabregas and Tomas Rosicky. This foursome's camaraderie was one element in the team's rise to the top of the Premier League, as they seemed as compatible on the field as they did off it. Perhaps it was an omen that Rosicky's last appearance that season was in late January, after which results took a turn for the worse. Certainly the three remaining players seemed to run out of steam at the same time, and it soon became apparent that Alex Hleb had his heart elsewhere, having reportedly met with Internazionale officials on the eve of Arsenal's Champions League second leg knockout match against Milan. Ultimately, Wenger decided to accept the inevitable and the £11.8 million Barcelona offered that went with it and reinvested the funds in a similar ball-player – Marseille's Samir Nasri. Like Flamini, Hleb went from a leading light at Arsenal to the reserves at his new club.

But the manager's notion of keeping his group together was being severely tested. He believed that everyone – even those he imported – would be loyal if they embraced the culture of the club. "Above all I believe in the virtues of a collective ethos," he explained, "and I believe that you can only maintain and develop that if you have a culture to impart; a culture that you can pass from generation to generation." Worthy words but the club's balance sheets painted a bleaker picture – the wage bill indicated that the manager was having to buy his treasured loyalty. Perhaps Wenger's rose-tinted glasses make him short-sighted whenever he looks at his boys. He hoped that he might be presiding over a golden generation which would bond, gather experience together and create a dynasty much as Giggs, Beckham, Scholes, the Nevilles and Butt had produced for Manchester United. But yesterday has gone and the time has passed when genuine world class stars – Vieira, Henry, Pires and Bergkamp – stay around for years and don't want to leave until Wenger shows them the door. Tony Adams feels that times have changed for the worse. "This Arsenal has lost just a little bit of being the top in some people's eyes," he said. "When you bring a player from abroad they don't have the same feeling for the club. They look at it as a stepping stone to the Real Madrids and Bayern Munichs."

If kids of 16 are prepared to leave their hometown club – even such institutions as Barcelona – and move abroad, how can Wenger reasonably expect them to show loyalty to him, to the club or indeed to anyone? As a football administrator, who has a lot of respect and affection for Wenger, ruefully observed, "Arsène Wenger thinks that their love of football will bind them together as they grow up but he forgets that there are very few people who genuinely love football with the intensity that he does. Only someone so completely in love with football could think that it would override culture, language, wealth and all the other differences between young players."

If Alexander Hleb had not already made his manager aware of the facts of life, then Emmanuel Adebayor underlined them for him. Overtures from Milan and Barcelona had turned the Togolese international's head and, endeavouring to exploit his exceptional 2007/08 season, he demanded pay parity with the world's top strikers. In response, Arsenal were prepared to let him leave, but at a price, one which deterred the interested parties, and so a new deal was eventually struck. (During an argument with a disgruntled fan, the striker revealed his weekly wage had risen to in excess of £100,000 a week.) The concession of a huge hike in salary at least ensured Adebayor would not be allowed to run down his contract in the way Flamini did, thereby providing the club with the reassurance that he would command the kind of fee commensurate with his ability if he left (30 goals in the 2007/08 season was an exceptional strike rate, even if his profligacy irritated those with half-empty glasses).

Over the course of six months, the departures of Lassana Diarra, Flamini and Gilberto – who was allowed to leave rather than see out the last year of his contract, and joined Greek side Olympiakos – severely depleted the midfield options. Prior to the start of the 2008/09 season Arsenal fans were anticipating the purchase of a top-notch name to partner Cesc Fabregas, and there was much speculation regarding Liverpool's Xabi Alonso. But Nasri aside, the only midfield arrivals were the unheard of 21-year-old Amaury Bischoff from Werder Bremen, a club for whom he had made a total of one appearance as a substitute, and Aaron Ramsey. At 17 years old, the young Welshman was one for the future, even if his £5 million price tag suggested he was already highly talented. Significantly, Arsenal's rivals for his signature, Manchester United, intended to allow him to remain at Cardiff before he was scheduled to go to Old Trafford in the summer of 2009.

A similar scenario affected defensive resources. Jens Lehmann returned to the Bundesliga with VfB Stuttgart and Philippe Senderos moved to AC Milan on a year-long loan deal. Having been a first-team squad member for four years, it seemed as if Wenger was paving the way for a new and better recruit. Thus when he purchased the injury-prone 31-year-old Manchester United reserve utility defender Mikael Silvestre for a token fee more than a few eyebrows were raised. The French international had made only a few first-team appearances for United in the previous two seasons, and was now very much surplus to requirements. Moreover, Silvestre seemed earmarked as cover for the left back position (rather than the crucial one of central defence), especially with Armand Traore being loaned out to Portsmouth. An atypical Wenger purchase, at least he might be someone William Gallas could talk to. At the end of August, *The Gooner* fanzine commented in its editorial with unfortunate prescience, "If he [Wenger] thinks the current squad have the quality to win enough of the key matches with the defensive options available, I fear senility is knocking on the door."

In the early days of the new season (2008/09), Wenger was taken to task by someone who was emboldened to inform him, "You need two six foot five world-class centre backs, an international goalkeeper, a midfield ball-winner and to make better use of the wings."

"I couldn't get the centre backs I was after," Wenger replied.

"And the goalkeeper?"

"If Almunia was English, he would be an international."

"That's a reflection on how poor English keepers are at the moment, and anyway he ain't no Schmeichel. And the attack?"

"You're right."

Yet the manager was still choosing to ignore the experience of his early years at Arsenal: the tough mature English professionals he inherited and the extra lease of life he gave them when he realised their value, the tall combative midfielders – Vieira and Petit – he bought and the resolution they all showed to right defensive wrongs and ensure that defence began in the midfield.

Undoubtedly the manager would have preferred to have had an extra central defender to add to Gallas, Toure and Johan Djourou, but he simply couldn't get the one he wanted. At the club's October AGM, he was questioned as to why he did not buy a centre-back after stating it was a priority at the beginning of the summer. "Football is not just like going to the supermarket," he responded. "You can't go in and say, 'I want one player who is six feet five inches with a good left foot and I want him to be delivered.'" Money was available – some £18 million – but with that seemingly insufficient one can only conjecture whom he had in mind. It would have been closer to the truth to say that he simply couldn't pay for his preferences. The players he wanted were available, but the manager's line was, "We have internal solutions" – sticking to what he had rather than buying someone who was not top of his list, so midfielder Alex Song had to be drafted in if more obvious defensive candidates were unavailable.

Song was also one of the options to partner Cesc Fabregas in the midfield. Aaron Ramsey may have been considered able enough to represent his country at full international level, but he was ultimately earmarked as a possible long-term replacement for Fabregas, who it was felt would inevitably leave at some stage. The other contenders for the position hitherto filled so capably by Gilberto and then Flamini were Denilson and Abou Diaby. The latter was injury prone and by and large struggled except when played as a support striker where his technique in tight situations together with his speed and energy found its optimum expression. (He was instrumental in a November 2008 victory over Manchester United and scored a couple of terrific goals against Fenerbahce and Aston Villa.) Song, unsurprisingly at 20, was inconsistent. Sometimes he showed flashes of the ability that his manager saw in him, but was too often wasteful in possession. So Denilson remained as the best of a less than vintage bunch, occasionally being moved wide to accommodate Song in the centre. Apart from Fabregas, who was much less effective than the previous season, no one displayed the requisite authority or consistency. Not only were fewer chances created but the defence lacked the protection it had previously come to take for granted.

Results reflected the reality of an inexperienced squad, with inconsistency their hallmark. Equally capable of beating Manchester United or Chelsea one week, but losing to Fulham, Stoke City or Hull the next, what had changed so much in a year? Then, Arsenal's title aspirations had remained intact until the final weeks of the 2007/08 campaign, yet next time around the wheels came off in the autumn.

The lack of experience, despite there being several players in their mid-20s and even older, was the key factor. Players far younger and less worldly were forced to replace their elders and betters. It was too much to ask. And Wenger knew it. 'Inexperience costs points,' he confided to a friend. The team, at times, visibly folded, confidence nowhere to be seen. This was not a case of one or two having an off day. The malaise had seemingly spread throughout the entire squad. There were whole matches when it was hard to believe this was an

Arsène Wenger team, so inept were they at even retaining possession.

The nadir – 'ahead' of several contestants – arrived in a narrow 1-0 home victory over Wigan. Emmanuel Eboue had gradually alienated the fans due to his perceived lack of contribution and unsporting conduct, specifically his propensity for diving and feigning injury. Eboue replaced the injured Samir Nasri before the interval and was not enjoying the best of games. However, as the final whistle approached, the team became progressively more agitated about hanging on to their slender lead. In the space of five minutes Eboue committed a series of howlers, culminating in effectively tackling his own teammate Kolo Toure and consequently surrendering possession. The manager felt compelled – as he had become a liability – to substitute his substitute even though only a couple of minutes remained. To add insult to the player's injured pride, the crowd first cheered when his replacement was announced, then booed loudly as he walked towards the touchline.

Eboue had been asked to fill Nasri's position on the left of midfield. That the manager felt a right-sided defender was the best option to take over in left midfield revealed the paucity of resources. Wenger required his charges to demonstrate they were exponents in the art of total football, but they were simply not up to the mark. It was an embarrassing day for the club, in spite of the collection of three points. The crowd had turned on one of the players and before long they would turn on the team and even the manager as sub-par performances way below the level the fans had come to expect followed one after another.

The Eboue fiasco was just one consequence of a number of seemingly quixotic managerial decisions. It was a bizarre situation to suggest that Carlos Vela might have to be sent out on loan again in order to gain experience when he was left on the bench against Wigan. Similarly, Aaron Ramsay and

Jack Wilshire, having started in the Carling Cup, were for the most part unused substitutes in the Premiership.

The prospect that the manager was facing the most difficult period of his 12-year reign was predicated by the sacking of the club captain William Gallas in November due to his revealing a split dressing room and criticising his teammates to the French media. It was one misdemeanor too many for Arsène Wenger and he appointed Cesc Fabregas as his new skipper. "There was a problem at half time in the 4-4 draw with Tottenham [at the end of October]," Gallas admitted. "The only thing that I could say was 'Guys, we resolve these problems after the match, not at half time'." The team lost concentration in the second half and ultimately allowed a 4-2 lead in the 89th minute to slip away. "When as captain," he revealed, "some players come up to you and talk to you about a player... complaining about him... and then during the match you speak to this player [assumed by the media to be Robin van Persie] and the player in question insults us, there comes a time where we can no longer comprehend how this can happen."

Outside the club, there would have been widespread sympathy with Gallas's observation that "big contracts can make you rest on your laurels" – an accurate description of some of his highly paid younger colleagues who had no requirement to install a trophy cabinet at home. "You know you've got to pay the money," former striker Alan Smith commented, "so you've got to trust in the individual and feel that you've done the right research into his character and that the money won't spoil him and take away his hunger. It's only human nature that some people are not the same once they are financially secure. The very best, however, retain their desire."

Gallas may well have hit the nail on the head with his statement, "We have to be warriors. That is how the team will forge their character and experience." And the lack of such an aptitude was probably why Arsenal could be overturned by less gifted teams with a more muscular approach. Gallas was directly suffering the consequences of the lack of physicality among his colleagues. The midfield was lightweight: Fabregas, Nasri and Denilson were all less than six feet and the taller men, Song and Diaby, simply did not win the number of aerial challenges that their height should have enabled them to do.

Wenger may have viewed Spain's European Championship-winning model as a benchmark for the future. But if so, he lacked the equivalents of Senna, Xavi and Iniesta to play alongside Fabregas (who could not even hold down a starting berth in his own national side). No successful team, whatever their size, did not possess a core of individuals who could respond in kind to rough treatment from their opponents. Wenger may have adored Dennis Berkamp for his consummate skill, but he must have been aware that the Dutch maestro was also mean and moody as well as magnificent. He knew creativity had to earn the right to put on a show. And perceived injustices were never ignored as the flurry of red cards bore witness. Presumably as justification for the right to express themselves, the manager turned a blind eye to his players' excesses on the field. Arsenal had evolved into smaller and less imposing physical specimens and the manager's priorities were not the positions where both neutrals and supporters perceived the team as under-strength, both literally and metaphorically.

Whether justified or not, with Gallas deposed, it was a case of 'the king is dead, long live the king', or *le roi est mort, viva el rey* as far as the dressing room was concerned. With the appointment of the 21-year-old Fabregas as skipper, some saw a parallel with that of Tony Adams back in 1988. However, Adams had more physical authority and – despite his tender years – had no compunction about organising those around him or reminding experienced professionals of their responsibilities. On one occasion he suggested to Dennis Bergkamp that his talent had not brought him the medal collection he should own. Fabregas was a far more considered and less vocal individual, what the French call a 'technical leader'. However, he indisputably enjoyed the respect of his teammates and his role in Spain's Euro 2008 triumph enhanced his burgeoning reputation. Nevertheless, due to the paucity of alternatives – Kolo Toure's form did not guarantee him a starting place at this time – Wenger had Hobson's choice when it came to selecting Gallas's successor. The manager used to talk about a team of leaders on the field, but those days were gone. Such was the lack of genuine contenders that – due to injuries to Gallas and later Fabregas – the armband was handed around like a hot potato. Nine different players captained the first team over the course of the season. (Set against Manchester United the comparison was invidious. In the prolonged absence of Gary Neville, experienced internationals Rio Ferdinand, Edwin van der Sar and Ryan Giggs stepped seamlessly into the breach.) So, on one level, the manager had his team full of captains in name if not in practice but the reality was that he still sought the natural successor to Tony Adams and Patrick Vieira, and the club had won nothing since the latter's departure.

Those captains exemplified the power and the desire – key characteristics of success in the Premiership – which, along with pace and technique, were the cornerstones of Wenger's philosophy. If the absence of muscular virility had been compensated for by an excess of attacking zeal, then maybe the deficiencies could have been glossed over but Fabregas and Samir Nasri apart, the lack of invention in midfield was reflected by the predictability of the approach work. Notably absent was the effortless zip and penetration of previous seasons. Too often, the one-touch play floundered against a massed defence, as the team was funneled into the centre where space was at such a premium that attacks were rebuffed with relative ease (a pattern that was aided by Wenger's choice of players on the flanks who preferred to cut in). It was instructive that the best displays tended to come against the better teams who played a more expansive game, thus allowing Arsenal more space and time in which to retain possession and fashion chances. But over the course of 38 games there were inevitably far more encounters against lesser teams where the absence of experienced professionals who coped with everything their opponents, the crowd and occasionally even the referees threw at them, came home to roost. As Tony Adams argued: "You have to beat a lot of teams. You can draw against Manchester United and Liverpool, they're irrelevant. If you beat the bottom ten home and away you'll win the league. So, if they come here and defend, go at them. Try and score in the first 20 minutes. I would get after them."

The inability to create opportunities continued with a succession of four league 0-0 draws soon after the turn of the year. It was the first time the club had endured such a pitiful sequence since the terminal decline of the George Graham era, and some fans with long memories even questioned whether the personnel were much better than their predecessors from that wretched 1994/95 season. The situation was exacerbated by the loss of the best player, Cesc Fabregas, to a knee injury in December and a three month stint on the sidelines.

As David Dein commented with dismay, "The crowd have started to turn against Arsène." There were a growing number of supporters who felt that the manager could no longer take the club forward. And even the less sensationalist media highlighted the issue. "Should Arsène Wenger Be Sacked?" asked *The Daily Telegraph*. Possession remained the manager's priority, but divorced from a cutting edge and with defensive deficiencies still apparent, few points were garnered. Unlike their main rivals, Arsenal could not seem to win on a habitual basis when they were under-performing. Doubts began to grow about whether – for the first time in over a decade – they might not finish in the top four and thus miss out on the lucrative Champions League the following season when Aston Villa overhauled them and slowly began to pull away as the curtain fell on 2008.

CHAPTER SEVENTEEN
TOO LITTLE, TOO LATE

Unlike the other major European leagues whose winter breaks allow them to concentrate more time on the transfer window, in England it was business as usual. Arsène Wenger faced the twin tasks of collecting sufficient points to qualify for the Champions League and securing the necessary transformation in his playing resources to make it happen. Pursuing his own course, contrary to what most fans thought the team urgently needed – a central defender and a midfield enforcer – Wenger enthusiastically chased Andrey Arshavin, the Russian international striker from Zenit St Petersburg. Even by normal standards, the first transfer Ivan Gazidis oversaw in his new job of Arsenal CEO was a baptism of fire. Arriving from the MLS, where central negotiating of players' contracts, salary caps and budgetary control are the order of the day, Gazidis was astounded by the lack of regulation. "One of the great attractions of the Premier League is that it is a bit like the Wild West," he observed. "It surprises me that we have allowed football to come to a point where there are so many unscrupulous operators and third parties taking money out of the game." Yet the Premier League was a well-oiled machine compared to Russia.

In autumn 2008, Ken Friar had set the ball rolling on the Arshavin negotiations for Gazidis. "I was involved from the beginning because Ivan Gazidis came in January and that deal started well before then," he confirms. With more experience than most in the whys and wherefores of the transfer system, Friar was fortunately on hand as the newcomer, who was now running the club on a day-to-day basis, came to grips with a very different sporting culture to that he had become accustomed to.

There were several reasons that the deal took a long time to resolve, not least a faulty fax machine in Zenit's club offices. "It wasn't just that," recalls Friar. "You had people in different parts of the world [involved in the process]. One gentleman was unfortunately in hospital and we had to contact him. Eventually, we had everything we should have had, but it was very near the final cut. [However] there was no question of it not being in on time," asserts Friar. "What the Premier League wanted to do, because it was a complex deal, was to satisfy themselves that everything was in order," which explains why the club only announced Arshavin as an Arsenal player some 24 hours after the necessary regulations had been complied with. Ken Friar explained that the delay "related to the structure of the deal for the player. They are personal details to him. The decision process at the other end was slightly more complicated." It was a euphemistic way of saying that Zenit St Petersburg's ownership structure may have struggled to pass even the Premier League's less than onerous conditions of their "fit and proper person" examination. What was certain was that Arshavin himself was desperately keen to become an Arsenal player and his decision to fly to the UK to ensure he was available for the required medical proved a wise one, as an exceptional snowfall ensured no one would be flying anywhere in England on transfer deadline day.

Being 27, Arshavin was a few years older than the usual Wenger acquisition. (Older still Mikael Silvestre had only arrived towards the end of the previous transfer window because of the manager's inability to bring in the quality defender he sought.) The two new faces were a tacit admittance on Wenger's part that he had relinquished too much experience too soon, and that – in Arshavin's case – creatively, he needed more quality and imagination. The side was in the midst of a lengthy unbeaten run in the league and FA Cup, but this was largely down to stemming the hitherto regular concession of goals, and the team worked hard to grind out results. Yet the new found solidity – William Gallas, relieved of the captaincy, played some of the best football of his Arsenal career – came at a price, as the appeal of Wenger's past teams was fast becoming a memory and a three-match sequence of 0-0 home draws in January and February produced boos at the final whistle. Lacking the inspiration of the still indisposed Cesc Fabregas, the team had seemingly run out of ideas going forward. Eduardo briefly returned and looked threatening, but was soon injured once again, whilst the other forwards were simply firing blanks. Former captain Tony Adams felt "the current forwards are not natural finishers" and those in the stands could only concur and reminisce about the likes of Thierry Henry and Ian Wright.

Fortunately Arshavin made an immediate impact. Whilst the understanding with his new colleagues was predictably somewhat lacking, on the ball he nevertheless began to live up to his high-class reputation. The impact he had was similar to that of Dennis Bergkamp, in that there were lengthy periods when it would seem he might as well not even be on the field, but then the few minutes in which he became prominently involved were frequently devastating. His presence buoyed his teammates, and it made a refreshing change to witness a true communicator talking constantly with those around him, who signalled his intentions when moves broke down so as to make a repeat error less likely. His evident maturity highlighted the lack of nous in a squad that leant too heavily on the younger element. Tony Adams emphasised what had been missing:

"When I came into the team, I had players with great experience around me, telling me, 'Don't do that there, do that, get that ball away', I don't see that in this current Arsenal team. I don't see people saying, 'Oi you Cesc! Don't do that there, you get your arse up there.' I don't see the experienced players at the club, and it's got to come from somewhere." Perhaps Arshavin drove the point home to the manager.

However, experienced and talented though Arshavin undoubtedly was, many observers felt the money could have been much better spent elsewhere. For some reason Wenger had departed from the successful physical ingredients of the past. Where was the pace and power that hitherto was a prerequisite for the midfield and defence? Commenting in *The Daily Telegraph* after yet another 0-0 draw with Tottenham in February, Alan Hansen suggested it was Wilson Palacios (who Tottenham bought from Wigan) rather than Arshavin, who Arsenal needed. "He [Palacios] is a 'not got the ball' type of player, whereas Arshavin is not", the most oblique footballspeak, but presumably Hansen meant someone who worked hard, tackled robustly and was combative for 90 minutes.

Luckily, Aston Villa started dropping points at the kind of rate no one could have foreseen. Under less pressure, and with Arshavin in the side, Arsenal gradually began to improve, eventually putting together an unbeaten sequence of 21 Premier League matches. However, the first 13 results in the run featured eight draws. In a season when Liverpool only suffered two defeats but still failed by four points to claim the title, wins were the currency that bought success, and Arsenal simply could not register enough of them.

Still, progress in cup competitions is about avoiding defeat, and going through to the last four of both the Champions League and the FA Cup stimulated some long overdue optimism. The improved defensive statistics suggested that the team had become much more difficult to beat than they had been a few months earlier and there was a genuine belief that what at times had seemed a nightmare season could have a positive denouement. Unfortunately having already played in the competition for his previous club, Arshavin was ineligible for the Champions League, so the FA Cup appeared to be the best chance of the first trophy after four barren seasons. (Even the Carling Cup would have been welcome, but Wenger had long since made it the province of his fringe players, with the likely failure to come out on top.)

Unexpectedly, the team selected for the first visit to the 'new' Wembley Stadium (where all FA Cup semi-finals are now held) to face Chelsea saw an astounding omission, namely Arshavin, who was relegated to the bench. Arsène Wenger subsequently attempted to justify his bewildering decision to forego the services of an experienced international in a rich vein of form. "I knew for the team that the [FA Cup] semi-final was a very important step [in order] to go through in the Champions League, and I knew that Arshavin wasn't available [for that]. In my calculation," he reasoned, "it would give the team the confidence to beat Chelsea, and [knowing I could] bring Arshavin on if needed, the team could then go on in the Champions League and know that it could win big games. It didn't work like that, and that was the only reason [he didn't start], not that he wasn't good enough."

Arshavin may have appeared with the score at 1-1, but only for 15 minutes. What the manager effectively did was to use the FA Cup semi-final as a dress rehearsal for a European encounter ten days later, demonstrating how little store he put by the competition. The supporters on the other hand, saw their best hope of a trophy carelessly squandered. They would have loved to have returned for the final, four days after the conclusion of any Champions League commitments, and believed any victory over Chelsea would have been no distraction to their European ambitions. Further, the long-term kudos of winning the FA Cup arguably compares more favourably to reaching a Champions League semi-final.

"Winning the first trophy makes such a difference," confirmed Tony Adams. "You get confidence that you're a winner. It changes your mentality." As it turned out, defeat in the 2009 FA Cup semi-final – with or without Arshavin – was poor preparation for the competition Wenger valued more. Arsenal lost 2-1 due to defensive errors with keeper Lukasz Fabianski, Emmanuel Eboue and Mikael Sivestre all culpable. Significantly, not one of the back five – Almunia, Sagna, Gallas, Djourou and Clichy – who had played in the previous meeting of the two sides (a 2-1 away win at Stamford Bridge) was present.

William Gallas was the key absentee, sidelined for the rest of the season due to injury. The inability to defend competently without him reflected poorly on the depth of the squad. In the 21 appearances Gallas made after being deposed as captain, the side conceded 13 goals. After his injury, 16 were yielded in the 11 remaining games of the season including four against Liverpool at Anfield. Three days after the FA Cup exit, Arshavin, as if to make a point about his minimal involvement at Wembley, had four attempts and scored with all of them. The scoreline might as well have read: Goals conceded by Arsenal's inept defence 4, Andrey Arshavin 4. What was worse for the travelling support was that their team looked to have won, going 4-3 up just seconds before injury time. A year on from their Champions League elimination on the same ground, the defence showed that it had not learned from the experience, and succumbed to an injury-time equaliser.

Another idiosyncratic managerial decision was to tinker with the formation at such a crucial stage of the campaign. Departing from the habitual 4-4-2 which had served him so well over the years, different formations were tried with players deployed in unaccustomed positions, such as Van Persie as a lone striker and Bendtner wide on the flanks. It was as if by the use of wacky tactical innovation the manager was attempting to camouflage the inherent deficiencies in his personnel. He experimented with a 4-2-3-1 formation, Cesc Fabregas playing as a shadow striker behind the target man (normally Emmanuel Adebayor) with two holding midfield players behind him. If it was an attempt to shore up the defence, the results were questionable, and there were doubts it made the attack function much better with Fabregas seemingly less influential than when played deeper. Of his new role, Fabregas said, "I've always faced the goal; looking backwards it is a little more difficult but I am learning a lot." Some might say if you are learning in semi-finals, the price to pay for the lesson may be progress to the final itself.

When Arsenal travelled to Old Trafford at the end of April for the first leg of their Champions League semi-final, the same back four – Sagna, Toure, Silvestre and Gibbs – who lined up against Liverpool were named to face Manchester United. With no Arshavin, they were played off the park, fortunate to only lose 1-0, largely due to an excellent display from returning keeper Manuel Almunia. They had progressed to the last four courtesy of knockout stage wins (via a penalty shoot-out) against Roma and an injury-ravaged Villarreal. At Old Trafford they were exposed as pretenders to United's crown of European champions. The manager was either unwilling or unable to explain the poverty of their performance and could only say that, "you will see a different Arsenal at The Emirates". Samir Nasri played as one of the holding midfielders in both games, despite only filling the role on two previous occasions, leading to suggestions that the manager was simply trying to find a formation in which he could field the maximum number of his more creative players. Wenger attempted to justify the decision by explaining "it's important to have possession, and I thought the combination [with Song] could create chances". Unfortunately, there was little evidence of that.

The lack of an away goal meant Arsenal had to keep a clean sheet in the return leg, or win by two clear goals if United scored. The manager's words – "the team will produce a magnificent performance and we will qualify" – came back to haunt him as the gulf between the two sides saw the visitors kill the tie stone dead by scoring twice in the opening 11 minutes, due to a defensive slip by 19-year-old reserve left back Kieran Gibbs and Almunia's inability to get his hands to a Ronaldo free kick from 40 yards out. United eased up, and won the match 3-1 at a canter. Gibbs's opposite number, Patrice Evra described the tie as "11 men against 11 kids. That's what made the difference. We have much more experience than them. Football is not only to play attractively with the ball." Tony Adams concurred, though his remedy bordered on the extreme. "I don't think Ronaldo got kicked until it was too late. You make a point of it. I would have told every one of them to take him out in the first ten minutes. Four yellow cards, job done." And Alex Ferguson had a different view on longevity to his opposite number. None of the 'old guard' from the generation that came through in the mid-1990s started the game, but the importance of their being integral members of the squad is undoubted by Adams, who sees a comparable absence as a weakness at Arsenal. "What you've not had is a continuity from all the old players," he states. "We all retired one by one and then [the team] fell away and the difference between Arsenal and Man United over the last ten years is that they've had some continuity. Scholes, Giggs, Gary Neville, they've had those kind of players. The timing's been a lot better. In the past there were players around who could teach the young guys. I don't see that now."

Wenger's dream, some would say obsessive quest, was over for another year. To add insult to injury, any lingering hopes of overtaking Chelsea to take third place in the league petered out by collapsing to their London neighbours the following weekend. The manager described it as "a strange game, down to the disappointment of losing to Manchester United in the Champions League". The 4-1 defeat at home brought the 21-match unbeaten league run to an end. Wenger was able to find some comfort from the statistics, asserting their sequence without defeat "was the longest in the league this year". But in truth the only other 'big four' side they had faced in that time was Liverpool. Without Arshavin (unavailable due to illness) Arsenal were incapable of landing more than a solitary strike against Chelsea. As if the manager needed any further reminder about the underlying problem with his team, it was the third occasion they had conceded four goals in the league that season.

Arsène Wenger had placed great store in the mental strength, intelligence, resilience, character and desire of his young squad, and frequently used this language to describe them. There was little evidence of it as one defeat after another ensured their campaign fizzled out in anticlimax. As in 2008, when the 2-2 draw at Birmingham presaged a collapse in the league and European elimination, so a year on, the FA Cup semi-final upset was soon followed by an abrupt end to their Champions League ambitions. Fortunately, they were at least safe in fourth place, on account of Aston Villa's even more dramatic loss of form.

By the season's end, Arsenal had scored as many goals (68) as champions Manchester United, but conceded 13 more (37). A year after finishing four points behind the title winners, they now found themselves 18 points adrift. The facts left no doubt as to where the team's problems lay. "The team lacks balance," says Tony Adams. "Defensively, it needs toughening up. If Wenger wants to attack with his fantastic full backs, you need some stability in the central areas, you don't need the midfield bombing on as well. If you've got so many players who think offensively, you're never going to get them to think defensively." Frank McLintock commented succinctly, "As individuals, the defenders are good but they don't perform as a unit." Adams continues, "You challenge these [opposing] players and see how good they are, you put them under pressure. Some of that mentality and power is not in [Wenger's] team at the moment and when I talk about balance it's not only defensively/offensively, it's height and stature as well. The people who come inside, the people who want to run, the people who need to defend – he's got to get that right and he knows that." But Arsène Wenger was never going to go public on his failings, and his reticence did not endear him to all, however good his intentions with regards to bolstering the self-belief of his players.

At the 2007 AGM, Peter Hill-Wood announced there would be an opportunity for shareholders to attend an annual question-and-answer session with Arsène Wenger. The first was held in May 2008, and passed off without incident. The timing of the 2009 event was somewhat unfortunate, coming four days after the 4-1 hammering by Chelsea, and nine days after the Champions League elimination and the realisation of one more year without a trophy. The shareholders, who had retained their stake ignoring the inducements to sell and earn a handsome return on their investment, were obviously true supporters of the club. They attended the meeting not because they were concerned about the value of their holding but because they intended to take the opportunity to cross-examine the manager. It was doubtless a commitment he wished he had never agreed to.

Earlier in the week, the Arsenal Supporters' Trust had been able to question Ivan Gazidis. He made a very positive impression and left the members with a real sense of optimism about the club's future direction. On the day of Wenger's inquisition, there had been a board meeting, and Gazidis, along with Peter Hill-Wood and Ken Friar, attended the shareholders' event and sat in the front row. The manager's demeanour was in total contrast to that of Gazidis, who had faced some tough questions but had responded with good grace and as much openness as he could. From the outset, Wenger was very defensive, so much so that one attendee later quipped his back four could have learned a thing or two from his performance. He gave the impression that he thought he was under attack, and treated even innocuous questions with a degree of wariness.

He acknowledged there was "massive frustration" over the manner of the European performances against Manchester United but reasoned that "overall, with the policy we've gone for with a young team, to finish in the position we did is not a shame." He added, "At the moment the vibes around the team are very negative, but I feel the Arsenal supporters should take a little bit of distance from that, and not get manipulated too much". Yet the media were taking their cue from what was being said on websites and on phone-in programmes; for the most part trenchant criticism that is unlikely to ever enter into the orbit of Wenger's day-to-day experience. The manager had created a situation where he had effectively placed himself and his players within a protective bubble. Fans rarely have any opportunity to encounter the playing staff, except in highly controlled situations with security staff hovering. Yet this was different. The questions were not vetted in advance and, exposed to unhappy fans, the bubble was burst. Arsène Wenger had to sit and listen to what the paying public thought of his players. And accused of being irresponsible and lacking fight, he immediately leapt to their defence.

"The players take responsibility when they are on the pitch," countered Wenger. "It depends what you call taking responsibility. We play in the best league in the world and I tell you,

you do not stay 21 games unbeaten if you do not stand up and you do not fight. People around the club know what is most important when you are a young team is to be supportive. It is easy to sit in the stand and say that they are not up for the fight. What they have done in this season in a negative environment shows that they will stand up and take responsibility. And it's my job to take the blame." Certainly, but what he failed to understand was that by paying his young players such ridiculous sums he had made them hostages to fortune. Moreover he has made a rod for their back and his own by raising expectations to a high level that previously he met with ease. Now though, over the last year or two diminishing returns had begun to set in. Under such circumstances fans have every right to be unforgiving when there is a palpable lack of quality, especially in experienced players and perhaps even worse when their more gifted colleagues show a continuous lack of commitment and are seemingly indulged by the manager.

Aside from the fanciful notion of the professional foul, where cynicism is permitted in the interest of gaining an advantage, professionalism, which the players are so fond of claiming they represent (as if they were comparable to doctors, lawyers and accountants), brings with it certain obligations, namely that they will be prepared to perform to their best mentally, physically and technically for the paying public. This is a minimum requirement. Any genuine love of the club, spirit of camaraderie and duty to their teammates is a bonus. By their own standards, Arsenal were unprofessional.

As far as Wenger was concerned, the impression he gave was that no one had a right to criticise his players and call themselves supporters. Unchallenged by the directors and his staff, he appeared oblivious to the notion that as a key employee in a plc he could be called to account by shareholders. His disinterest was exemplified by a run-in he had with a fan at Stamford Bridge. "We win at Chelsea after a disastrous game at Man City," he recalled. "I go to the loo after the game, and a guy says, 'Well done Arsène, we won today, but we will not win the championship this year,' and this was in November. I said, 'Sorry, to me you are not an Arsenal fan'. He said, 'Of course I am an Arsenal fan'. I said, 'We are just a team with the oldest player 21 in midfield, and we beat Chelsea, who are a mature team with a massive investment, and the only thing you can say after the game is we will not win the championship. You cannot say to me you're a fan because you don't even believe in your own players.' That's a responsibility as well, because people say 'I am a fan, but only if it all goes well, you win 38 games on the trot, and win all the trophies, then I am a fan.' I'm sorry, but that is easy."

For most of his life as an Arsenal fan, it hadn't been "easy" for Steve Mono. Yet he has never left before the final whistle and under no circumstances would ever contemplate booing his team. A mild-mannered professional man who has been an Arsenal supporter for longer than Arsène Wenger has been alive (a season ticket-holder for 50 years and a shareholder for 45) Mono freely admits to being an admirer of Wenger who, he says, has brought him more pleasure in supporting his team than he ever believed was possible.

Perplexed at the manager's preference for youth over experience, he felt he had some legitimate points to make at the shareholders' Q and A. He began, after trying to reassure the manager, telling him that he was among friends, by expressing his failure to understand what Wenger had in mind before the 2008/09 campaign kicked off.

Mono: "It's very difficult to understand how we lost five international midfield players when we started last year, including Rosicky. Three of them captains. How was your thinking that we could possible compete in the Premiership having lost those players? I don't think it's fair to the younger players, especially Fabregas, I just don't understand your mindset. Also I can't understand the virtual swapping of Senderos with Silvestre. The policy has always been not to give older players contracts and it seems totally against your philosophy to allow a 23-year-old centre half to go and to bring in – I could almost refer to Silvestre as a geriatric centre half – and he's been unfit for half of the season, but when he was up against class players he's been totally inadequate."

Wenger: "I do not accept the statements you make about our players. Are you a shareholder?"

Mono: "Yes."

Wenger: "And you speak like that about our players. I'm sorry, I cannot accept that, the way you speak about the players of your own club."

Mono: "What I said was about one individual player."

Wenger: "You should not use these terms about the players, you should see him [Silvestre] in training every day."

Mono: "I'm sure he's a very nice man and behaves very well but up against very high standard players he's been found wanting."

Wenger: "I can't understand how we lost five internationals?"

Mono: "I'm including Diarra."

Wenger: "How many games did Diarra play last year?"

Mono: "He was at the club."

Wenger: "He left in January."

Mono: "I said last year."

Wenger: "And who are the other four?"

Mono: "Well I'm including Rosicky. Then Hleb, Flamini and Gilberto."

Wenger: "Gilberto played 13 games last year. He was 33 years old."

Mono: "Yes, but we still lost that experience."

Wenger: "We lost experience because we did not know that Rosicky . . ."

Mono: "You lost five international players."

Wenger: "We did not know that Rosicky would not be available and we did not want Flamini to go. We did not want Hleb to go. Do you know the rules of the modern game? After three years a player over the age of 28 can buy his contract out. You cannot stop him. Hleb had completed three years. We did not want him to go. He came in with the transfer request and we cannot stop him."

Mono: "I understand that you did not want him to go but how could you possibly not bring in replacements? How did you think you could possibly compete in the Premiership without these five international players?"

Wenger: "Because we had plenty of young players who we used."

Mono: "You have wonderful young players and I'm not attacking you."

Wenger: "You are attacking the players – that is much worse. Today we had a training session. Do you know how many injured players we had? Eleven. Do you want me to give you the names?"

Mono: "You misunderstand me."

Wenger: "No, I don't misunderstand you. You cannot say on one side, 'Why do you not play Walcott' and on the other side say, 'Why do you not play experienced players?' You cannot say on one side, 'Leave out Fabregas' and on the other, 'Why do you play a 30 year old guy in his place?' I know. I am 30 years in this job, I know a guy who is 30 years will make less mistakes than a guy who is 20 but you must accept as well that you will lose the young players. We lose a Walcott. We lose Fabregas. When he came here he wanted the chance to play. I accept – if you say the players are too young – that's your view. Everybody has an opinion until he is in the position to show what he can do with his opinion. But what I do not accept is that is if we have come from this position in agreement with the board, what I don't like is for you to say, 'You go wrong with these players, you will never go anywhere.' I say that is your belief, but I don't believe it. But people always criticise the players and if they go somewhere else in two or three years you will say, 'Why did you let Diaby go, why did you let Song go? Why did you let Walcott go? They are all great players' They will show you that they are great players."

To be rebuked by the manager and (in the press) by the chairman and subsequently misrepresented by the media was both deeply upsetting and a serious piece of miscasting. The exchange probably represented a lowpoint in the manager's relationship with the supporters. Wenger doubtless believed that they should endorse all his selections, and his response gave the impression that he considered them, in the words of blogger and shareholder Vic Crescit (who gave an account of the meeting online) as "ill-considered and ill-informed. Some he seemed to regard as outright impertinent."

After the Q and A with Wenger, in an amiable conversation with Mono, Gazidis admitted that maybe Arsène takes too much on his shoulders. With his intimate knowledge of American sports where the media have far more access than Arsenal or indeed any Premier League club are prepared to concede, and where the customer is king rather than being taken for granted, this was a public relations exercise that seriously backfired. Even worse, in this case, the customers were part owners of the company. And as a final insult to injury, the session was edited before being broadcast on Arsenal television, the more critical exchanges including Steve Mono's and Wenger's defence of Adabayor in response to diving allegations ('a great player who has done fantastically well for the club') were unsurprisingly omitted.

Wenger was obviously affected by the experience. Bob

Wilson, who chaired the meeting commented, "The general tenor was constructive, [but] the comments singling out players upset Arsène like I've never seen him before." The following week at his pre-match press conference Wenger reflected, "There is criticism I accept with respect, but disrespect I don't accept. I accept everyone's opinion, but what was not enjoyable in that meeting was that it was disrespectful to some players and I don't accept that. If we lost 38 games on the trot I would not accept that. The club have moved forwards, not back, since I came to Arsenal. I was disappointed because I believe especially the shareholders cannot complain. In October 1996 the share price was around £400 and now it is £10,000. I would prefer it if the fans complained than the shareholders. I could understand that more." But all the shareholders present at the meeting were also fans (as one succinctly put it, "It's Henry who excites me, not the price of shares.") and probably voiced their concerns in a far more civil manner than a meeting with the rank and file would generate, as a cursory look at the independent websites or a flick through the pages of *The Gooner* would tell Wenger. But his only regular exposure to the opinion of supporters is probably the occasional booing he hears on a matchday when things have not gone well.

Although he himself had described the 3-1 Champions League defeat as "the most disappointing night of my career" he felt that there had been some over-reaction to his team's failure to rise to the big occasion. "When you look now at people assessing the situation, it has just become ridiculous. Every year, every day you feel like you killed somebody. It is unbelievable. If you do not distance yourself from it you think, 'What kind of world are we living in?'"

The club decided he should see some supportive messages emailed to them from those in the stands who backed him. The response was partly prompted by the media in Spain and the UK picking up on an interview for *Telefoot* on TF1, the main French television channel for whom Wenger is a consultant. Questioned about Florentino Perez's candidacy for the Real Madrid presidency, and his subsequent plans if elected, Wenger responded, "With Perez, the project will be obviously interesting for any coach." Would he be tempted? He replied, "I'm a coach." Had he been in contact with Perez? "Allow me to remain discreet on that matter," said Wenger. Asked by the presenter Christian Jeanpierre how he found Arsène, the interviewer, David Astorga, replied "*tendu*" (uptight). With two years until the end of his current contract, it could have been a coded warning to the club, and possibly its supporters, that he should not be taken for granted and that he might be more appreciated elsewhere. On his return to England, he had an extended lunch with Peter Hill-Wood and Ivan Gazidis at the club's training ground, doubtless discussing plans for the summer, and quite possibly confirming that he was as committed as ever to the club – or at least that was the media's interpretation.

Wenger had held discussions with Perez in 2003, at a time when his budget had been severely cut ensuring he missed out on possible signings such as Cristiano Ronaldo. Since then, Roman Abramovich's fortune had catapulted Chelsea to the forefront of English and European football, whilst Manchester United continued to speculate on players and accumulate trophies at a rate Arsenal could only dream of in the far-flung future. Arsène Wenger was still fighting the odds, only in the face of such a financial disadvantage – in spite of the club's phenomenal turnover – he was not actually beating them anymore.

CHAPTER EIGHTEEN
NOW OR NEVER

"If we buy, it certainly won't be players who lack experience. We have enough of those." When Arsène Wenger outlined his intentions for the summer a few days after his team's exit from the Champions League at the hands of Manchester United, there would have been a loud chorus of "hear, hear" from Arsenal fans. "I do what I can with what I have available and you have never heard me complain," he said, "but I do not accept that people think I'm stupid enough that I have £100million at my disposal and I put it in the bank because I am scared to spend it," contradicting his response to Peter Hill-Wood and Danny Fiszman who, when asked what he would do if he was given such a windfall, were promptly told, he'd hand it right back again. Then, for good measure, Wenger added, "I believe the more everybody shuts up inside the club, doesn't talk about anything and works hard is [for] the best." It was perceived as a clear message that he did not want to hear any more "Arsène can afford to buy any player he wants, he only has to ask," statements from board members.

But it was too late. The manager had long ago let the cat out of the bag. The popular assumption that he was happy enough to construct a young team through choice had been seized upon by the board for their own purposes. Better to let Wenger face the brickbats from the supporters and the media than admit that the club could not afford to buy the stars who would increase the likelihood of success.

Certainly all the tickets may have been sold, but the poor fare on offer was turning the public away. So when it was habitually claimed, over the course of the 2008/09 season, that 60,000 were in attendance (amounting to over 99 per cent matchday stadium utilisation – the highest in the Premier League) even though there were clearly empty seats all around the ground, people believed the evidence of their own eyes and no longer trusted the official line. Yet if the club had issued the true numbers who had passed through the turnstiles, the illusion that demand continues to outstrip supply would not be so easy to maintain. That many season ticket holders were not even bothered about occupying seats they had paid so handsomely for should be a matter of grave concern. The next logical step would be that they will not be bothering to renew them. After the anticlimactic finish to the 2008/09 season, a significant number decided to do just that, with others opting to subsidise their outlay by renting their seats. The novelty of the Emirates is over. Fans now know they can easily get tickets to go six or seven times a season, which is sufficient for many of them. The market for selling seats, generally at face value, already flourishing through the unofficial supporters' chatrooms, forums and email lists is set to continue to expand. Of course it is tougher to get a ticket when Manchester United are in town, but for Bolton it's a breeze, especially if the game is televised. Even the added attraction of Champions League participation is not always enough to fill the stadium.

The Champions League semi-final elimination at the hands of Manchester United encapsulated the season. Arsène Wenger talked up his team and they let him down. They were simply not good enough. Supposed to come of age for the second leg, the biggest game the Emirates had hosted so far, the evening fell flat early on in the proceedings and there was a steady exodus of fans by half time.

In the final that United reached at Arsenal's expense, Barcelona took care of the English champions in a way that Wenger must have wished his team could emulate, with a style that he has always aspired to but, more and more of late, has consistently failed to produce. "We are convinced, [myself and] the directors, that we are doing the right thing," said Wenger adamantly, "Because we want to run the club by respecting the financial balance, by developing the idea of the game played how we want it played, and by developing the players who we bought, who have been at the club for five years. If we do not get there next year, or the year after, then I will be responsible and stand up for it, don't worry."

Looking to the future, the relationship between the manager and new CEO Ivan Gazidis – a man with new ideas and methods – is key. A few months into the role, Gazidis's work can now begin in earnest. The initial signs augur well with Wenger revealing, "I see Ivan as someone who can help me achieve my targets, and we have a shared vision as to how the club has to be run. As much as you can say, 'if we don't win, I am responsible,' I want to say, 'If we don't win, he is responsible!'" Gazidis's experience in the buying and selling hundreds of players for MLS should enable the manager to take more of a back seat once he has identified a target, proposing more and disposing less. Wenger may have been overprotective of his squad, but he will not be able to shield them from the evaluation of the CEO. "My focus is going to be very, very laser sharp on what we do to improve the performance of the team," said Gazidis.

Whether Wenger continues to be master of all he surveys will be interesting to observe. Gazidis, although fully supportive of the manager, will have noted that he is unchallenged by his staff and his fellow directors. David Dein was fond of repeating that the manager had a job for life at the club but a human resources department is about to be established because "As we now have over 400 employees we require that," said Gazidis, admitting, "I was surprised when I came in that that didn't exist. It's one of the key areas in any size of organisation." Undoubtedly such a move will challenge the wisdom of the current arrangement whereby Arsène can do what he wants with a budget of £100 million provided he delivers Champions League revenue every season (expected to pull in the highest amount ever for 2008/09). But Gazidis set a loftier benchmark when he pronounced, "This is a club that aims higher than 4th place. We don't believe that's good enough, this club wants to win things."

Given that Wenger is 59 and Gazidis 45, the long-term future of the club could well lie with the CEO rather than the manager. At least he is likely to be more hands on than anyone Wenger has had to work closely with before. The immediate tasks are to fill glaring vacancies on the coaching side with the proviso that, as Gazidis admits, "If Arsène doesn't believe it, then how are you going to push someone in there and make it work?" And the manager seems perfectly content with his existing set-up. He leans a lot on Boro Primorac who was himself a coach in the French first division before joining Arsenal soon after Wenger arrived in England. Ken Friar explained how the duo worked together. "Boro sits up in the stand for all the first team games and will go down and analyse things both at half time and at full time. And then the following day, even if it's a Sunday, they will have the tape of that match and they will be sitting there for hours between them analysing the game. So that works out well too. They complement each other. I've never known them to have a disagreement. I'm sure that's a good partnership." But could the same be said about Pat Rice? Would he have met the criteria for a good number two if Gazidis had been involved in the appointment?

Just as important, do either Primorac or Rice ever challenge their boss?

Perhaps, as Frank McLintock has commented, "Wenger should have kept Don Howe around." The former England coach, one of the most revered defensive organisers in the game, instead of being installed as Wenger's number two, was employed in the youth academy with Liam Brady. Not that he wasn't successful but, like Wenger, Brady carefully controls his territory so Howe's scope was limited and, besides, his forte was working with experienced players. As an elder statesman he would have been no threat to Wenger but someone who, just as when Bob Wilson was his goalkeeping coach, at least would have provided expert specialist advice. Martin Keown, a younger and more forceful personality, worked with the squad in 2006 whilst preparing for his UEFA coaching licences. With Eboue, Toure, Senderos or Campbell and Flamini forming an improvised back four was it a coincidence that the defence was set to go all the way to the Champions League final? Perhaps Keown preferred the comfort of the BBC's pundit sofa or maybe he was seen as a barrack room lawyer, more of a threat than the compliant current set-up.

At least there is now someone in the boardroom willing to talk to Arsène Wenger about his methods. Ivan Gazidis was asked about his interaction with the manager.

"I speak to Arsène about anything I want to speak about and ask him what I consider to be the difficult questions. I've never found him resistant or defensive to those questions. I've never felt that he's not willing to examine his modus operandi and think about things with an open mind. I think we have very full, frank, open discussions."

"Have you disagreed with him?"

"Of course. But if it comes to somebody's judgment about what's happening on the pitch, I trust Arsène Wenger's judgment a lot more than I trust my own."

"But you can propose and allow him to dispose."

"We have interesting discussions on a lot of different issues and I've never found him resistant to that."

In getting to know Arsène Wenger, Gazidis is sure he's got the best man for the job. Nevertheless, he concedes, "I do think he takes a lot on his shoulders. He doesn't take the easy way out, which is to point fingers of blame in other directions. He's so instrinsically entwined with the club and so involved in the formation of our strategy, that he will not disavow it. We're embarked upon a journey that has evolved, not signing superstar players, clearly not in the Real Madrid or Chelsea or Manchester United model. These are the questions that maybe we need to look at, the strategy that we've adopted. That's what the club has been doing, and I think Arsène, to his eternal credit, has never sought to divorce himself from that direction. Instead he's sought to embrace it and to do the best he can within it. My view is that at this club, we have stability through being self-sufficient. We are not reliant on outside sources of financing. That's a very challenging path to walk down. It's difficult and it creates a lot of short-term competitive challenges for us. But long-term I'm confident that the club will be strong and one of the best clubs in England and the world. And we're not pushing ourselves into an unsustainable business model."

Because the landscape of English football has changed so much since the arrival of Roman Abramovich, and attained a further dimension with the acquisition of Manchester City by the Abu Dhabi United Group Investment and Development Limited, Arsenal are no longer competing on the level that existed when the Emirates was planned and the funding arranged. The board and Wenger continue to argue for the long-term benefits of financial self-sufficiency, but with Chelsea and Manchester United spending 70 per cent and 20 per cent respectively more on salaries and with the summer of 2008 and the January 2009 transfer window showing the highest levels of expenditure yet recorded (Manchester City had a gross spend of around £80 million), it is becoming more difficult with every passing year for Wenger's men to stay ahead of the chasing pack. "Arsenal are not a bad side, but they are not good enough to win a major trophy anymore," ruefully observed a long-standing supporter, asking, "Have they accepted that finishing fourth and balancing the books is the preferred option?"

In 2007, expecting the Highbury Square treasure trove, Wenger was anticipating a positive financial landscape by the summer of 2009. Now that the stagnation in the housing market has put paid to that idea, it is up to the board to ensure the manager has sufficient funds to buy the *savoir faire* the squad is crying out for. Since the Emirates opened plenty of money has been made by past and present directors through share dealing, but little has seen its way back into the club. Perhaps, if they are not able to donate some of their fortune or provide 'soft' (interest-free) loans as other more altruistic owners have done, they could contemplate the notion of a rights issue to raise funds in the way that new shares were created when ITV [then Granada] purchased a 9.99 per cent stake (eventually bought by Stan Kroenke). But with the current board owning less than 50 per cent of the club, the idea of further diluting their holding is not an appealing one unless they wish to clear the way for Stan Kroenke to invest the millions more necessary to own the club outright. However, should he fail to do so, in the event of a rights issue Alisher Usmanov could step into the breach by increasing his shareholding to such a level that he might not even need to form an alliance with Lady Nina Bracewell-Smith in order to take control.

Some fans might actually welcome this development, as long as it meant greater investment in the team. In the event that Alisher Usmanov does flex his muscles and decide to test the water with a bid, perhaps making the kind of offer that even the board's major shareholders would find it difficult to resist, the one thing he is adamant on is that the incumbent manager remains.

That Wenger is one of the most in-demand managers in world football and could probably walk into any job he fancies indicates the universal respect for him held by his peers. As a consequence of his philosophy, football fans all over the world watch televised matches in anticipation of another vintage Wenger-inspired Arsenal display. The manager is all too well aware of this, confirming, "I want to win trophies, but I think that you cannot survive a long time as a club, or have a world reputation without a style of play."

The infrastructure may be in place, but until the debt becomes less of a burden and more money is spent on the finished articles rather than potential, the club must be wary of being overtaken and falling back into the pack. They are attempting to chase those ahead of them at the same time as looking over their shoulder. So if Wenger needs eyes in the back of his head, he must first admit to seeing what is staring him in the face, and take the appropriate measures. Perhaps he will be prompted by Ivan Gazidis, who observes, "I don't have rose-tinted spectacles on with respect to where our team is, at the same time I do think it's a team that, despite its youth, is growing up. Now that doesn't necessarily mean it doesn't need to be supplemented and that we don't need to look at that but I think it's probably further along than people give it credit for." And the CEO adds pointedly, "If we don't deliver success Arsène is under the same pressure as anyone in that position."

And success means trophies: another season without them could see a long and happy marriage end in an amicable divorce. Arsène, though devastated, would probably understand if it came to pass. "I always say that a manager has a love story with the club," he said in April 2008, "and he has to behave like it will be a love story forever. But not be stupid enough to believe it will never end."